SCHLEIERMACHER IN PLAIN ENGLISH

STEPHEN D. MORRISON

BELOVED PUBLISHING · COLUMBUS, OH

Copyright © 2019 by Stephen D. Morrison

All rights reserved.

No part of this book may be reproduced in any form or by any electronic or mechanical means, including information storage and retrieval systems, without written permission from the author, except for brief quotation.

Print ISBN: 978-1-63174-175-3

eBook ISBN: 978-1-63174-176-0

Cover design and illustration copyright © 2019 Gordon Whitney Media (www.GordonWhitneyMedia.com)

Beloved Publishing · Columbus, Ohio.

CONTENTS

Abbreviations   v
Introduction   vii
Biography   xv

PART I
CHRISTIAN FAITH

1. Election, Community, and Grace   3
   Sermon: One Greatly Extended Community   19
   Sidebar: The Spirit-Filled Church   23
2. The Triune God of Love   31
   Sidebar: Sabellius Reconsidered   41
   Sidebar: God Hidden and Revealed   49
3. Christ Our Redeemer   59
   Sidebar: Death and Resurrection   75
   Sermon: Eternal Life   81
4. The Entrance Hall and Boundary Line   85
   Sidebar: On Scripture   107
5. Conclusion to Part I   113

PART II
MAJOR WORKS

6. On Religion   125
7. Christian Ethics   133
8. Hermeneutics   141
9. Luke and The Life of Jesus   151
10. Brief Outline of Theology as a Field of Study   159

Afterword   171
Key Themes   175
A Brief Reading Guide   183
About the Author   193
Also by Stephen D. Morrison   195

ABBREVIATIONS

BO — *Brief Outline of Theology as a Field of Study, Third Edition* by Friedrich D. E. Schleiermacher; translated, with essays and notes, by Terrence N. Tice. Louisville, Kentucky: Westminster John Knox Press, 2011.

CE — *Selections from Friedrich Schleiermacher's Christian Ethics* by Friedrich D. E. Schleiermacher; edited and translated by James M. Brandt. Louisville, Kentucky: Westminster John Knox Press, 2011.

CF — *Christian Faith: A New Translation and Critical Edition* by Friedrich D. E. Schleiermacher; translated by Terrence N. Tice, Catherine L. Kelsey, and Edwina Lawler; edited by Catherine L. Kelsey and Terrence N. Tice. Louisville, Kentucky: Westminster John Knox Press, 2016.

iCE — *Introduction to Christian Ethics* by Friedrich D. E. Schleiermacher; translated by John C. Shelly. Nashville, Tennessee: Abingdon Press, 1989.

OG — *On the Glaubenslehre: Two Letters to Dr. Lücke* by Friedrich D. E. Schleiermacher; translated by James Duke and Francis Fiorenza. AAR Texts and Translations Series number 3; Chico, California: Scholars Press, 1981.

OR — *On Religion: Addresses in Response to its Cultured Critics* by Friedrich D. E. Schleiermacher; translated, with introduction and notes, by Terrence N. Tice. Richmond, Virginia: John Knox Press, 1969.

INTRODUCTION

The best that can be said of me is that I am not what they take me to be.[1]

— Schleiermacher

History is often unkind to its most original thinkers. Because they challenge us so deeply, we seldom have the patience required for understanding them. Hegel's often-quoted saying is apt: "A great man condemns the world to the task of explaining him."[2] The greatness of a work does not guarantee it will be understood. The opposite is often the case. We are more likely to misunderstand great thinkers than to acknowledge their complexities and take the time to learn from them.

It may be an overstatement, but I can think of no figure in recent theological memory misunderstood more severely than Friedrich D. E. Schleiermacher. His legacy is strangely divided. Although few critics deny his significance, he is rarely celebrated. He was an undisputed architect of the modern era, one to whom we all owe a debt, yet his work is often discussed as if it were the root of all our woes. But I am here to say he is not who you think he is. Schleiermacher is not the "villain" of modern theology. That old, marred image is in dire need of revision.

Among the numerous reasons for the vilification of Schleiermacher is the influence of Karl Barth, the great twentieth-century theologian and a famous critic of Schleiermacher's theological program. Historical theologians often take Barth's own account of their relationship at face value, that Schleiermacher turned theology into a subjective meditation on human emotions, and

Barth saved theology by returning its focus to the Word of God. This is the familiar story I once accepted uncritically. I even passed it along in the first book of this series.[3]

But the best thing that can be said of Schleiermacher still today is that he is not what his critics take him to be.

My goal for this book is simple: I want to reevaluate Schleiermacher and come to a new understanding of his legacy, to show how vital his work is for theology today and how severe our loss whenever we ignore him. This will require not only the difficult task of understanding him rightly but of unlearning what we were once taught.

From Barth to Schleiermacher: My Journey

My theological education has been dominated by Karl Barth.[4] So it should be no surprise to learn that the first image I held of Schleiermacher was that of an enemy—before ever reading him for myself. What led me to write this book? The previous titles in this series (on Barth, Torrance, and Moltmann) follow a "Barthian" trajectory.[5] So it may seem out of character for a Barthian to now turn his attention to one of Barth's favorite opponents.

But the first thing I learned about Schleiermacher was that he can be—and perhaps *must* be—appreciated from the Barthian perspective. The truth is Barth's theology has more in common with Schleiermacher than he dared to think possible (though he hoped it might be true), and Barth owes a lot to Schleiermacher's perspective, far more than he was willing to let on. There are still a lot of things they disagree about, certainly, but there are too many convictions they share to ignore. So we should banish every suspicion of Schleiermacher as Barth's enemy. At the very least, their relationship is far more complicated than it appears at first glance.

But this is not a book about Karl Barth, and I only mention him for two reasons. First, because my own experience with reading Schleiermacher has been so decisively shaped by Barth. Much of what I had to re-learn about Schleiermacher was a correction of what Barth led me to believe about him. Second, because this is probably a familiar story for many theology students. Barth's enormous influence over twentieth- and twenty-first-century theology has led to Schleiermacher's neglect. So by turning my attention to Schleiermacher and examining him from the Barthian perspective, it is not in the sense that I will repeat any of Barth's criticisms of Schleiermacher—on the contrary, I hope to overcome the damage his critique has done to Schleiermacher's name.

Barth's Critique

Barth's stance against Schleiermacher particularly and liberal theology generally was summarized best in 1928: "One can *not* speak of God simply by speaking of man in a loud voice."[6] This polemic exemplifies Barth's early theology, and it sets the course for much of his later thought. Barth sought to do theology again from the basis of God's Word, rather than human intuition. For Barth, Schleiermacher's theology was little more than anthropology in disguise. That is, he saw Schleiermacher's God as the projection of human feelings in the echo chamber of empty subjectivism.

Schleiermacher's doctrine of the Trinity is another major point of criticism, particularly its placement in the Conclusion of his dogmatics. Barth takes this to mean that the Trinity has no "constitutive significance" for Schleiermacher's theology.[7] In contrast, Barth wished to give the Trinity a place of controlling and determinative importance. In other words, Barth believed Schleiermacher's doctrine of the Trinity was non-essential to his theology, included merely to offer lip-service to the appearance of a truly *Christian* dogmatics. Barth argued that Schleiermacher had constructed a philosophical, subjectivist theology that failed to be thoroughly Christian but only Christian in part. The doctrine of the Trinity was added only as an afterthought—as nothing more than a Christian mask to cover up a philosophical, speculative core.

All things considered, however, Barth never thought of himself as Schleiermacher's absolute enemy. In contrast with Brunner—who famously set fire to all the books he owned by Schleiermacher after publishing his critique—Barth considered Schleiermacher a brother and life-long conversation partner. He always "tried to be a loving student and not an enemy" and never thought of Schleiermacher as a heretic.[8] He even praised Schleiermacher, saying, "[T]here has never been a systematician in modern times like Schleiermacher. He knows the beauty of theology. The rest do not."[9] Just a few years before writing *The Epistle to the Romans,* Barth stood before his congregation in Safenwil and called Schleiermacher "one of the deepest Christian thinkers of all times, full of devotion to and understanding of Jesus."[10] His polemic was not a hostile attack, but above all, it was one of respect and admiration. To this day, on the staircase of Barth's residence in Basel, a portrait of Schleiermacher hangs in a place of honor, and a bust of the great theologian was ever watchful in Barth's classroom. It is clear that Barth greatly admired Schleiermacher, despite his fierce criticisms.

Terrence Tice, an outstanding Schleiermacher-scholar and translator, once met with Barth to discuss his relationship with Schleiermacher. He recounts their conversation:

One day after I had returned to Switzerland (1962-65), we had been talking for some time in his study. I told him that despite the differences and what I regarded to be his serious misreadings, he of all the theologians since Schleiermacher was Schleiermacher's truest heir and had overall been the most faithful to what Schleiermacher was trying to do. At this, he rocked back and forth in his chair and for some minutes loudly laughed and laughed. After a thoughtful pause he said, with great earnestness, 'I would wish that to be true, I hope it is.' Then he spoke again of his love for Schleiermacher, of his having viewed him dialectically in light of modern trends traced to him, of his regrets, of his critical position's having become softer in tone, of his wishing for a chance to talk it all out with him in heaven, and of its being perhaps too late to go back and try again, that others must do that.[11]

Why read Schleiermacher as a Barthian? *For Barth's sake.* Barth's relationship with Schleiermacher was profoundly ambivalent. He expressed a great appreciation for Schleiermacher, praising him as one of the most significant theologians since Calvin, yet he was also one of the most fervent critics of his work. Barth would be disappointed to learn that so many Barthians refuse even to read Schleiermacher, let alone offer him a fair reading. Schleiermacher is, of course, well worth reading in his own right. He was a brilliant, influential man, and his multi-faceted contribution to theology is enormous. But the idea that we cannot appreciate Schleiermacher if we also appreciate Barth is false. Barth would fiercely disagree with such a dichotomy.

It will also be helpful for us to recognize two critical conclusions scholars have reached. First, Barth and Schleiermacher have more in common than often thought, as we have already noted. There are, of course, irreconcilable differences between them, including sharp disagreements over Christology, the atonement, the Trinity, the divine attributes, and scriptural authority. But many of their core convictions are shared, such as their dedication to placing Jesus Christ at the center of theology, their emphasis on divine grace, their ethical commitments, and their non-speculative approach.

Second—and perhaps most important for our study—it has been well established that Barth *misreads* Schleiermacher. Both Schleiermacher-scholars *and* Barth-scholars have recognized this.[12] Barth's interpretation of Schleiermacher's theology as a subjectivistic and humanistic construction is a poor misreading. This book is my attempt to offer a reevaluation of Schleiermacher from the Barthian perspective. As such, one of my primary aims is to overcome the plethora of misunderstandings that surround Schleiermacher's life and thought, many of which come from Barth.

Surprised by Schleiermacher

I do not want to give the impression that this book will be more about Barth than Schleiermacher. Above all, my goal is to present Schleiermacher on his own terms, to celebrate his work, and to offer him every opportunity at a fair reading. I have therefore set out to read Schleiermacher with a *charitable* lens, against the Barthian tendency to paint him as a villain. As I began to read his work for myself, I discovered just how much there is to agree with Schleiermacher about, how much beauty he packs into his systematic cohesiveness, and how much strength there is in his perspective. In short, I often found myself "surprised by Schleiermacher," to mimic a phrase from C. S. Lewis.

Schleiermacher himself would remind us that approaching a text with the illusion of absolute objectivity, of being free from all preconceived ideas, is an impossibility. A "pure" reading is beyond us. We cannot escape ourselves. So I offer no apology for coming to Schleiermacher from the Barthian perspective, but I *do* make every effort to ensure this perspective in no way hinders my reading of his work.

But I was not the first to "discover" any of this, nor will I pretend that my reading of Schleiermacher is an altogether original one. The secondary literature available on Schleiermacher is of the "highest order," as far as scholarly accounts are concerned. It would be impossible to write this book if it were not for the work of masterful writers and translators who have devoted so much of their time to Schleiermacher. So I must offer up my sincerest gratitude and indebtedness to Terrence N. Tice, Catherine L. Kelsey, Robert W. Williams, Daniel J. Peterson, and Shelli M. Poe—to name only the most helpful individuals from a long list of interpreters I have benefited from. Daniel and Shelli were kind enough to offer valuable feedback on early versions of this book, and for their help, I am especially thankful.

An Outline of this Book

I will spend most of this book examining Schleiermacher's theological masterpiece, *Christian Faith*. Part I aims to give a fresh reading of Schleiermacher's dogmatics against its many misreadings. I do not follow a chronological outline of the text but examine it somewhat in reverse. This is on purpose, to shed new light on Schleiermacher's essential arguments before the more controversial elements are discussed. If you have a particular concern about his controversial methodology—i.e., the "feeling of absolute dependence"—then feel free to skip ahead to chapter four. But I have not begun there intentionally so that a better reading of his work may come forward.

In the meantime, here is a helpful rule of thumb to avoid misunderstanding Schleiermacher's methodology: The "feeling of absolute dependence" and "Christian religious self-consciousness" always refers to the relationship God establishes with us by grace. It is not a subjective "feeling" but a perception controlled by and originating from God's self-revelation, Jesus Christ. If we think of these terms relationally, then we will be much closer to understanding Schleiermacher's point.[13]

As in the previous books of this series, I support the chapters of Part I with "sidebar" and "sermon" sub-chapters. Sidebars aim to explore a particular idea more in-depth, to analyze a point of interest constructively, or to clear up a specific misconception. Examples from Schleiermacher's sermons help contextualize his theology into the realm he believed it must be situated in, the Church.

Part II examines the major works of Schleiermacher, although only those works directly related to his theology are studied. We could have discussed his philosophy, pedagogy, or his work on Plato just as well, but I have limited myself to analyzing those texts that have direct consequences on his theology. My limitations as a writer are the primary reason for this. I am less informed in these areas than I am in theology and have little to contribute by examining those texts. But this should not be taken to indicate their lack of importance.

Schleiermacher's thought is so vast and interconnected that there is always the risk of missing the forest for the trees. So I will conclude by outlining a few key themes from Schleiermacher's work. These are highlighted throughout, but I wanted to give them separate consideration because of how vital they are for understanding Schleiermacher rightly.

Finally, I provide a brief reading guide in the hopes that you may come to appreciate Schleiermacher by reading him for yourself. I suggest three possible ways to read *Christian Faith* and explore other notable works of a primary and secondary nature.

On Charity

Schleiermacher's theology and its major impulses have shaped modern theology in numerous ways. Whether or not we agree with the specific ideas Schleiermacher developed, we cannot help but appreciate the significance of his contribution. As B. A. Gerrish writes, "It is the direction he took, more than the conclusions he reached, that makes him the father of modern theology."[14] He casts a long shadow over the theological landscape, and his influence remains strong today, in spite of the numerous criticisms he has suffered.

Many of my readers are likely to come to Schleiermacher from a critical point-of-view, Barthian or otherwise, and so it is helpful to approach his work with a mindset of charity. His legacy is not easily ignored, and if we take the time to understand him correctly, it will only be to our benefit. But to do this, we must give him the "benefit of the doubt." We must read him charitably.

Schleiermacher's own approach to reading those whom he disagreed with is well worth learning from:

> [A]mid the various conflicts which I am necessarily exposed to in my career, and amid the numerous misunderstandings of the extreme parties on both sides, through which I am obliged to wind my way, it is ever a great encouragement to me when I discover even a faint glimmer that leads me to think that we hold the same goal in view, and are labouring for the same end. [...] Thus at least I learn to unite, quietly within myself, with many who believe themselves far distant from me, and herein dwells a peculiar life-giving energy.[15]

Reading with charity is an important hermeneutical mindset, but it is especially beneficial when we are dealing with a figure so controversial—and so misunderstood—such as Schleiermacher. May we seek first to understand and appreciate what he accomplished before we take up the old pitchforks, so that we may, perhaps, realize how unnecessary they were all along.

Stephen D. Morrison
Columbus, 2019

---

1. OG, 36.
2. I initially found this quote in H. R. Mackintosh's *Types of Modern Theology,* 1 (London: Nisbet and Co. LTD, 1937). But I was unable to locate its origin in Hegel—even though others have attributed it to him—so it may be a misquote.
3. *Karl Barth in Plain English*. Columbus: Beloved Publishing, 2017.
4. As I have noted in previous volumes, I am thoroughly an "amateur" theologian. With this, I mean I have no formal training in theology, and so the "education" I refer to is a self-taught regiment of reading. The root of the word "amateur" is the same as "lover." I often call myself an amateur because I am passionate about theology, hold no formal qualifications, and write with a popular-level approach.
5. It is worth noting why the term "Barthian" is problematic. Barth himself strongly disliked it, since he had no desire to form any such "school" after his theology (a conviction he shared with Schleiermacher). To call oneself a "Barthian" is to be at odds with the very heart of Barth's theology, namely, the non-objectifiablity of God. Accordingly, Barth stressed the inability of humans to create a "system" of theology, even calling systematic theology a "contradiction in terms." But the "Barthian" label may be useful for describing those who have been influenced by his work. So in this regard, it is not wrong to say that I am a "Barthian," and that the books in this series have been written from a "Barthian" point of view. Although, the term should be used with caution.
6. *The Word of God the Word of Man,* 196. New York: Harper & Brothers, 1957.
7. *Church Dogmatics* I/1, 303. Peabody: Hendrickson Publishers, 2010.
8. *Barth and Schleiermacher,* 49. Philadelphia: Fortress Press, 1988.
9. Ibid., 50.
10. Quoted in Matthias Gockel: *Barth and Schleiermacher on the Doctrine of Election,* 5.

(Oxford University Press, 2006.) Barth's pronouncement is from a sermon preached on January 19, 1913—six years before publishing *Der Römerbrief* (1919).
11. *Barth and Schleiermacher*, 55-6. Philadelphia: Fortress Press, 1988.
12. Most, if not all, Schleiermacher-scholars agree that Barth misreads Schleiermacher, though fewer Barth-scholars do. The best essay on the subject is James Gordon's "A 'Glaring Misunderstanding'? Schleiermacher, Barth and the Nature of Speculative Theology." (*International Journal of Systematic Theology*, vol. 16 number 3, July 2014; pp. 313-330.)

    One of the most notable figures bridging the gap between Barth and Schleiermacher (from the Barthian-perspective) is Bruce McCormack, whose work on Barth is groundbreaking and influential, if also controversial. See McCormack, *Orthodox and Modern*. (Grand Rapids: Baker Academic, 2008.) Also see Alice Collins, "Barth's Relationship to Schleiermacher: A reassessment." (*Studies in Religion* 17/2, 1988, pp. 213-224.)
13. For example, Robert Williams notes that "the feeling of utter dependence signifies a mode of coexistence with other, and as such discovers and presupposes the other. It can only be understood as a correlation between self and this distinctive other" (*Schleiermacher the Theologian*, 37; Philadelphia: Fortress Press, 1978). So it is an inherently relational concept, not a subjective emotion, yet Schleiermacher's critics so often fail to recognize this distinction and misread him accordingly. The God to Whom we depend absolutely has priority over the self that feels absolutely dependent; it is thus a perception controlled by God and not by the self. So the feeling of absolute dependence is at once the experience of *grace*, and as I will continue to argue throughout this book, Schleiermacher is preeminently a theologian of God's grace.
14. *A Prince of the Church*, 69. Philadelphia: Fortress Press, 1984.
15. *The Life of Schleiermacher: as Unfolded in His Autobiography and Letters*, Vol. 2, 323. London: Smith, Elder and Co., 1860.

BIOGRAPHY

Friedrich Daniel Ernst Schleiermacher was born on November 21, 1768, in Breslau (modern-day Wrocław, Poland) in the Prussian region of Silesia, and he died on February 12, 1834, in Berlin. He was the son of Gottlieb Schleiermacher, a Reformed Church chaplain in the Prussian Army, and his grandfather, Daniel Schleiermacher, was also a Reformed pastor. It is notable that Schleiermacher represents the third generation of Reformed pastors in his family lineage. He spent his life upholding the principles of the Reformed faith as a preacher, professor, and theologian.

Schleiermacher's life could be divided into three major periods. First, his childhood and schooling with the Moravians and later studies at the University of Halle. Second, his time among the romantics in Berlin from 1796-1802, which culminated in the publication of both *On Religion* (1799) and his *Soliloquies* (1800). Third, his systematic period as a professor and pastor up until his death in 1834, which culminated in the publication of his masterpiece, *Christian Faith* (1821/22, second ed. 1830/31), alongside other notable works of systematic character. We will examine Schleiermacher's life in these three periods. They may be loosely described as a developmental period of growth, an early constructive period, and a late systematic period.

1. Developmental Period: Childhood and Education (1768-1795)

Schleiermacher's early development was indebted to the Herrnhuters, or "Moravians," as we say in English. Among the Herrnhuters, Schleiermacher experienced his first spiritual awakening, and it was in their midst that he became an honest doubter who learned to think critically. So it is worth beginning with a brief history of the Moravian Church.

We often think of the Moravian Church according to its renewal under Count Zinzendorf in the eighteenth century, but its history actually traces back to Jan Hus in the early fifteenth century. The Hussite Church predated Martin Luther's German Reformation by one-hundred years and was one of the first Protestant churches to rebel against Rome. The "Bohemian Reformation" is less known but no less significant. Arguably, Hus instituted the very first Protestant Church. He was burned at the stake for his teachings in 1415, and his ashes were thrown into the Rhine River to avoid veneration. But this only led to further rebellion against Papal authority, leading to the Hussite Wars. Hus' influence was so profound that in the sixteenth century a majority of the Bohemian and Moravian lands were Protestant. But after widespread political changes in the region, which took place in the time leading up to the eighteenth century, the Protestant Hussites were heavily persecuted and forced underground. This set the stage for the Church's revival under the leadership of the most famous Herrnhuter, Count Zinzendorf.

Zinzendorf used his estates in Berthelsdorf to establish a model Christian community. His concern for the poor led him to welcome a settlement of persecuted Protestants from Moravia on his lands. These were the remnants of Jan Hus' Protestant Church in Czech, and it is why we call them the "Moravians" still today. Under Zinzendorf's guidance, the Moravians became a thriving community dedicated to personal piety, prayer, and missions. A revival broke out, in which the Spirit moved powerfully among them as in the days of Pentecost. As a result, the community multiplied.

Their radical approach to missions and prayer are notable examples of the Moravian spirit. The community was committed to continuous, uninterrupted prayer, which endured for over one-hundred years. The Moravians are forerunners of modern-day prayer houses and movements, such as the International House of Prayer in Kansas City. Likewise, their missionary efforts are a source of inspiration for modern missionary movements, such as Youth With a Mission (YWAM). The Moravians were so radical in their evangelical efforts that some willingly sold themselves into slavery to reach lost souls on new continents. From the slave-boats, they would shout their anthem: "May the Lamb that was slain receive the reward of His suffering!" Their emphasis on piety, missions, prayer, and devotion to the blood of Christ remained hallmarks of the community throughout Schleiermacher's time with them.

The Schleiermacher family first became acquainted with the left-wing Reformed Herrnhuter Brethren Church in 1778. Gottlieb Schleiermacher had a profound conversion experience with the Herrnhuters, and Friedrich himself had a similar experience at the age of eleven. Many sleepless nights of unrest resulted in Friedrich's first inner transformation, which was chiefly an awakening to God's saving grace. Schleiermacher's theology is, perhaps above all else, a theology of grace, though this fact has often been poorly neglected. The grace of God so envelops his entire outlook that only a poor reading of his theology ignores its significance. Even at the young age of eleven, God's grace was *the* hallmark of his life.

Schleiermacher writes reflectively about his awakening to a "higher life" in 1802:

> [H]ere my consciousness of the relation of human beings to a higher world first arose [...] Here there first developed that mystical disposition which is so essential to me and has saved and preserved me under all the assaults of skepticism.[1]

At the age of fourteen, only a few months after a second transformative experience in Gnadenfrei, Schleiermacher was sent to Niesky to study with the Herrnhuters. Sadly, he would never see either of his parents again. His mother died later that same year (1783), and while he regularly corresponded with his father up until his death in 1794, he never saw him again in person.

Life with the Herrnhuters was initially very productive and fruitful for Schleiermacher. The community participated in four daily services, and the immediate presence of God in the innermost-self was stressed with exceptional vigor. Zinzendorf and his followers had rejected the outside world, and so severe restrictions were enforced, including the prohibition of card games, swimming, and chess. Academically, however, there was a degree of freedom permitted, which gave Schleiermacher space to discover his love for classical Greek literature and philosophy. This passion continued for the rest of his life —including his favorite philosopher, Plato, whom he first discovered later at Halle.

In 1785, Schleiermacher left to attend the Herrnhuter's theological school at Barby, walking for five days with ten of his classmates through the Prussian wilderness. His education was far less free in Barby than it was in Niesky. He was no longer permitted to read poetry or literature, since everything from the outside world was deemed impure and thus rejected. But Schleiermacher persisted through strict censorship and formed a small group of students who met secretly to study classic and contemporary literature, including recent texts of enlightenment philosophy. They called themselves the "independent thinkers." The book that seemed to impact them the most was Goethe's *The Sorrows of Young Werther*. The humanism of that text, and other lofty books like it, offered a radically different perception of the world than the one taught by the Herrnhuters. The Herrnhuters had so heavily emphasized the sinfulness of human beings that the humanistic picture presented in Goethe was nothing short of a revelation.

At the age of nineteen, Schleiermacher found himself in sharp conflict with the community and its teachings, but also with his father. He had become an honest doubter, but the strict education of the Moravians had no tolerance for uncertainty. For them, doubt was the expression of a sinful will. Uncertainty regarding the divinity of Christ and the necessity of a blood atonement put him at significant odds with their teachings. Schleiermacher's honesty regarding his struggles led to him eventually leaving the Brethren to attend Halle University.

Schleiermacher never renounced his religious training completely, as he later wrote in a letter, "I have become a Herrnhuter again, only of a higher order."[2] Likewise, in *On Religion,* he famously described his early piety:

> Now piety was, as it were, the maternal womb in whose sacred obscurity my young life was nourished and prepared for a world still closed to it. Before my spirit had found its distinctive sphere in the search for knowledge and in the mature experience of life, it found its vital breath in piety. As I began to sift out the faith of my fathers and to clear the rubbish of former ages from my thoughts and feelings piety supported me. As the childhood images of God and immortality vanished before my doubting eyes piety remained.[3]

Schleiermacher's first great book argued that the essence of religion is not what we do or think but *piety* itself, a "sense and taste for the infinite" (OR, 82). In other words, it is in the relationship God forms with us by grace, not by any works we perform or doctrines we subscribe to, that religion thrives. His doubts about certain doctrines of faith, those vanishing beliefs of his childhood, were not the *end* of his faith but its transformation into something "higher." Piety remained, and with it, the consciousness of God's grace, but the doctrines themselves faded away. This distinction between the *knowledge* of faith and faith itself (its *essence*) is vital. Did Schleiermacher lose his faith during this time? No, his faith remained secure. What he lost, however, was the childish acceptance of what he had been taught to believe. In short, he was becoming a critical thinker. His faith, however, did not rest on a foundation of intellectual agreement with a system of belief but on the grace of God.

This distinction was lost on his father, however, in a heartbreaking exchange of letters between 1786 and 1787. Schleiermacher first tested the waters, so to speak, by asking his father about those who harbor doubts about certain doctrines. His father presumed he was referring to another student, when in fact Schleiermacher was referring to himself. Finally, Schleiermacher confessed that these doubts had arisen in him:

I confessed to you, in my last letter, my dissatisfaction with the limited scope of my position here, and pointed out how easily, under such circumstances, religious doubts may, in our times, arise among young people. I thus endeavored to prepare you for the intelligence that these doubts have been awakened in me, but I did not attain my object. You believed that your answer had set me at rest; and for six whole months I most unjustifiably remained silent, because I could not find it in my heart to destroy this illusion.

Faith is the regalia of the Godhead [i.e., God's royal due], you say. Alas! dearest father, if you believe that, without this faith, no one can attain to salvation in the next world, nor to tranquility in this—and such, I know, is your belief—oh! then, pray to God to grant it to me, for to me it is now lost. I cannot believe that He, who called Himself the Son of Man, was the true, eternal God; I cannot believe that His death was a vicarious atonement, because He never expressly said so Himself; and I cannot believe it to have been necessary, because God, who evidently did not create men for perfection, but for the pursuit of it, cannot possibly intend to punish them eternally, because they have not attained it.[4]

Schleiermacher signed, "Your distressed and most dutiful son." Much to his dismay, the letter was not well received by his father, and a discord developed in their relationship. The doubts he confessed were taken to mean the renunciation of his faith, when, in fact, Schleiermacher was merely expressing doubt in the *thoughts* of piety and not renouncing piety itself. Admittedly, he could have been more clear about this, but perhaps he could not articulate the difference yet, which he later expressed so well in *On Religion*. A reconciliation eventually took place between father and son, although the letters that detail this have been lost. Gottlieb's uncle, Samuel, wrote to this perplexed father with some words of advice. He said that honest doubting deserves its proper time and must be dealt with gently. It seems this opinion swayed Schleiermacher's father, and they were reconciled. Not much is know beyond this, however.

We should not read Schleiermacher's letter as a dogmatic indication of his mature theology. While these uncertainties may have remained and could possibly be seen in his mature work, he does not outright reject the doctrines mentioned above. Doubt does not mean denial. Instead, he remained faithful to the original intentions of these doctrines, to their *spirit*, without restricting himself to their *letter*. He was at once faithful *and* modern in his approach.

Schleiermacher benefited a great deal from his time with the Moravians, even if he left their care slightly disillusioned. He learned Hebrew, Greek, Latin, English, and French. This profound grasp of languages was an indispensable resource for Schleiermacher as a scholar. He later wrote that because of his schooling, both independently and among the Brethren, he "learned to contemplate the world from an idea out."[5] In other words, he was given the tools to think. It is unfortunate, however, that the same people who taught him to think for himself were dissatisfied with the results. So he outgrew them and sought a new environment to continue his education.

Schleiermacher left Barby for Halle University in 1787. He lived with his uncle, Samuel, who was a professor at the university. Schleiermacher was a good student, but he seemed to prioritize his own independent studies over university lectures, which he rarely attended. A critical focus of these independent readings was his study of Kant. He devoted himself to understanding the famous philosopher. He even met him once, though it was an uneventful occasion for both men. Schleiermacher's relationship with Kant is a complicated one, but it seems to have been at once appreciative and severely critical. The extent to which it is more the former or the latter is up for debate. Schleiermacher was also introduced to Plato and Aristotle at Halle. Plato, far more than Kant, should be considered the most significant philosopher in Schleiermacher's thought. At the very least, Plato was his favorite. He once expressed as much in a letter, writing, "There is no author who has affected me as much and who has initiate me into the holiest of holies—not only of philosophy, but of all humanity—as this divine man."[6]

Schleiermacher received "good" or "very good" scores on all his exams, except, ironically, for his exam in dogmatics, which received "satisfactory" marks. From 1790 until 1793, Schleiermacher lived in Schlobitten and worked as a private tutor for the pious and aristocratic family of Count Dohna. Before this move, he briefly lived in Drossen, but it was a time of profound depression and skepticism. Schlobitten, however, was a fruitful time of spiritual and intellectual recovery.

While the daily events of his tutoring position were mundane, the life he lived among the family rejuvenated Schleiermacher and taught him a new outlook on life. He described it to his father:

> Here my heart is properly nurtured and need not wither under the weeds of cold erudition and my religious feelings do not die under theological speculation. Here I enjoy the family life for which man is made and this warms my heart [...] I am coming to know both myself and others.[7]

Here Schleiermacher learned the value of community, that life is best *shared*. The dialectic of an individual bound to the community and the community to an individual is a major theme of his theology and philosophy. Humanity is inescapably interconnected. During this time, Schleiermacher also discovered a love for preaching, and he slowly crafted his skills. He would send weekly sermons to his father and uncle for correction and comment.

Differences in political and theological opinions with the Count put an end to Schleiermacher's time with the family, though the departure was mutually cordial. He went back to Drossen initially, though he soon took up the position of an assistant pastor in Landsberg, which lasted from 1794 until 1796. Schleiermacher had to complete his second theological exams before he could begin, which he did in 1794, receiving once again only satisfactory marks in dogmatics. Schleiermacher's father died during his first year at Landsberg, which deeply moved him. Their relationship had become very warm.

At the age of twenty-eight, Schleiermacher accepted his first pastoral assignment at the Charité Hospital in Berlin. His inaugural sermon was preached on September 18, 1796—signifying the end of his developmental period. But it also marked the beginning of his first constructive period, which produced several important philosophical and theological works, including his first major book, *On Religion*.

2. Early Constructive Period: Berlin and On Religion (1796-1802)

From 1796-1802, Schleiermacher lived in Berlin and actively participated in one of the dominant intellectual movements of the era: German Romanticism. But we must not misconstrue Schleiermacher as a Romantic thinker himself. Schleiermacher's *On Religion* addressed these "cultured despisers" as an *outsider*. Ultimately, he did not wish to be molded by Romanticism but to shape it himself. It is just as improper to designate him as a "Romantic" as it would be to call him a "Kantian" (though he has been called both). In the same way that Schleiermacher's relation to Kant was at once critical and appreciative, so was his relationship with the Romantics. *On Religion* was a *counter-cultural* book—not the passive product of its environment but a catalyst for its reform. It is important to remember that Schleiermacher was, above all else, a pastor and minister of the Gospel. He was an outsider among the Romantics. Although there was undoubtedly some degree of romantic influence on his thinking, Schleiermacher never wanted to be anything else but a servant of the Word.

This was also a very productive time for Schleiermacher. On top of his pastoral duties, Schleiermacher wrote articles, translated English sermons and travel books, and developed new friendships. In 1799 and 1800, he published essays that defended the full civil rights of women and Jews, showing a concern for social issues in a way that was far ahead of his time. He also fell in love, tragically, with a married woman. Eleonore von Grunow was unhappily married to a Lutheran pastor, and Schleiermacher waited six dreadful years for her to make up her mind about him. He tried to convince her to leave her husband and marry him, but he also gave her space to make the decision for herself. Finally, she decided to remain married. The mixture of this loss and the still recent death of his father set Schleiermacher into a whirlwind of productive activity. Schleiermacher was a remarkably disciplined writer, but he displayed an even more profound output than usual in this period of his life.

It was during this time that Schleiermacher also started his most significant translation project, a critical German edition of the works of Plato. The project began with the help of his friend and brief roommate, Friedrich Schlegel. Eventually, however, the burden fell entirely on Schleiermacher. His work as a Plato scholar often goes unnoticed, but it remains influential still today. According to Julia Lamm, "Now, almost two hundred years later, his translation not only dominates sales of paperback editions of Plato in Germany but also remains an authoritative translation for scholars."[8]

All this productive energy culminated in his first great work, *On Religion*. It was written in just two months, between February and April 1799. He published it anonymously, although it was not long before he was discovered to be its author. Less than a year later he published a complementary volume, his *Soliloquies*, written in less than a month in the fall of 1799. It was released as a "new year's gift" in 1800. These two books make up a kind of manifesto for his early life and career, though the rhetorical style of both works is sharply distinct from his late systematic style. On top of all this productivity, he was faithful to his pastoral duties, which included daily prayer visits to the sick and poor at the hospital and preaching every Sunday.

The impact of *On Religion* was profound, not only for his circle of friends in Berlin but all throughout the theological world. Daniel Schenkel describes the book's impact: "The *Speeches* [OR] went off like Congreve rockets into the paper tabernacles of the prevailing Enlightened theology."[9] Schleiermacher's book threw down the gauntlet on rationalism and supernaturalism. Rationalism was dominant among the Enlightenment theologians, who had restricted faith to reason. Supernaturalism was dominant among the more conservative theologians, who had argued for a supernatural interpretation of faith and its doctrines. Schleiermacher found himself standing against both tendencies for the rest of his life, implicitly arguing against them in his mature work, *Christian Faith*.

Accordingly, it is worth noting that Schleiermacher never considered to be himself a liberal theologian. He would, perhaps, call himself a *centrist*. He stood opposed to the radical opinions of both the liberal and conservative thinkers of his time. While today we often call him the father of modern liberal theology, this is a title Schleiermacher would have rejected. He thought of himself as a moderate. Neither the reductionistic rationalism of the Enlightenment nor the reactionary traditionalism of the supernaturalists would do. As Walter Wyman notes, "It is conventional to call Schleiermacher the father of liberal theology; [but] he saw himself as a centrist, working out a third alternative between the extremes of rationalism and supernaturalism."[10]

Because Schleiermacher proposed such a paradigm-shattering interpretation of religion, he was often misunderstood by his peers. He was deemed a Spinozist, a pantheist, and even an atheist because of *On Religion*. He denied all these claims. Yet, in spite of these controversies, the fact remains that Schleiermacher's book did have a significant impact on the spirituality of his generation. According to Redeker:

> If there is to be a new inquiry into Schleiermacher's theological significance it must recover one insight above all which recent Schleiermacher criticism has either forgotten or overlooked, namely, that a large number of his contemporaries, particularly the younger generation of theologians around 1800, did not see Schleiermacher at all the way we do. In the course of their lives many of them repeatedly acknowledge his decisive influence on their faith and theology.[11]

In his autobiography, the Lutheran theologian Claus Harms reflected on Schleiermacher's impact, "In my final academic years I read Schleiermacher's *Speeches*; they killed rationalism for me. I cannot say it more clearly: here began what I call the hour of birth for my higher life."[12] Others credit Schleiermacher's writings—especially his sermons, both preached and written—as important catalysts for their spiritual lives. In fact, Schleiermacher was more revered as a preacher during his lifetime than he ever was as a dogmatic theologian. Today we acknowledge his contribution to dogmatics, but in his own day, he was, first and foremost, a preacher of the Word. He admitted as much himself, declaring, "I always have [wished] to be nothing but a servant of this divine Word."[13] The impact of his work, especially *On Religion*, is seldom considered—or if it is, it is only as a secondary factor after his academic contributions. But undeniably, the book was a catalyst for the religious development of many, and recognizing this will give us the proper perspective on Schleiermacher and the impact his work had on the public.

In 1802, Schleiermacher took up a pastoral assignment in the small, Reformed congregation of Stolp, situated along the Baltic coastline. The romantic environment of Berlin faded away, and Schleiermacher focused on his sermons. Schleiermacher writes about his growing determination as a preacher:

> This calling has become more and more dear to me, even in its unpretentious form and in its unhappy relation to the spirit of the times. If I had to give it up I believe I would grieve even more deeply than for all that I have now lost.[14]

He also worked diligently on two significant, methodologically intensive, philosophical projects. Both endeavors were highly self-critical, however, and reflected a new sense of growth. Schleiermacher was beginning to realize that the need was now for systematic thought, not rhetorical flourishes. This is arguably the major difference between his early and late constructive periods. The former was rhetorical and prose-oriented, while the latter was more methodologically intensive and systematic. This shift began to develop in Stolp.

The first text he worked on was his translation of Plato, but the second is often considered to be his first great scholarly work, *Outlines of a Critique of Previous Ethical Theories* (1803). This text took eleven months of strenuous work to complete. The result was a sharply critical piece that examined previous ethical systems, with only Plato and Spinoza receiving even slightly favorable judgments. But the book had little to no effect on philosophy at the time, which disappointed Schleiermacher greatly.

The newly formed Würzburg University invited Schleiermacher to be a professor of ethics and pastoral theology in 1803. He was hesitant at first, but finally accepted their offer when it was promised that he could still pursue his great love of preaching. But he never made it to Würzburg. The Prussian throne intervened and called Schleiermacher to Halle instead, offering him both the position of *Professor Extraordinarius* and University Preacher. After a year at the university, Schleiermacher became a full member of the faculty, *Professor Ordinarius*.

The Prussian government had two motivations for appointing Schleiermacher to Halle. First, they wanted Halle to become the most distinguished Prussian university, and second, they hoped to foster unity between the Lutheran and Reformed Churches. The University of Halle was predominantly Lutheran, as was all of Prussia at the time, and so Schleiermacher, as a prominent Reformed churchman and theologian, was a fitting appointment. Halle became the first integrated faculty.

Today, the Reformed character of Schleiermacher's theology is often debated, but in his own time, there was no question about it. Schleiermacher was among the minority with his Reformed faith, and there was no mistaking the distinction.

1803 and 1804 are overlapping years between Schleiermacher's early and late periods. His early period ends with the publication of a final rhetorical work, *Christmas Eve,* in 1804. His late systematic period begins with the publication of his first great academic work, *Outlines of a Critique of Previous Ethical Theories,* in 1803. In his transition to life as an academic, these two works bookend the two periods of his adult life.

Christmas Eve was written rapidly in three weeks after a sudden bolt of inspiration in December 1804. He gave it to his friends as a Christmas gift, but they encouraged him to publish it, which he did in January 1805. *Christmas Eve* contains elements that hint towards Schleiermacher's new systematic pathway, even though its form remained tied to the rhetorical attempts of his early period. Accordingly, Richard Niebuhr considered the text a good entry-point for his study of Schleiermacher. The book was written after the style of the Platonic dialogues, in which a group of friends gather for a Christmas Eve celebration and discuss the meaning of the incarnation. Niebuhr rightly notes that when we read this text, we should refrain from trying to find Schleiermacher's voice in any one character. Each character, at times, reflects Schleiermacher's personality and thoughts. Its message is found in *dialogue,* not in any one monologue.

Ultimately, the text's central theme is joy in the arrival of the Christ child. Terrence Tice notes, "Schleiermacher carries the incarnational idea further than many theologians have, by stressing what Jesus's sharing of his life with others unto death has actually effected within the human community."[15] Christ's effect on the community is displayed by the joyful celebration of Schleiermacher's characters. As Niebuhr writes, "The theme of this Christmas symposium is, then, the new life released in the nativity of Christ and the inward appropriation of the same as joy and peace through the feast of Christmas."[16]

Schleiermacher's late systematic period was just as multi-faceted as it was productive. But at the center of his complex theology remained one simple emphasis: Jesus Christ our Redeemer. This was already present in Schleiermacher's *Christmas Eve* and continues all the way until his theological masterpiece, *Christian Faith*. As such, Schleiermacher's systematic period is at once his Christomorphic period, in which everything has its reference point in Christ and redemption.

3. Late Systematic Period (1803-1834)

Schleiermacher's professorship at Halle lasted until 1806. His lectures centered around New Testament studies, which he considered essential to every student's theological development. This included extensive work on Paul's letters. His course on Galatians was one of his most popular, with 120 regular attendants. Schleiermacher wanted to understand Paul as much as he had come to understand Plato. He also lectured on Christian ethics, dogmatics, and Church history. In between lectures, he worked on his Plato translation.

On October 17, 1806, Napoleon's army invaded Halle and effectively put an end to the University. Schleiermacher tried to remain in Halle without his post, but he could no longer sustain himself and returned to Berlin in 1807. He published a critical study of 1 Timothy, applying the historical-critical method of Biblical interpretation to the text. He also published, in 1808, an essay entitled *Occasional Thoughts on Universities.* This text led to his direct involvement in the founding of the University of Berlin, where he would remain for the rest of his life.

Although Schleiermacher is not always recognized as a founder of the University (because he did not play an original role in its planning), he was nevertheless instrumental in determining how the University of Berlin came to be organized. And because of how influential the University became (it is often referred to as the "Humboldtian model of higher education"), Schleiermacher's influence helped determine how modern universities are organized still today.

Wilhelm von Humboldt founded the University of Berlin in 1809. He implemented several key ideas from Schleiermacher's essay and regularly sought his guidance as a collaborator. Schleiermacher opposed technical schools of higher learning and favored schools that stressed the development of the individual in a wide variety of fields. This was the first idea the University adopted from Schleiermacher. Its aim, therefore, was holistic: To represent the totality of knowledge, not just one particular aspect of it. Schleiermacher wrote, "There is no productive scientific capacity in the absence of the speculative spirit."[17] Empty speculation is not meant here, but rather a higher consciousness of knowledge as a totality rather than an isolated focus on one part. Accordingly, the philosophical faculty became predominate over all others because philosophy deals with the very nature and act of learning itself. Whenever a university today devotes itself to the development of a well-rounded person rather than to merely a skilled tradesman, then this is the influence of Schleiermacher and the University of Berlin.

The second idea Humboldt implemented from Schleiermacher was the connection between research and teaching. The professor should be a mediator between pure academia and technical practice. The university should, therefore, encourage students not merely to repeat a specific list of facts and figures, but to become captivated by the very idea of knowledge itself within the vast array of specializations. To be *learners,* not merely the learned, is the goal of higher education. But only if professors themselves are given the freedom to remain learners can this message be conveyed, and so they must be free to continue their research alongside teaching.

Finally, Schleiermacher's third contribution was to stress the importance of the separation of state and university. The state must give the university its proper space and freedom to pursue research and teaching.

Schleiermacher's primary influence on the University of Berlin, however, was his own work as a scholar and professor. He was named the first dean of the theological faculty in 1810. He taught on a wide range of subjects during his time there. In theology, he lectured on just about every conceivable topic, except for the Old Testament. In philosophy, he taught dialectics, ethics, psychology, pedagogy, aesthetics, and hermeneutics. In addition to his daily lectures, Schleiermacher was a faithful preacher every Sunday at Trinity Church, an avid correspondent with friends and family, an administrator for the University, and a productive writer. He would often stay up late into the night reading or writing by candlelight, which led to poor eyesight later in life. Since his lectures always began early in the morning (6 AM), we might estimate that he slept, on average, just four or five hours a day. His determination to pursue such a wide range of fields, and with such excellence, is staggering.

In addition to his busy schedule, Schleiermacher, at the age of forty, married Henriette von Willich (1809). She was the widow of his friend, Johann Ehrenfried Theodor von Willich. Together they had four children in addition to the two from her previous marriage.

In 1811, Schleiermacher published one of his most important works, *Brief Outline of Theology as a Field of Study*. This text set out to organize the field of theology into an ingenious three-part schema: philosophical, historical, and practical theology. It set out to survey both the unity and diversity of the field from a single point of view, namely, that theology's primary goal is to serve the Church. Every division of the field, therefore, works towards that end.

It was also during this time that Schleiermacher likely began thinking about the construction of his masterpiece, *Christian Faith*. The primary impulses of that system were starting to take shape, and it is likely that he had a working outline formed in the back of his mind in the ten years between *Brief Outline* and the first edition of *Christian Faith* in 1821. The Church-oriented perspective articulated in *Brief Outline* was one such impulse. Another conviction of Schleiermacher's dogmatics was his refusal to engage in empty speculation. He sought to ground dogmatics in the concrete experience of the Christian community. This impulse is arguably one of the most significant innovations of his theology. It includes Schleiermacher's dedication to the non-objectification of God and thus the refusal to anthropomorphize God. The significance of this impulse, as well as the content of his dogmatics, will be examined in Part I of this book.

As an academic, Schleiermacher's influence was and remains widespread. Tice notes, "[I]n the modern era as a whole, scarcely any area of theology has failed to be touched by his work."[18] But his influence was not limited to the realm of theology. He also decisively shaped an entire discipline (hermeneutics), as well as contributing much to philosophy and politics. Philosophical ethics, dialectics, and Platonic scholarship, to name just a few fields, are all indebted to Schleiermacher's work. He casts a massive shadow over the modern era.

During his lifetime, however, Schleiermacher was celebrated most of all as a preacher. When he died on February 12, 1834, a tenth of the city of Berlin attended his funeral. It was practically a day of mourning, as Martin Redeker writes, "His death moved the entire population of Berlin."[19] It is estimated that as many as twenty thousand people followed his casket through the streets. Even Prussian royalty, including the Queen, paid their respects. There is no doubt that some of the attendants were theology students or those who had read his dogmatics, but it is far more likely that such a massive crowd gathered to pay their respects to Schleiermacher the preacher, not necessarily the theologian.

Schleiermacher's death is a fitting testimony to the enduring legacy of his life. On February 2, 1834, he preached his last sermon at Trinity Church. Ten days later he died of pneumonia at the age of sixty-five. He was urged by friends and family to rest and not continue with his lectures, but he stressed how important his work was to him, especially the work of preaching the Gospel. On February 6, he delivered two lectures, attended a catechizing of the youth, and saw to a few administrative duties at the University. Towards the end of the day, he was very hoarse and suffered from chills. On the night of February 11, he asked his wife to read a hymn to him. His friend and colleague, Dr. Friedrich Lücke, recounts what took place the next day and in his final hours:

> The last days and hours of his life were pervaded and irradiated by the presence of religion. [...] Affectionately mindful of children and friends, and, in proportion as he drew nearer to the important moment, more profoundly immersed in love, as the inmost spring of his being, he said, 'To the children I leave the saying of St John, 'Love one another!' [...]
>
> The last morning, his suffering visibly increased [...] [After sending away the children,] he laid his two forefingers upon his left eye, as he often did when reflecting deeply, and began to speak: 'We have the reconciliation-death of Jesus Christ, his body and his blood.'—While he thus engaged, he had raised himself up, his features began to grow animated, his voice became clear and strong, and he said with priestly solemnity, 'Are ye one with me in this faith?' to which his friends replied with a loud 'Yea!' 'Then let us celebrate the Lord's Supper! But there can be no talk of sacristan. Quick, quick! Let no one stumble at matters of form!' After that which was necessary for the purpose had been fetched [...], he began, with increasingly radiant features, and eyes in which there had returned a wonderful, indescribable brightness, nay, a sublime glow of affection, with which he looked upon those around him,—to utter a few

words of prayer and of introduction to the sacred service. After this, addressing in full and aloud, to each individual, and last of all to himself, the words of the institution [Matt. 26:26; 1 Cor. 11:23-29], he first gave the bread and the wine to the others who were present, then partook of them himself, and said, 'Upon these words of Scripture I abide; they are the foundation of my faith.' After he had pronounced the benediction, his eye first turned once more towards his consort with an expression of perfect love, and then he looked at each individual with affecting and fervent cordiality, uttering these words,—'Thus are we, and abide, in *this* love and fellowship, *one!*' He laid himself back upon the pillow. The radiance still rested upon his features. After some minutes he said, 'Now I can hold out here no longer;' and again, 'Give me another position.' He was laid upon his side; he breathed a few times; life came to a stand. The children had entered the room in the mean time, and surrounded the bed, knelling. His eye gradually closed.[20]

This moving account of Schleiermacher's final day summarizes well the central obsession of his life: Jesus Christ. That his last desire was to take Communion, in the company of his beloved friends and family, is a fitting testimony to the spirit of his life and thought. Above all else, Schleiermacher was a Christian. And for him, that meant living in the fellowship of others. These two things—his friends and his faith—were the anchors of his life.

Schleiermacher's legacy is not without controversy. But even the harshest critic cannot help but marvel at his devotion, determination, and the accomplishments that sprung forth from his unquenchable spirit. Above all else, he was a minister of the Gospel.

---

1. Quoted in Terrence Tice: *Schleiermacher (Abingdon Pillars of Theology)*, 2. Nashville: Abingdon Press, 2006.
2. *The Life of Schleiermacher: as Unfolded in His Autobiography and Letters,* Vol. 1, 284. London: Smith, Elder and Co., 1860.
3. OR, 47-8.
4. *The Life of Schleiermacher: as Unfolded in His Autobiography and Letters,* Vol. 1, 46-7. London: Smith, Elder and Co., 1860.
5. Quoted in Terrence Tice: *Schleiermacher (Abingdon Pillars of Theology)*, 3. Nashville: Abingdon Press, 2006.
6. Quoted in Julia Lamm: "Schleiermacher as Plato Scholar," 209. *The Journal of Religion* Vol. 80, No. 2 (Apr. 2000), pp. 206-239.
7. Quoted in Martin Redeker: *Schleiermacher: Life and Thought,* 19. Philadelphia: Fortress Press, 1973.
8. "Schleiermacher as Plato Scholar," 207. *The Journal of Religion* Vol. 80, No. 2 (Apr. 2000), pp. 206-239.
9. Quoted in Martin Redeker: *Schleiermacher: Life and Thought,* 63. Philadelphia: Fortress Press, 1973.
10. "Sin and Redemption," *Cambridge Companion to Friedrich Schleiermacher,* 146. Cambridge University Press, 2005.
11. *Schleiermacher: Life and Thought,* 34. Philadelphia: Fortress Press, 1973.

12. Quoted in Martin Redeker: *Schleiermacher: Life and Thought,* 34. Philadelphia: Fortress Press, 1973.
13. *Servant of the Word,* 211. Philadelphia: Fortress Press, 1987.
14. Quoted in Martin Redeker: *Schleiermacher: Life and Thought,* 73. Philadelphia: Fortress Press, 1973.
15. "Editor's Introduction," *Christmas Eve Celebration,* xxvii. Eugene: Cascade Books, 2010.
16. *Schleiermacher on Christ and Religion,* 43. New York: Charles Scribner's Sons, 1964.
17. Quoted in Martin Redeker: *Schleiermacher: Life and Thought,* 96. Philadelphia: Fortress Press, 1973.
18. *Schleiermacher (Abingdon Pillars of Theology),* 17. Nashville: Abingdon Press, 2006.
19. *Schleiermacher: Life and Thought,* 212. Philadelphia: Fortress Press, 1973.
20. *Reminiscences of Schleiermacher,* 84-6. Columbus: Beloved Publishing, 2018.

PART I
CHRISTIAN FAITH

1

ELECTION, COMMUNITY, AND GRACE

SUMMARY: Schleiermacher's innovative doctrine of election establishes two essential points. First, he is preeminently a theologian of grace. Second, his theology is tremendously community-centric and forbids individualistic interpretations of faith. Schleiermacher stands out as one of the first theologians to offer an innovative revision to the doctrine of election since Augustine.

IN SCHLEIERMACHER'S OWN WORDS:

Community is something essential to human nature.[1]

[O]ne cannot speak, in particular, of a divine decree concerning each individual person. Rather, we can say that there is only *one* decree by which God determines what will become of each and every human being and thus that this decree is not at all different from the order according to which the dead mass is quickened by the divine Spirit.[2]

[T]he election and reprobation of individuals are simply the two contrasted yet in each instance correlated aspects of one and the same decree, whereby through divine power, yet in a natural way, the human race is to be transformed into the spiritual body of Christ.[3]

SECONDARY QUOTES:

> Schleiermacher, like the Moravians, attributed the awakening of religious feeling not to the initiative of the believer but to the free grace of God—in other words, he viewed religious awareness as depending upon and arising from grace. It is surprising how often superficial evaluations of Schleiermacher fail to grasp the profound sense of grace that suffuses his whole theology. [...] Indeed, Schleiermacher's well-known definition of religion as the feeling of absolute dependence is perhaps best understood as the awareness of the utter 'givenness' of faith. Schleiermacher was a theologian of grace.[4]
>
> — C. W. CHRISTIAN

Introduction

There are three reasons why I want to begin by considering Schleiermacher's doctrine of election. First, and most simply, when I began my own research into Schleiermacher's thought, I was surprised to discover just how profound his doctrine of election was but also how little I had heard about it. I quickly came to suspect that Barth owed an unspoken debt to Schleiermacher for some of the major impulses behind his ground-breaking work in *Church Dogmatics* II/2.[5] In this sense, Schleiermacher is a kind of midway point between Calvin and Barth, and his work on election should be taken just as seriously as theirs. As B. A. Gerrish notes, Schleiermacher was actually the first theologian since Augustine to develop the doctrine of election into something new (since Calvin mostly followed Augustine).[6] Furthermore, Alexander Schweizer argued that Schleiermacher effected the revival of particularly *Reformed* theology with his doctrine of election.[7] Even though it is often overlooked, it is a significant contribution, and so we will begin with Schleiermacher's doctrine of election for the sake of recapturing its significance for theology today.

Second, I want to begin here to combat what is likely the most substantial misunderstanding surrounding Schleiermacher's theology, namely, his supposed "subjectivism." The standard interpretation goes something like this: "Schleiermacher based his theology on the subjective feelings of human beings, which in turn makes God the highest projection of the human spirit. Schleiermacher was unorthodox and denounced his faith. He retained Christian elements in name alone, but his system was fundamentally philosophical and speculative. Schleiermacher speaks of God by speaking of humanity in a loud voice—that is, by projecting the human spirit into the cosmos and calling it 'God.'"

This is not only a poor misreading of Schleiermacher but, as I hope to show, it is plainly wrong. One of the first steps in overcoming this misunderstanding is to recognize just how completely the doctrine of grace permeates Schleiermacher's theology. The doctrine of election, then, solidifies the fact that it is not the individual who seeks God, but it is God who seeks the individual. God is always before us. Christ is the author and perfecter of our faith. Schleiermacher's infamous "feeling of absolute dependence" will be misunderstood whenever we fail to recognize that Schleiermacher was, perhaps above all else, a *theologian of grace*. That God is gracious towards us as the One to whom we depend absolutely is the most basic statement of his theology; thus, the fundamental theme of Schleiermacher's theology is grace.

Third, beginning here will help emphasize a vital presupposition of Schleiermacher's thought, that community is essential to human nature. To be human is to be related to others. This results in a community-centric approach to theology, which can be seen in Schleiermacher's doctrine of election but also his doctrine of sin.

Finally, I want to be clear that I am not attempting to hold up the doctrine of election as an interpretive key for the rest of Schleiermacher's theology. The incredible nuance of his work would be devalued if we attempted to subdue it under one doctrine. Election is not the central doctrine of his theology, however vital it may be.[8] In fact, Schleiermacher offers fewer than forty pages in *Christian Faith* to describe it (out of a thousand). Just because this is a helpful place for us to start does not mean it will remain the most important.

General Overview in Contrast with Calvin and Luther

What makes Schleiermacher's doctrine of election significant? Recognizing the key differences between Schleiermacher, Calvin, and Luther will best display the innovation of his approach. So we will begin by contrasting Schleiermacher's position against these classical conceptions of election.

Who does the divine decree address?

- CALVIN AND LUTHER: Individuals.
- SCHLEIERMACHER: Humanity.

Is it a single or double decree?

- LUTHER: A single decree of those whose faith God foreknows.
- CALVIN: A double decree of election and reprobation.

- SCHLEIERMACHER: A single decree for all humanity.

Who are the elect?

- LUTHER: Those whose faith God has foreseen.
- CALVIN: Those preordained to election due to God's good pleasure.
- SCHLEIERMACHER: All humanity.

Who are the reprobate?

- LUTHER: Those who resist faith.
- CALVIN: Those preordained to reprobation.
- SCHLEIERMACHER: Temporarily, those not yet regenerated. Eternally, no one.

What is death's role in election?

- LUTHER AND CALVIN: Death is the final cut-off point.
- SCHLEIERMACHER: Death is a stage of development. A person's state of being at death is not permanent, and those who die as reprobates will not remain so eternally.

Is salvation universal or particular? Does God will for all to be saved?

- LUTHER: God's will is universal but the success of salvation is particular. Only some will be saved.
- CALVIN: God's will is particular and the success of salvation is particular. Only some will be saved.
- SCHLEIERMACHER: God's will and the success of salvation are both universal, what God wills God does. All will be saved.

Four points highlight the originality of Schleiermacher's doctrine of election:

1. The divine decree is directed towards *humanity,* and only as such does it refer to individuals. God does not elect individuals but the totality of the human race.

> [O]ur presentation knows of no unconditioned decree concerning any

individual as such, in that all that is of an individual nature is mutually conditioned. Instead, it recognizes only *one* unconditioned decree—that is, one by which the whole, viewed in its undivided interconnectedness, exists in the way it does by virtue of divine good pleasure.[9]

2. Reprobation is a historical/temporal reality, not an eternal one. The reprobate are "passed over" only for a time, but they will not remain in such a state of being forever.

> [A]nd as long as divine predestination has not yet come to light in them [the reprobate], they are, purely and simply, where the whole church also was at one time. On account of this fact, we too can never cease to view them as objects of that divine activity by which the church is gathered and as included with us all under the same divine predestination.[10]

3. There is only *one* unconditional decree: the election of all humanity to redemption in and through Jesus Christ.

> [T]he redemptive power of Christ [...] is sufficient to save the totality of the new creation contained within the human race from shared perdition.[11]

4. Death is a stage of development. The possibility of redemption does not end with death. How exactly this works and what it looks like is beyond the scope of dogmatics and lapses into speculation. But we have a firm hope that those who die as reprobates will not remain eternally outside the scope of Christ's redemption.

> Suppose that instead we proceed based on the presupposition that all who belong to the human race would, sometime or other, be taken up into community of life with Christ. Thus, this one divine predestination would remain. In no way would we conclude from the claim that this predestination would not yet have been accomplished during a given individual's lifetime that some other destination would be accomplished through that individual's death. Rather, even the condition one would have at death would at that point be simply an intermediate one.[12]

Election on an Empirical Basis

Now that we have grasped the basic outline of Schleiermacher's doctrine of election, we will look more closely at the arguments that have led to these conclusions.

The first thing we have to consider is the question of dogmatic placement.

Where does the doctrine of election fit within systematic theology? For Barth, election was part of the doctrine of God. For Calvin, it was treated in book three of the *Institutes,* on personal salvation. For Schleiermacher, however, it belongs in the doctrine of the Church. Therefore, the essential question behind Schleiermacher's doctrine of election is not about God (Barth) or about an individual's salvation (Calvin), but about the historical Church. That is, Schleiermacher does not ask why some individuals are saved and others are not, nor does he ask what election means for God, but why some people are Christians *already* while others have *not yet* become ones. Election serves the purpose of answering why the Church is the Church and not the world (or why the world is the world and not yet the Church).

Since the divine decree is *one* and undivided, it cannot be directed towards individuals. Instead, it expresses God's will for the totality of the human race. That is what makes Calvin's placement unacceptable, for Schleiermacher.[13] The question is not why some *individuals* are saved and others rejected, but why the Church is constituted as it is in contrast with the world. Likewise, Schleiermacher might consider Barth's placement of election in the doctrine of God far too speculative; thus, Schleiermacher limited himself to dealing with the question of divine election only on an *empirical* basis, that is, by thinking through the actual historical appearance of redemption in the Christian Church.

Because predestination is singular, then the only difference between the elect and reprobate is "simply the difference between being taking up into the reign of Christ earlier or later."[14] Reprobation is not ordained by God, and those living as reprobates presently are nevertheless objects of divine love. There is no double predestination but one, single decree for the whole of humanity. So election is a question of *timing*, of the natural, gradual emergence of the Church. It considers how humanity will be transformed, through natural means,[15] into the spiritual body of Christ. So for Schleiermacher, the reprobate are not *eternally* condemned but passed over only for a time. Gradually, all will be taken up into the reign of God.

This also means reprobation is a historical event that *assists* in the one divine decree for the election of all humanity, and it should be thought of as a temporal stage included in that decree. That is, the reprobate are passed over temporarily, not in spite of, but for the sake of the eventual redemption of all humanity. Reprobation is part of God's one eternal decree only to the extent that it serves election. Reprobation is the natural, historical outworking of God's gracious election, a *stage of development* and not an eternal status. Schleiermacher writes:

> God's will is always active, because every stretch of time runs its course only in fulfillment of God's will. Moreover, whatever might seem to resist or

repulse God's will is always simply contributing toward its temporal fulfillment.[16]

Even in their reprobation, those still unredeemed *contribute* to the fulfillment of God's will for their redemption. Election and reprobation are *temporal* distinctions, only election is eternal. So the possibility of redemption persists after death.

Schleiermacher's revision is significant because it universalizes the divine decree and connects election with redemption. It is no longer a matter of isolated persons chosen at random, but according to the divine government of the world, all persons, sooner or later, will be taken up into the reign of God and share in Christ's redemption. Predestination is singular. With this, Schleiermacher has overcome the problematic particularism of traditional doctrines of election.

But it is not in some fatalistic sense that election is universal, it is Christ's work. Election and redemption are intrinsically related. All humanity is predestined to redemption in Christ.[17] And because of Schleiermacher's Christomorphic doctrine of creation (more on this in chapter four), we can say that to be God's creature *is* to be elected to redemption in Jesus Christ. The whole interconnected process of nature is teleologically oriented to redemption and the new creation of all things. Election is not a question of God choosing some individuals over others, but the gradual unveiling of the reign of God over all creation. The only difference is being taken up in the reign of God sooner or later, election or reprobation.

On Religions

On a brief, somewhat unrelated note, this insight offers a profound basis for reckoning with the appearance of other religions. Schleiermacher's conviction that faith is always communal and, accordingly, that election is community-centric helps us think about the relationship of Christianity with other non-Christian cultures. Especially for many Eastern religions, such as Hinduism, there is an unbreakable bond between religion and culture. To give up one's religion would be to renounce one's heritage and community, and thus one's self. It would be a form of social suicide. A person's unique upbringing, including their community, culture, and language, determines so much of the religious landscape in the world today. For example, those brought up in America, with a sizable Christian population, are far more likely to become Christians themselves than someone born in Indonesia—the largest Muslim country in the world, with an estimated 227 million devotees.

A Christian faith that altogether ignores these cultural factors, which significantly contribute to religious diversity, would be a Christianity unequipped for the modern world. We should see other religions not as enemies to God's will but as essential and necessary stages in the development of humanity towards its complete redemption in and through Jesus Christ. These other faiths, according to Schleiermacher, are made up of reprobate people, temporarily passed over for the sake of God's one eternal divine decree. They are God's elect people even in their present state of reprobation, and we must trust that they will not eternally remain in such a state but will eventually be taken up into the reign of God.

The fifth speech of *On Religion* acknowledges this point. Schleiermacher writes:

> No man can come into actual existence as a single human being without also at the same time and through the same act being set within a world, within a definite order of things and among particular objects.[18]

Schleiermacher's doctrine of election offers profound hope for those who presently live in a state of being "passed over" by God. These reprobate individuals are included in the single, all-embracing divine decree of election. We may hold out hope for their redemption.

Universalism

Returning to Schleiermacher's argument, it may be apparent already that this understanding of election as a single, community-centric, universally oriented decree leads, necessarily, to universalism. But there has been some debate over the extent of Schleiermacher's universalism. One argument states that Schleiermacher's relationship with universalism is similar to Barth's. That is, he accepts the *possibility* of universalism but denies it dogmatically.[19] There is some weight to this, since Schleiermacher, like Barth, refused to allow for empty speculation and stressed the human limitations of dogmatics. But this conclusion forces inconsistencies onto Schleiermacher, and so it is flawed. Instead, I agree with Daniel Pedersen's conclusion: "Schleiermacher not only does, but *must*, on pain of incoherence, hold to universal salvation."[20]

Schleiermacher's system requires universalism. He even goes so far as to argue that if universalism is *not* the outcome of human history, then the bliss of salvation is threatened. In other words, redemption will not be complete until it is shared by all. Redemption involves the perfection of our humanity, moving from a state of selfish hatred of our neighbor to selfless love for others, and therefore, the loss of any one person in hell would be eternal grief for those perfected in love. The very existence of "hell" is a continual threat to the bliss of "heaven." Such a dualistic outlook is logically excluded from

Schleiermacher's theology. So it is entirely appropriate to deem Schleiermacher a universalist.

Murray Rae highlights the strength of Schleiermacher's universalism, noting, "[T]here is something profoundly important in his refusal to accept a concept of salvation that is careless of the plight of one's neighbor—and even one's enemies."[21] Would it not result in a hopeless state of self-contradiction if we thought salvation included becoming cold-hearted towards our unredeemed neighbor? Concern for our neighbor is an essential part of who we are as human beings. We are communal by nature. Christ's Sermon on the Mount exemplifies the high point of our redemption, to love God and each other. But do Christ's ethics only matter for our lives *on earth*? Will the command to love our neighbor as ourselves cease after death? If so, then the afterlife would not be an *improvement* of our nature—we would not be *more* compassionate and loving after death—but instead, it would signify the detriment of our existence, being worse off than we were before redemption. If we find that our theology causes us to be *less* compassionate towards others—even towards our enemies—even towards *God's* "enemies"—then we have not yet understood Christ's gracious redemption.

Schleiermacher writes, "Thus, there is no way to overcome this discordance if, proceeding from our Christian consciousness, we are supposed to consent to assume that a portion of our human race would remain entirely excluded" (CF §118.2, 777). In other words, if there is any part of the human race that will be eternally excluded from redemption, then a permanent discord will remain, disrupting our state of blessedness. It would no longer be a state of blessedness at all. The dualistic picture of humanity divided into those who suffer eternal damnation and those who take joy in eternal salvation is logically unsustainable. If humanity is communal by nature, then this must be true. The joy of salvation is disrupted by the knowledge of damnation; thus, belief in heaven cannot exist alongside belief in hell. Schleiermacher writes, "I know of no way in which [hell] can be reconciled with the universal love of God."[22] So not only would a permanent discord remain in us but also in God, a dispute between God's love and justice, if any portion of creation is unredeemed. All humanity must be redeemed, or none of it ever will be. Redemption must be total, or God would not be a faithful creator. This is the crux of Schleiermacher's argument for the eventual salvation of all.

Schleiermacher summarizes his point:

> If we now consider eternal damnation in its relation to eternal blessedness, it is easy to see that if eternal damnation exists, eternal blessedness cannot continue to exist. That is to say, even if the two domains were totally separate externally, such an elevated state of the blessed, already regarded in itself,

could not be conjoined with complete ignorance of others' lack of blessedness [...] If we accordingly apply to the blessed some knowledge regarding the condition of the damned, this knowledge cannot be imagined to be devoid of feeling for them. This is so, for if the perfecting of our nature is not to have retrogressed, this feeling must embrace the entire human race [...] Hence, we surely ought, at the very least, to grant equal right to that more moderate outlook of which there are also still some traces in Scripture,[23] namely that by the power of redemption a general restoration of all human souls would eventually occur.[24]

Schleiermacher is clear: In the end, either all will be redeemed, or no one will be. Eternal blessedness is threatened by even the slightest knowledge that some portion of humanity remains unredeemed. The perfection of our nature necessitates *more* empathy, not less. The redemption of all is a presupposition of Schleiermacher's theology.

Conclusion

By considering Schleiermacher's doctrine of election, we have taken the first step past the common misreadings of his theology. The feeling of absolute dependence is best understood in the context of God's gracious election of all. It is not a subjective emotion or private experience but the effect of God's grace. God remains first even in our consciousness of God. We perceive ourselves as having been posited in this interconnected world but of not positing ourselves, and thus, we are conscious of an "other" to Whom we depend absolutely. This is grace: that God chooses us. As I will continue to argue, the presence of divine grace permeates Schleiermacher entire theology.[25] The doctrine of election is merely the first step towards realizing this, as Kevin Vander Schel writes, "Schleiermacher's revisionist account of the doctrine of election clearly upholds the Reformed emphasis on the primacy and indispensability of grace."[26]

Furthermore, Schleiermacher's doctrine of election is a significant improvement over previous attempts. It resolves many of the problematic tendencies in both Calvin and Luther. By shifting the focus from individuals to the community, stressing the unity of God's will and action, arguing for a single decree for all, and asserting that redemption remains a possibility after death, Schleiermacher has constructed a profoundly original interpretation of God's gracious election. Conflicts with the reformed tradition aside, he faithfully upholds the Reformation impulse. As Schleiermacher proclaimed: "The Reformation still goes on!"[27]

Calvin himself once pointed out that the difference between a "disciple" and an "ape" is that the former builds on their teacher's insights and goes *beyond* them, while the latter merely repeats what they have said.[28] In this sense, Schleiermacher is a greater heir to the Reformation than those who just repeat and regurgitate either Luther or Calvin's system. Schleiermacher's doctrine of election is not perfect, but it is a favorable development in the history of Christian thought. In its originality and systematic cohesiveness, it is a profound testimony to the spirit of the Reformation, and ultimately, it deserves more attention than it receives.

The Doctrine of Sin

It may seem odd to end this chapter by considering the doctrine of sin, but it is necessary to emphasize Schleiermacher's conviction that human nature is inherently communal. This presupposition significantly affected how he formed the doctrine of election, but it is also crucial for how he deals with sin and many other subjects.

Schleiermacher fervently rejected theological individualism. Errors are inevitable if we focus on individuals stripped from their community, culture, and history. To be human is to be relational, to exist in a particular time and place, and to be bound to a given environment. We cannot escape ourselves or our situation any more than we can jump over our own shadow. Faith, too, is communal, as Schleiermacher stressed in the fourth speech of *On Religion*: "Religion must be social if it is to exist at all. It is man's nature to be social. It is pre-eminently the nature of religion to be so" (OR, 208).

Regarding sin, Schleiermacher writes, "[S]infulness is of a thoroughly collective nature" (CF §71.2, 428), and "sin is to be conceived correctly only as the collective act of the human species" (CF §77.1, 483).

Schleiermacher was one of the first theologians to stress the communal nature of sin. In this sense, liberation theology owes a debt to his work. The idea so central to liberation theology, that an entire culture can sin through its systemic racism, classism, or sexism, can be traced back (albeit indirectly) to Schleiermacher's doctrine of sin.

If we begin with an unrealistic picture of humanity, then we will arrive at an understanding of sin unfit for humanity's plight. Schleiermacher's doctrine of sin is an improvement over traditional interpretations because it is more attuned to human nature. A purely "spiritualized" doctrine of sin is like a pair of shoes three sizes too small, it is unfit for reality. If humanity is indeed sinful, then sin is social just as much as it is spiritual and ethical.

I will not attempt a complete study of Schleiermacher's doctrine of sin here, but it is worth recognizing one of its key points. For Schleiermacher, the "complete knowledge of sin comes to us only in and through the Redeemer's utter lack of sinfulness and his absolute strength of spirit" (CF §68.3, 413). In other words, it is only in the light of redemption that we can adequately see sin for what it is. Systematically, Schleiermacher treats sin first, but the consciousness of grace, of redemption in and through Christ, arises *before* the consciousness of sin.[29] Christ's perfect God-consciousness reveals our lack of God-consciousness. Schleiermacher's doctrine of sin is closely connected with his doctrine of redemption.

Every individual is irrevocably bound to their community and inherits the collective sinfulness of humanity. By unavoidably participating in the systems and social structures that actively hinder perfect God-consciousness, the individual is unable not to sin. Here Schleiermacher develops the doctrine of original sin in a unique way. While the mythological image of the fall of Adam is rejected, he nevertheless retains the essential components found in that doctrine. We at once contribute to the sinfulness of the community and inherit its collective sins. The community is sinful because of its individuals, and the individual sins because of their community.

Schleiermacher further distinguishes between original sin and "actual" sin. Original sin is what we socially inherit from the collective sinfulness of humanity, but actual sin is what we contribute to collective sinfulness. Sin is social "God-forgetfulness," but it is perpetuated because of each individual's own God-forgetfulness. The community as a whole is guilty, and each individual is guilty. Original sin is the social situation of the collective human race, a position that actively hinders God-consciousness. Actual sin is each individual's lack of God-consciousness and therefore their contribution to its social hindrance. By stressing the communal nature of sin, Schleiermacher in no way downplays the responsibility of each individual for their own sinfulness.

Schleiermacher also proposes a re-interpretation of humanity's original perfection. Original perfection is not a mythological, primordial state of being free from sin before the fall, such as in the Garden of Eden. Instead, the original perfection of humanity means our innate *capacity* for God-consciousness. Even in our sinful state, we remain capable of receiving grace and developing God-consciousness. That is, we are redeemable. In this sense, the fellowship of the faithful in the Church of Jesus Christ is the communal answer to the original, collective sins of the community. God-consciousness is strengthened by the influence of Christ through the common spirit of the Church. Sin is overcome through fellowship with Christ and in the new creation. The reign of God overtakes the reign of sin in the human community.

This brief survey of Schleiermacher's doctrine of sin provides a clear example of his conviction that human nature is inherently communal. This conviction greatly influenced his doctrine of election, which began not with the individual but the whole human community, and it will continue to be vital as we further discuss his theology.

Finally, recognizing how Schleiermacher understands the communal nature of sin, we can now see why he so fervently rejected an individualistic doctrine of election. We cannot think of God's will as if it were directed in a piecemeal fashion towards one individual over another. Instead, God's will is one and undivided in desiring the redemption of all humanity in and through Jesus Christ. God does not elect individuals but the totality of the human race. Schleiermacher's doctrine of sin highlights his conviction regarding the interconnectedness of all creation. It is impossible to separate individuals from their community. Just as an individualistic doctrine of sin errs by failing to understand that human nature is inherently communal, so an individualistic doctrine of election fails by considering individuals apart from their community.

Individualism Destroys the Very Nature of Christianity

Schleiermacher's commitment to a community-centric vision of faith is so ingrained in his theology that he considered individualism ("separatism") one of the greatest threats to Christianity. He writes:

> [T]wo views are thereby excluded. The first view supposes that a person could take part in redemption and become blessed through Christ outside the collective life founded by him, so that a Christian could do without this collective life and, as it were, be alone with Christ. To be sure, we have to designate this separatism as fanatic. [...] Moreover, logically, such separatism [...] *destroys the very nature of Christianity.* It does so, in that it postulates Christ's having an effect without mediation in time and space, and, at the same time, it isolates itself in such a way that no continuing effect of what has been accomplished in him can ever occur.[30]

The importance of this claim and how Schleiermacher implements it will continue to unfold as we progress further into his dogmatics. It is vital for rightly understanding him. Indeed, an individualistic mindset not only leads to a flawed concept of election but to a faulty Christianity altogether. Schleiermacher's work is an essential reminder of Christianity's fundamental focus on community.

The perception that Schleiermacher's theology is merely subjective is also invalidated at this point. Whenever he speaks of religious self-consciousness or the feeling of absolute dependence, he presupposes the essential interconnectedness of all creation. As Niebuhr writes, "The developed God-consciousness unites the religious man with other being; it does not isolate him in the mystery of his own existence."[31] It is never the self *alone* but always the self in relation. Few theologians have presented such a profoundly communal vision of Christian faith as Schleiermacher.

---

1. CF §110.1, 723.
2. *On the Doctrine of Election*, 73. Louisville: Westminster John Knox Press, 2012.
3. Ibid., 76.
4. *Friedrich Schleiermacher (Makers of the Modern Theological Mind)*, 36. Waco: Word Books, 1979.
5. Gockel writes, "Barth's theology is not just a repudiation of Schleiermacher but an expansion of his predecessor's work in a new framework" (*Barth and Schleiermacher on the Doctrine of Election*, 13; Oxford University Press, 2006). And he notes their shared grace-centric outlook: "For both theologians, the doctrine of election stresses the indispensability of God's grace" (ibid.).

    The similarities are most prominent, however, in Barth's two early attempts at reconstructing the doctrine of election. *The Epistle to the Romans* and *The Göttingen Dogmatics* present a doctrine clearly influenced by Schleiermacher. In *Romans*, for example, Barth writes that God "rejects, in order that he may elect" (347). So reprobation is included in election and is not its opposite. In *The Göttingen Dogmatics*, he writes that the "point" and "goal" of predestination is "always election, not rejection, even in rejection" (460). These indicate a continuation of Schleiermacher's doctrine, which emphasizes single predestination, the one divine decree of election. In *Church Dogmatics* II/2, Schleiermacher's influence remains present as Barth considers the election of the community (§34) before the election of the individual (§35), though both are rooted in and proceed from the election of Jesus Christ (§33).

    For a complete study of their similarities and differences, see Matthias Gockel, *Barth and Schleiermacher on the Doctrine of Election*.
6. See *Tradition and the Modern World*, 99-150. Chicago: The University of Chicago Press, 1978.
7. See Gerrish, ibid. Schweizer referred to Schleiermacher as the "reviver of the Reformed consciousness in the modern era" (quoted in *The Blackwell Companion to Modern Theology*, chapter 9; Blackwell Reference Online, 2017).
8. Niebuhr argued, "The doctrine of the eternal decree that elects men in and through Jesus Christ is the most encompassing single statement of the principle of the interconnection of the doctrinal contents of *The Christian Faith*" (*Schleiermacher on Christ and Religion*, 248; New York: Charles Scribner's Sons, 1964).
9. CF §120.4, 793.
10. CF §119.2, 782.
11. CF §119.3, 785.
12. CF §119.3, 783.
13. It is worth noting that Schleiermacher saw himself in basic harmony with Calvin except for one point: He rejects Calvin's assumption that those passed over in time will remain reprobates eternally. He begins from the perspective of the whole of humanity, rather than from particular individuals, and speaks of a single decree instead of a double decree. In Schleiermacher's essay, *On Election*, he argues against the Lutheran position in favor of the Calvinist position of election, although he makes this significant qualifying alteration to Calvin: single, not double predestination. But he is still closer to Calvin than often thought.
14. *On the Doctrine of Election*, 78. Louisville: Westminster John Knox Press, 2012.
15. A central theme of Schleiermacher's theology is that the "supernatural becomes natural." Here, the supernatural decree of election is naturalized in the form of the historical Church as the reign of God gradually unfolds in time. Divine grace is naturalized as God acts through the interconnected process of nature. The natural and the supernatural are harmonized. Julia Lamm writes, "[A]ccording to Schleiermacher, grace arises immediately out of, and is the continuation of, the incarnation" ("Schleiermacher's Treatise on Grace," *The Harvard Theological Review*, Vol. 101, No. 2, Apr. 2008, 140).
16. CF §54.4, 314.

17. Gockel notes, "The fact that Schleiermacher says 'predestination to salvation in Christ' and not simply 'predestination in Christ' underlines the redemption-centered character of his approach" (*Barth and Schleiermacher on the Doctrine of Election*, 87; Oxford University Press, 2006).
18. OR, 296.
19. Matthias Gockel and Anette I. Hagan argue this point, and their reasons are noteworthy. As Hagan states: "Partly because of the insufficient scriptural evidence for both and partly because of his premise about what constitutes a doctrinal proposition, Schleiermacher did not afford a doctrinal status either to universalism or to twofold foreordination" (*Eternal Blessedness for All?*, 151; Eugene: Pickwick Publications, 2013).

    In this sense, they are correct. Schleiermacher does not treat universalism as a doctrine of faith. Yet I believe we must go further. Just because it is not a matter of faith-doctrine does not mean it is not essential to his system. Schleiermacher's dogmatics would be incoherent without presupposing the eventual redemption of all to blessedness. Even if, like other "prophetic" doctrines, it cannot be part of faith-doctrine, this does not mean it is not a necessary *conclusion* of faith-doctrine. As we will see in the sidebar to chapter three, eternal life is also not a matter of faith-doctrine, but it is nonetheless a necessary conclusion to it based on Christ's immortality. Rightly, universalism is not a doctrine of faith because, according to Schleiermacher's dogmatic limitation, we cannot extrapolate it from Christian religious self-consciousness. But it is a necessary conclusion to it, just as eternal life and God's threeness are also important conclusions.

    Another argument states that Schleiermacher developed from his election essay, which openly embraced universalism, to a more calculated approach in *Christian Faith*. But this is denied by Schleiermacher's own reference to that earlier essay at the beginning of §118n1 (771). He writes, "Once and for all, for this point of doctrine I make reference to my essay on the doctrine of election."
20. *The Eternal Covenant*, 146; Berlin: Walter de Gruyter, 2017.
21. "Salvation-in-Community," *All Shall Be Well*, 197. Eugene: Cascade Books, 2011.
22. *On the Doctrine of Election*, 77. Louisville: Westminster John Knox Press, 2012.
23. Schleiermacher cites 1 Cor. 15:25, 53, 55.
24. CF §163.PS.1, 997-8.
25. Julia Lamm argues that grace is "fundamental to Schleiermacher's mature theology [...] so that his dogmatics cannot be properly understood without careful attention to it. In that sense, the *Glaubenslehre* [faith-doctrine] could be said to be a *Gnadenlehre* [grace-doctrine], since everything in it is an explication of the Christian experience of having been redeemed by Christ, which is an experience of grace" ("Schleiermacher's Treatise on Grace," *The Harvard Theological Review*, Vol. 101, No. 2, Apr. 2008, 135).
26. "Election in Christ in Schleiermacher's *Christian Faith* and *Christian Ethics*," Open Theology 2015; 1, 341.
27. Quoted in Martin Redeker, *Schleiermacher: Life and Thought*, 198. Philadelphia: Fortress Press, 1973.
28. See B. A. Gerrish, *Tradition and the Modern World*, 48. Chicago: The University of Chicago Press, 1978.
29. On this point, Barth agrees with Schleiermacher, writing: "But this real knowledge of sin takes place in the knowledge of Jesus Christ. [...] The fact that man is a sinner, and what his sin is, is something that in the last resort we can measure properly and fully only by that which on the New Testament understanding is man's salvation, the redemptive grace which comes from God to man" (*Church Dogmatics* IV/1, 390-1; Peabody: Hendrickson Publishers, 2010).
30. CF §88.3, 547; emphasis mine.
31. "Schleiermacher and the Names of God," *Schleiermacher as Contemporary* (ed. Robert Funk), 185. New York: Herder & Herder, 1970.

SERMON: ONE GREATLY EXTENDED COMMUNITY

> [T]he reign of God does not consist in the relationship of individuals to the Redeemer [...] the Redeemer has not descended simply to enter into the hearts of particular human beings and in that way to bless or save each individual. Rather, he also came to bless or save them in that he collected them within one greatly extended community. He would have to kindle a new collective life generally throughout the earth and in this way transform the entire world by his existence in it, bringing them, with his Spirit, into a new life. [...] [T]he Redeemer's appearance is for us the decisive turning-point over the entire history of the human race.[1]
>
> — SCHLEIERMACHER, IN A CHRISTMAS SERMON FROM 1820

Jesus was not sent to save individuals. But our staunch individualism has tainted the good news so severely that Jesus Christ has become *our* personal Lord and Savior rather than *the world's*. Schleiermacher's vision of a community-centric Christianity is a profoundly counter-cultural message that we need to hear in the Church again today. Jesus is the Lord and Savior of *all* people, not a personalized salvation-dispenser.

An apparent universalism arises from this, which Schleiermacher articulates later in the sermon. If we faithfully proclaim Christ to be the Savior of the world, then we should not be afraid of this term "universalism," since it is the natural offspring of our confession that Jesus is Lord. Schleiermacher argues that the Word of redemption is "just as strong and efficacious as that commanding Word which called the external world into existence!"[2] In other words, the same power that created the world is, in both scope and effect, the same Word that redeems humanity. There are not two Words of God but one.

In the same way that we had no vote in our natural birth—no one can decide *not* to be born—so we do not get a vote in whether or not the new creation will come to be. The appearance of the Redeemer has ushered in the reign of God, and it will continue to spread until grace encompasses the whole world. Therefore, to imagine redemption as anything *but* total and all-embracing is to misunderstand God's will for creation.

The same Word that created the world is also the Word of election. Creation in the beginning set in motion the appearance of the Redeemer. God did not will one thing and do another. Whatever God wills God does. So for God to create *is* for God to elect. God's Word appears divided whenever we believe that some are created just to be rejected eternally. But God's Word is not divided. The new creation will be just as all-embracing as creation in the beginning.

Schleiermacher finds it inconsistent to say that God creates human beings in a state of sin without also electing them for redemption in Christ. For Schleiermacher, the so-called fall of humanity in Adam was merely a poetic expression of our innate sinfulness, not a historical event. He considers it a given that human beings were created sinful from the beginning.[3] Accordingly, for God to create someone and *not* elect them for redemption would be a contradiction in God's will. But Schleiermacher insists that what God wills God does, and therefore, whomever God creates God also elects to redemption in and through Jesus Christ. So if we ask, "Who are the elect?" The answer is: "Whomever God creates, God wills to redeem and redeems. The scope of election is all-embracing."

God Will Lose Nothing and No One

In another sermon, Schleiermacher again expresses his conviction regarding the election of all people to redemption in Jesus Christ. In 1823, with John 16:23 as his text, Schleiermacher declared:

> We may not doubt that what he so decidedly proclaimed to be the will of the Father who sent him is true. We whose hearts are full of longing and faith in the Redeemer may doubt least of all. For he takes up as a special part of the end for which the Father sent him that dearest hope that has somehow arisen and spread in every race of humankind. And he assures us that he will raise all whom the Father

has given him at the last day because he shall lose nothing he has given to him.[4]

And he concluded with this prayer:

We firmly believe that you, who gave your Son all authority in heaven and on earth, also know how to take care that he lose nothing you have given to him; for none of your eternal and blessed decrees can go unfulfilled. Yes, through him and for his sake you will lead all to salvation, because we know that you sent your Son into the world not to judge the world, but to save it.[5]

Just as God has faithfully guided us to redemption in Christ, so we can trust that God will guide all people to redemption. Our Christian self-consciousness of redemption in and through Christ does not limit the scope of redemption, but rather, it should be the basis from which we hope for the redemption of all who have not yet become part of the Church. The belief that God has elected us *over* others is nothing less than pride rearing its ugly head. It implies that we somehow "deserve" redemption while other people do not.

It is not our responsibility, then, to speculate why some are saved and others appear as if they are not. Instead, we must recognize that God will accomplish what God has decreed. If God decrees the redemption of humanity in and through Jesus Christ, then we can trust that it will be achieved. Our question now becomes why some are included earlier and others later, and this is precisely what Schleiermacher's doctrine of election sought to answer. It necessitates leaving the door open for regeneration after death, although Schleiermacher never gives specifics about what this might look like. Because all will be redeemed, reprobation is always a temporal development, and therefore, we have no reason to assume this development ends with death. The question of election is not one of *status* but *timing*. At the root of Schleiermacher's doctrine is the assurance that what God wills God does. Or, in the words of his sermon: God will lose nothing and no one.

---

1. "The Transformation That has Begun From the Redeemer's Appearance Upon the Earth," 16; trans. by Terrence Tice in *Schleiermacher: The Psychology of Christian Faith and Life*, 15-39. Lanham: Lexington Books, 2018.
2. Ibid., 27.
3. For Schleiermacher, it is necessary to conclude from this that God is the author and originator of sin and that sin is rooted in divine causality, inasmuch as sin is included in the interconnected process of nature. See CF §61n1, §79, and §81.2. This does not, however, mean God approves of sin or even causes it directly but that God is its originator as it relates to redemption, though he is the originator of redemption differently than of sin. Pedersen notes, "God only ordains the whole as a whole, along with all the particulars that

world entails" (*The Eternal Covenant*, 146; Berlin: Walter De Gruyter, 2017). Sin is a particular ordained in relation to the whole, and the whole (what God wills) is nothing less than the redemption of all creation. Sin is not caused by God even in its being (consequently) ordained by God. Therefore, for Schleiermacher, sin is not real for God, it is not willed by God, and thus it does not exist. Sin is the negation of being itself. It is only necessary in relation to its being overcome in Christ.

4. *Servant of the Word*, 203. Philadelphia: Fortress Press, 1987.
5. Ibid., 208.

SIDEBAR: THE SPIRIT-FILLED CHURCH

> Thus creation is supernatural, but it afterwards becomes the natural order. Likewise, in his origin Christ is supernatural, but he also becomes natural, as a genuine human being. The Holy Spirit and the Christian Church can be treated in the same way. Therefore, I would prefer that one devise for me a position where what is supernatural can at the same time be natural.[1]
>
> — Schleiermacher

It may be surprising to learn that Schleiermacher's ecclesiology (his doctrine of the Church) is the longest section of *Christian Faith*. His Christology, the true "heart" of his theology, spans one-hundred and seventy-eight pages. In contrast, his doctrine of the Church spans two-hundred and forty-one pages. It includes three subdivisions: the emergence of the Church, its continuance and coexistence in the world, and its consummation. Schleiermacher's doctrine of election is found in the first subdivision and spans only a handful of pages. We have already stressed the significance of the Christian community for Schleiermacher, but I want to constructively consider the possibility of reading Schleiermacher's theology as a theology of the third article (the Holy Spirit). This was a possibility Barth hinted towards but quickly discredited. Yet perhaps there is more to it than he thought possible. So we will examine Schleiermacher's doctrine of the Church and Spirit to see if he might be read in such a way.

A Theology of the Third Article

Barth's published lectures on Schleiermacher were given in 1923/24 at the University of Göttingen. In a postscript written in 1968, the final year of Barth's life, he reflects on his career-long engagement with Schleiermacher. He is warm towards him and shows how deeply he appreciates him as a theologian. Barth borrows a line from Mozart's *The Marriage of Figaro* to express their ambiguous relationship: Despite being so critical of his theology, he nevertheless felt, "An inner voice always spoke to his advantage."[2] Furthermore, Barth expresses how open he still feels towards Schleiermacher, after all these years of criticism. He writes, "The door is in fact not latched. I am actually to the present day not finished with him."[3]

Even more surprising is how Barth finds himself hoping to be "at one with Schleiermacher," though he expresses doubt that such unity could be possible.[4] He then lists five conditions that could, perhaps, facilitate this union, and these appear in the form of unresolved questions.

The first and second questions deal with Schleiermacher's relation to philosophy. Barth misreads Schleiermacher as having grounded his system *on* philosophy, rather than *borrowing* from it, which is a common error we will address in chapters four and five. The third question asks, that when he speaks of human beings and their relation to God, whether it is in "relationship to a reality which is *particular* and concrete" or in a generalized, abstract sense.[5] The fifth question is self-reflective, as Barth wonders whether he has been fair to the intentions of Schleiermacher's theology.

Finally, it is the fourth question that I want to focus on here. This is where Barth offers up a possible reading of Schleiermacher as a theologian of the Holy Spirit. Barth writes:

> [W]hat I have occasionally contemplated [...] [is] the possibility of a theology of the third article; in other words, a theology predominantly and decisively of the Holy Spirit. [...]
>
> I would like to reckon with the possibility of a theology of the Holy Spirit, a theology of which Schleiermacher was scarcely conscious, but which might actually have been the legitimate concern dominating even his theological activity.[6]

In short, Barth proposes a solution to his misreading of Schleiermacher, namely, that he would have been more successful if he had built his system as a theology of the Holy Spirit rather than as a philosophical construct in Christian clothing. Barth has come so close to understanding Schleiermacher, yet he is still so far away. His final remark is strange, in which Barth claims, without offering any proof, that Schleiermacher was "scarcely conscious" of a theology of the Holy Spirit. But my proposal is this: What if he actually *was* aware of such a possibility? And not only aware but actively pursuing it? Could Schleiermacher's theology be read as a theology of the third article, as Barth speculated? Barth himself was doubtful, but recent scholars are more optimistic.

Terrence Tice thinks Barth was on the right track with his "largely correct" suggestions, including his idea about a theology of the Holy Spirit.[7] In fact, Richard R. Niebuhr has already gone so far as to characterize Schleiermacher's theology as "a theology of grace and sanctification, of life within the 'kingdom' of grace or the *Spirit-filled church*."[8] Niebuhr further explains the importance of reading Schleiermacher's terminology of consciousness or feeling according to its essential "neediness for that which is other, that which is not self."[9] In other words, Schleiermacher's "feeling of absolute dependence" *is* a clear indication of his theology of grace. The feeling of absolute dependence begs the question, "To *Whom* do we depend absolutely?" A theology of the feeling of absolute dependence *is* a theology of the Holy Spirit and grace.

Because Schleiermacher's theology is neither semi-Pelagian or Arminian, we must remember that God's sovereign grace is central. Even when Schleiermacher discusses, at great length, the complexities of consciousness and feeling, he remains committed to the grace of God. In fact, so much time is spent on human consciousness *because* of that conviction, not in spite of it. It is because God has elected, in grace and love, for us to be God's own people that we feel absolutely dependent on God. But God retains primacy. Religion as "feeling," in Schleiermacher's usage, denotes an immediate existential relationship of which we are not the authors. God is first in our consciousness of God. God-consciousness is not self-generated.

It may be easy to imagine that Schleiermacher is doing theology from below, so to speak—as if he *begins* with human beings and abstracts their psychological reflections to develop a theology of God, which is indeed nothing less than anthropology. That was Barth's critique. But when we recognize the preeminence Schleiermacher gives to *grace*, especially to the gracious action of God as the Whence of our existence, then this misreading becomes invalid. Schleiermacher's theology is "from above." It is with this in mind that we can read Schleiermacher as a theologian of the Holy Spirit.

Church and Spirit

What does all this have to do with Schleiermacher's ecclesiology? For Schleiermacher, the Church and the Spirit are intimately connected. The editors of the new critical edition of *Christian Faith* offer a helpful summary of his doctrine of the Holy Spirit and its connection with the Church. They write:

> §116.2-3 refers to the Holy Spirit as the 'common spirit' that indwells the community of the faithful. [...]
>
> This common spirit *is* the divine Spirit that, through its gifts, is constitutive of the church over its entire existence, development, and consummation. It, like Christ, represents 'the supernatural becoming natural' [...] and, for that reason, is called 'holy.' So, the actual nomenclature 'Holy Spirit' is not a name or title but the designation of a continuing redemptive, sanctifying process, which, in turn, stems from God's 'one eternal divine decree.'[10]

The common spirit is God in communion with the Church, the presence of divine grace in the fellowship of those redeemed in and through Christ. In the same way that "God was in Christ" indicates the being of God in Him, for Schleiermacher, so the "common spirit" indicates the being of God in the Church.

This is why Schleiermacher's doctrine of the Church is so essential for rightly understanding him. Schleiermacher was a theologian of the *Church,* in the fullest sense of the word: Church-centric, Church-oriented, and Church-serving. As we will later see in his Christology (chapter three), Schleiermacher considered the Church *so essential* to Christianity that he argued if it were to disappear from the face of the earth, Christianity could no longer exist. The very proclamation of the Gospel depends on the communication of Christ's sinless perfection in and through the "common spirit" of the Church. Redemption is possible only in the Spirit-filled Church. It would be impossible for someone to discover Christ's redemption by reading a book or having a private spiritual experience. Just as everything we say about Christ depends on the presence of God in Him—that is, His absolutely strong God-consciousness—so in the Church, everything depends on the common spirit to communicate the "power of new life" (CF §121.2, 801). The common spirit is the redeeming presence of God in the Church, or, in other words, it is what makes the Church the "body of Christ" and the "fellowship of Christ."

Schleiermacher's three doctrinal propositions on the Holy Spirit are worth quoting in full:

> *First Doctrinal Proposition:* The Holy Spirit is the uniting of the divine being with human nature in the form of the common spirit that animates the collective life of faithful persons.[11]

Second Doctrinal Proposition: Every regenerate person partakes of the Holy Spirit, so that there is no vital community with Christ without an indwelling of the Holy Spirit, and vice versa.[12]

Third Doctrinal Proposition: In its purity and fullness the Christian church, being animated by the Holy Spirit, is formed as the perfect image of the Redeemer; every regenerate person is a complementary constituent part of this community.[13]

The Church's entire existence, development, and consummation are determined by the presence of God in and with it in the form of its common spirit. The Holy Spirit is "naturalized" from the supernatural, so to speak, into the common life of the Christian community. The common spirit of the Church thus makes up its vital center.

In his lectures on the life of Jesus, Schleiermacher writes, "Christ's oneness with the Father is to be explained in light of our oneness with him."[14] Accordingly, the common spirit—God's presence in the Church, or our "oneness" with God—is a theological parallel to God's presence in Christ. In the same way that God was in Christ, the Holy Spirit is present and active in the Church. Schleiermacher is hesitant, however, to directly say that Christ is God or that the common spirit is God. Instead, he stresses that these terms indicate the active being of God in Christ and in the Church. This retains God's livingness so that God does not become an object of human control, even while describing God's activity in our midst.

Schleiermacher considered John 1:14 ("And the Word became flesh and lived among us…") a key text for understanding his dogmatics. It is, in his mind, "[T]he basic text for all dogmatics, just as it should be for the conduct of ministry as a whole" (OG, 59). This concept of the supernatural becoming natural is a significant theme of his theology, and it is exemplified here in his doctrine of the common spirit of the Church. In the Church, God is active and present in and through our fellowship with one another.

The main point to take away from all this is that Schleiermacher's theology is deeply committed to the Holy Spirit. And considering the Church's importance to his dogmatics, the Spirit is an essential element in his theology—so much so that it is not a stretch to call his dogmatics a "theology of the third article." Schleiermacher's system was built in such a way that the least essential elements appear first and the most essential ones come later—although this is not a rule but a tendency of his arrangement. These later doctrines (such as God's love and wisdom, the Trinity, the Church, and the doctrine of Christ) are the true ground and basis for his whole system. Schleiermacher's great work was designed to reach its highest point with its Conclusion. It was written logically from the most abstract and least essential to the most concrete and vital. Schleiermacher's placement of the doctrine of the Church towards the end of his dogmatics indicates its vitality to the whole work.

It is perplexing to consider just how little attention Schleiermacher's ecclesiology receives,[15] but I hope this section has shown how vital it is for understanding his theology. It is in this sense that we could feasibly read Schleiermacher as a theologian of the third article, the Spirit-filled Church. Every nagging doubt we feel about his supposed subjectivism will be relieved. We are now in a place to recognize that "the feeling of absolute dependence" has its ultimate basis in the Spirit of God who acts graciously towards us in Christ and in the fellowship of His people, the Church. Schleiermacher's theology is profoundly pneumatological.

On Election

The same "supernatural becoming natural" principle that Schleiermacher applies to the Spirit and the Church is present in his doctrine of election. In fact, these points are closely related. Brandt explains:

> Election, the doctrine of divine grace as the gift of salvation given unconditionally in Christ, is an important lens for understanding the church. In his discussion of election, Schleiermacher emphasizes the church's 'natural' operation; election occurs in history as persons are drawn into the church. Election is not, from this point of view, something hidden from human sight in the mystery of God's decree, formulated from eternity and inaccessible to mortals. Schleiermacher identifies a single divine decree (the goal of which is complete communion of all humans with God), made known in Christ and gradually working itself out in human history. Thus Schleiermacher emphasizes the natural means by which divine election is effected: 'What proceeds from the *one* point is only gradually spread out over the entirety of space.'[16]

Election in the Church is the "naturalized" expression of God's undivided decree. It is the supernatural manifested in and through the natural. It is not an abstract, unknowable decision, the content of which we can only speculate, but a concrete act of God in time and space through the interconnected process of nature. Its natural manifestation is the Church, and Christ is its basis, both historically and presently through His self-presentation.

Schleiermacher's theology disavows every trace of speculative content in favor of natural phenomenon rooted in divine causality. What God wills God does, and therefore, natural occurrences are the means through which God acts. So the question the doctrine of election asks is not about an arbitrary decree for certain individuals over others, nor is it a speculative one regarding God, but it is about a specific natural phenomenon, namely, the Church.[17]

Conclusion

Schleiermacher's pneumatological ecclesiology is not likely what Barth envisioned when he proposed a theology of the third article, but it is also not too far off. I am not deluded into thinking Schleiermacher's work aligns with what Barth imagined a theology of the Spirit might look like. But Barth is entirely mistaken to assert that Schleiermacher was unaware of a theology of the Holy Spirit. Instead, I would argue that the Holy Spirit is absolutely vital to his theology, especially his doctrine of the Church. Understanding this also sheds light on the controversial "feeling of absolute dependence," which we will unpack more completely in chapter four.

---

1. OG, 89.
2. *The Theology of Schleiermacher*, 267. Grand Rapids: William B. Eerdmans Publishing, 1982.
3. Ibid., 274.
4. Ibid., 175.
5. Ibid., 276.
6. Ibid., 276-8.
7. *Barth and Schleiermacher*, 57. Philadelphia: Fortress Press, 1988.
8. Ibid., 34; emphasis mine.
9. Ibid., 37.
10. CF §116 n1, 763; emphasis mine.
11. CF §123, 807.
12. CF §124, 813.
13. CF §125, 818.
14. *The Life of Jesus*, 269. Philadelphia: Fortress Press, 1975.
15. For example, I find it strange that *The Cambridge Companion to Friedrich Schleiermacher* —an otherwise superb introduction—overlooks ecclesiology almost entirely. Although some essays do allude to its importance, it is not treated at length.
16. *Schleiermacher and Sustainability*, ed. by Shelli M. Poe., 18. Louisville: Westminster John Knox Press, 2018. Citing CF §117.1, 767.
17. Kevin Vander Schel notes the significance of this move: "[Schleiermacher] centers his treatment [of election] on the historically conditioned unfolding of redemption in human living: the historical outworking of grace. This innovative and challenging understanding of grace and history reveals Schleiermacher not only as a pioneering figure of modern theology but as an agile and innovative thinker who remains a creative interpreter of the Protestant tradition" ("Election in Christ in Schleiermacher's *Christian Faith* and *Christian Ethics*," Open Theology 2015; 1, 341).

2

THE TRIUNE GOD OF LOVE

SUMMARY: Schleiermacher is a profoundly Trinitarian theologian, despite the often repeated claim that he disregards the doctrine. Furthermore, the high point of his doctrine of God is the assertion "God is love." That God is love and Triune are essential to his entire dogmatics.

IN SCHLEIERMACHER'S OWN WORDS:

[O]nly love and no other divine attribute can be equated with God.[1]

[W]e now justifiably regard the doctrine of the Trinity [...] as the copestone of Christian doctrine.[2]

SECONDARY QUOTES:

Rather than a sign of the insignificance of the doctrine, Schleiermacher's placement of the Trinitarian Treatise is actually a result of his desire to revitalize it within Protestant theology.[3]

— SHELLI M. POE

According to the critical experiential principle, God cannot be separated from the world, and a *Glaubenslehre* [faith-doctrine] has no basis for speaking about God beyond or in separation from his actual relation to the world. God's being is not to be separated from his act.[4]

— Robert R. Williams

Introduction

It is commonly said that Schleiermacher denies the Trinity or holds it in low esteem. So it may surprise us to read what one early translator and interpreter has said to the contrary:

> With regard to Schleiermacher's view as a Trinitarian, I can truly say that I have met with scarcely any writer, ancient or modern, who appears to have a deeper conviction of, or more hearty belief in, the doctrine of the real Godhead of Father, Son, and Holy Spirit. This is the basis on which the whole super-structure of his Christian system rests.[5]

— Moss Stuart

This chapter will focus, in part, on correcting this misconception. Schleiermacher's Trinitarianism is more thoroughly ingrained into his dogmatics than it appears at first glance. The difficulty we have in recognizing this, however, rests on the fact that Schleiermacher conceives of the Trinity in a highly original form. The originality of his Trinitarian theology has led to misunderstanding his intentions. Furthermore, the placement of the doctrine in the Conclusion of his dogmatics has contributed to its perceived devaluing.

A secondary focus of this chapter will be Schleiermacher's doctrine of God, particularly his conviction that God's essence may only be equated with love. We cannot *define* God in Godself (the hidden God), we can only *describe* God for us and with us (the revealed God). Yet Schleiermacher is also convinced of the complete coincidence of the God hidden and revealed, the harmony of God's being and act. His method is aimed towards the removal of all speculative content from the doctrine of God. The proposition that God's essential being is love is the high-point and culmination of Schleiermacher's doctrine of God, everything before it is subsidiary.

The Triune God

Why did Schleiermacher place the doctrine of the Trinity in the Conclusion of his dogmatics? Schleiermacher's *Christian Faith* may be thought of as a pyramid. The beginning sections—the infamous Introduction and Part One

—are the most abstract, the broadest. Although, unlike a pyramid, these sections do not establish a foundation for the rest of the construction, but rather, these are the boundary lines that must be set before the proper work of dogmatics can be done. In fact, the pyramid is upside down. The peak or culmination of the work is its true foundation and basis, that which holds the whole project together. Part Two contains reflections on those doctrines immediately conveyed by the consciousness of sin and grace.[6] And the "copestone" is the doctrine of the divine threeness, the Trinity. It is the point towards which everything else leads. By placing the doctrine of the Trinity in the Conclusion of his dogmatics, Schleiermacher is not attempting to downplay its significance but, on the contrary, to highlight its vitality.

Schleiermacher also believed the doctrine of the Trinity needs to be reformed, and he proposed a few avenues for its revision. One of the main goals for this arrangement was to retain what is essential in the doctrine while paving the way for a revision of its form. As Shelli Poe writes, "In part, Schleiermacher concludes rather than begins with the Trinity because he wanted to show how one might maintain the essential elements of the doctrine of the Trinity without espousing it in its conventional form."[7] With this, Schleiermacher initiated a revival in the doctrine of the Trinity. As Carol Jean Voisin writes, "Not since the Nicean and Constantinopolitan Councils and Augustine has the doctrine been acknowledged as such a pivotal and creative part of the Christian doctrine of faith. To be sure, no Protestant made such a claim for the Trinity before Schleiermacher."[8] As we will soon discover, the "revival" of Trinitarian theology in modern times did not originate with Barth but with Schleiermacher.

Redemption is the key component in Schleiermacher's doctrine of God. So it is fitting that he begins his reflection on the Trinity by establishing its connection with redemption. He notes how the doctrine was developed in defense of the view that "nothing less than the divine nature was in Christ and indwells the Christian church as its common spirit" (CF §170.1, 1020). Because the same God who indwells the Church was in Christ, we are lead to reckon with divine threeness. Subordinationism is ruled out—in which the Spirit or the Son is less than divine—because the consciousness of redemption in Christ and through the common spirit of the Church cannot be subordinate forms of God-consciousness. It was by reflecting on the Church's collective experience of redemption that the early theologians developed a doctrine of the Trinity. Recognizing this connection is vital for understanding Schleiermacher's point. He writes:

> By virtue of this interconnection we now justifiably regard the doctrine of the Trinity, insofar as these features are lodged within it, as the copestone of Christian doctrine.[9]

A "copestone" is a stone placed along the peak of a sloping roofline. In German, the word is closely related to conclusion (*Schlußstein* = copestone; *Schluß* = conclusion). Shelli Poe argued that *Schlußstein* is better translated "keystone," the stone that holds together two sides of an arch, which highlights how Schleiermacher's doctrine of the Trinity holds the whole work together and is truly its essential, concluding element. However we translate it, the Trinity is of great importance to Schleiermacher's dogmatics. The doctrine was not simply added on later for the sake of offering vain lip-service, it is truly *essential* to Schleiermacher's entire presentation.

But Schleiermacher also recognized that the doctrine of the Trinity is not an immediate expression of Christian self-consciousness; instead, it is its necessary conclusion. This is why he stressed the connection between redemption and the Trinity. It was in *defense* of redemption in and through Jesus Christ that the Early Church developed the doctrine. It is not as if we could do without the Trinity—we can not—however, it is not an immediate expression of redemption, but a conclusion redemption necessitates.

In all this, Schleiermacher has established his congruence with the orthodox tradition of the Chalcedonian and Athanasian theologians. He has done this by indicating the boundary for what can and cannot be said about God, which was also an essential function of those early formulas.[10] He stands sharply against the same heresies the Early Church opposed, namely, Arianism and subordinationism. Schleiermacher emphasized the real Godhead of Father, Son, and Spirit. The experience of redemption in Christian religious self-consciousness depends on the being of God in Christ and in the common spirit of the Church. For the Son or the Spirit to be in any way less than divine, or divine but subordinate, would be to deny redemption itself. Redemption necessitates the doctrine of the Trinity and is incomplete without it, even if it is not *immediately* conveyed in religious self-consciousness. In what they opposed and the basis from which they built, both Schleiermacher and the theologians of the Early Church stand united regarding the Trinity.

These points are easy enough to understand, and they show why the common critiques of Schleiermacher's doctrine of the Trinity are misguided. But difficulties arise when we begin to consider Schleiermacher's conviction that the doctrine of the Trinity needs to be reformed, especially his proposed avenue of reconsidering Sabellius. Schleiermacher highly values the doctrine, but he is critical of the ways it has been conceived in the past. He is faithful to the *spirit* of the orthodox tradition but does not feel bound to the *letter* of its exact formula. Schleiermacher calls for reform in the doctrine of the Trinity. This is another reason why he placed the doctrine in the Conclusion of his dogmatics. He wanted to show how the Trinity can be essential to a system without forcing adherence to the formulas of traditional orthodoxy.

He retained its essential function while stressing the need for new expressions.

Sabellius' Non-Speculative Path

For Schleiermacher, the doctrine of the Trinity is long overdue for reformation. It survived the Protestant Reformation without alteration, but Schleiermacher suggests its revision is necessary to secure the future of Christian theology. But he does not construct a revision of the Trinity himself, he merely highlights the need for one. He offers a few possibilities but ultimately leaves the question open.

One such possibility is to reconsider Sabellius' doctrine of the Trinity. Schleiermacher does not mean we should adopt modalism, which is often linked with Sabellius. Instead, Schleiermacher argues that the Early Church misunderstood Sabellius, and he offers a new reading of his work. Fiorenza summarizes Schleiermacher's relationship with Sabellius well:

> When Schleiermacher suggests that Sabellius as well as Athanasius should be a resource for future doctrinal progress, he is not making Sabellius the endpoint but is suggesting that one should develop an understanding that goes beyond the contrast between Athanasius and Sabellius. Indeed, he suggests, and especially underscores in the second edition [of CF], that Christian theology needs to develop the Trinity in a way that takes into account the Reformation impulse, thereby going beyond Athanasius and Sabellius.[11]

What Schleiermacher finds attractive about Sabellius is his refusal to speculate about God's being in Godself. Sabellius considered speculation regarding an antecedent Trinity inappropriate because such speculative methods trespass beyond our reach as humans. Therefore, he sought to speak of God only in accordance with God's acts towards us in history.

Schleiermacher's doctrine of God is a noble attempt to speak only within the limits of piety, that is, within the confines of Christian self-consciousness. He restricted himself to describing the actual state of Christian consciousness, of God's relationship with us, rather than speculating about the being of God in Godself. This non-speculative tendency is a major impulse of Schleiermacher's dogmatics. He writes:

> [W]e have no formulation for the being of God as such distinct from the being of God in the world.[12]

This does not equate God with the world (pantheism) but recognizes that the knowledge of God is never abstracted from the actual conditions that make revelation possible, namely, the Word made flesh. In other words, God cannot be thought of apart from the world to which Christ came. Because we are bound to the earth, God's gracious self-revealing is never without the being of God in the world, the Word spoken in and to human flesh.

Schleiermacher's method is often misunderstood as a subjectivist attempt to re-center our God-talk around the feelings of human beings, but this is not the case. At its core, his method is non-speculative. It is not a celebration of speculation but its undoing. He strives after an *empirical* system—having to do with a real, historical phenomenon.

The doctrine of the Trinity needs to be reformed along these lines. The doctrine has suffered its fair share of bad analogies and anthropomorphic images. Perhaps more than any other doctrine, it has become a spectacle of abstraction. Schleiermacher aims to construct an empirically-grounded doctrine of the Trinity in the place of these vain speculations.

In this sense, Schleiermacher takes the doctrine of the Trinity far more seriously, in his earnestness to improve it, than those theologians who merely repeat the common formulas unthinkingly. We cannot treat the doctrine as if it were settled and finished, perfect in every way. No, the doctrine of the Trinity remains, like every doctrine, a human, time-bound reflection. So it is equally susceptible to error. If we have learned anything from the "revival" of Trinitarian theology in the past century, it is that Schleiermacher was right, the Trinity needs to be reformed. Moltmann, Pannenberg, and Barth are just a few examples of theologians who have attempted their own reformations of the doctrine. Schleiermacher reminds us:

> [N]o definition of a doctrine that is conceived, even in the most complete state of community, can thus be viewed as unreformable and valid for all times on that account.[13]

The Christian faith is a *living* faith, not an unchanging, dead reflection. We should expect fresh interpretations of our faith to develop with each and every generation. The doctrine of the Trinity is not exempt from this rule.

In the sidebar following this chapter, we will examine more thoroughly Schleiermacher's essay on Sabellius. For now, we will move on to discuss the doctrine that God is love. Unlike anything else we say about God, this is the one thing that can be said regarding God's innermost essence that does not lapse into empty speculation.

God is love

The high point, the most exhaustive statement of Christian piety is that God is love. Every other attribute[14] culminates in divine love and is included in it.

Schleiermacher argues that "only love and no other divine attribute can be equated with God" (CF §167.1, 1008). Love is God's essential being, and every other attribute must be held in relation to divine love. But what is love, for Schleiermacher? He offers a clear definition: "Love is the orientation of wanting to unite with others and wanting to be in the other" (CF §165.1, 1004). It is the "underlying disposition" in the process of redemption and the reign of God. Through Christ's redemption, God reveals Godself as love. It is *the* expression of the divine nature, the only attribute that can be equated with the very being of God. Love is the truest expression of God's being in such an exhaustive way that it may be substituted for the very name "God."

This means God's activity is not arbitrary but motivated and intentional. Love denotes God's intentionality, while divine power denotes the effectiveness of God's loving will. Neither aspect of God's being can be isolated. God's love and power are mutually dependent. Abstract power without love makes God a demonic, lifeless force, but love without the ability to fulfill its intentions is equally meaningless. As Niebuhr writes:

> Divine activity is *motivated* or *intentional* activity. Any term or phrase that is incapable of indicating this intentional aspect of God's power is theologically defective, so far as Schleiermacher is concerned. [...] 'Love' designates the intention of God's activity. 'Almightiness' designates the effectiveness of that activity. Neither is of interest apart from the other.[15]

God is love, and God's love achieves its goal, namely, the redemption of all creation in Jesus Christ. It is this almighty love that motivates God's acts of creation, election, redemption, and consummation. What God wills God does. God achieves the redemption God desires for the beloved. It is who God is, God is love.

But what about the other attributes discussed in *Christian Faith*, such as divine omnipotence and eternity? Schleiermacher writes that, in themselves, these attributes would be only a "shadow of faith," and as such, they would express only the kind of faith "devils too can have" (CF §167.2, 1009).[16] Every attribute takes a subordinate position to the doctrine that God is love. For example, while Schleiermacher discusses divine omnipotence and eternity in Part One, their fullest expression is found in the context of divine love. So omnipotence is the "almighty love" of God, and God's eternity is God's "eternal love." Apart from divine love, God is an abstraction.

Divine wisdom is the counterpart to divine love. The attributes of love and wisdom are the culminate expressions of God's being, though only love may be identified with the essence of God. We cannot say "God is wisdom" in the same way that we say "God is love." Divine wisdom is the expression of God's relation to the world. Wisdom is divine love as it orders and preserves all things. For Schleiermacher, the Christian belief that "everything is created with a view to the Redeemer" means "everything is already ordered by means of creation" (CF §164.1, 999). God's loving wisdom has arranged creation for the sake of redemption.

The divine will is *singular,* as Schleiermacher writes, "[T]here is no division or contrast in the divine causality anywhere and we can view the divine government of the world only as *one* causality, directed toward but *one* aim" (CF §164.3, 1001). The unity of love and wisdom means there is no ordering, creating, and preserving apart from love, and there is no love apart from the wisdom that orders, creates, and preserves the world. God's love and wisdom together reflect God's will to be *our* God, to bind Godself to the world. Schleiermacher writes that "these two attributes are not divorced, not in any way whatsoever, but are so totally one that one can also view each attribute as already contained in the other one" (CF §165.2, 1004). God's love and wisdom are in perfect harmony. The world itself is the "theater of redemption." The divine wisdom grounds the world in such a way that it is a form of the divine self-communication, "the absolute revelation of Supreme Being" (CF §169, 1013). Divine wisdom is the "unfolding of divine love" (CF §169.3, 1017), the "art […] of bringing the divine love to its complete realization" (CF §165.1, 1004).

Schleiermacher admits there is a certain anthropomorphic risk in saying God is love, but it is worth this danger to express the Christian consciousness of redemption. We may misinterpret the love of God as a human attribute with personal connotations, but it is worth allowing some error to express the culminating experience of the Christian faith, God is love.

Conclusion

The fundamental conviction of Schleiermacher's dogmatics is that God is the Triune God of love. His entire system leads to this conclusion and is incomplete without it. It is vital we do not miss this point. Together with the doctrine of Christ the Redeemer, which necessitates divine threeness and reveals the divine love, this is the heart of Schleiermacher's *Christian Faith*. In chapter four, we will explain why Schleiermacher's dogmatics was arranged like this, but for now, it is important we recognize the essential place he gives to these doctrines.

---

1. CF §167.1, 1008.
2. CF §170.1, 1021.
3. *Essential Trinitarianism,* 54. Bloomsbury T&T Clark, 2017.
4. *Schleiermacher the Theologian,* 182. Philadelphia: Fortress Press, 1978.
5. "Introduction by the Translator," *An Essay on the Trinity,* 4. Columbus: Beloved Publishing, 2018.

6. Julia Lamm: "Schleiermacher identifies Part Two as the heart of the entire dogmatics and describes Part One [...] as an abstraction from the experience of having been redeemed by Christ, [thus] it would follow that the second aspect of Part Two ('explication of the consciousness of grace') is, structurally speaking, the center and foundation of his dogmatics; methodologically speaking, it is the departure point" ("Schleiermacher's Treatise on Grace," *The Harvard Theological Review*, Vol. 101, No. 2, Apr, 2008, 138).

    This further confirms the fact that Schleiermacher's theology is preeminently one of divine grace, as it also shows how those doctrines treated explicitly in Part Two are the center of the whole work. The culmination, or Conclusion, of Schleiermacher's dogmatics is the doctrine of the Trinity, its doctrinal "copestone" or "keystone."
7. *Essential Trinitarianism*, 59. Bloomsbury T&T Clark, 2017.
8. "A Reconsideration of Friedrich Schleiermacher's Treatment of the Doctrine of the Trinity," 142-3 (unpublished dissertation); quoted in S. Poe: *Essential Trinitarianism*, 61. Bloomsbury T&T Clark, 2017.
9. CF §170.1, 1021.
10. See Sarah Coakley: "What Does Chalcedon Solve and What Does It Not?" in *The Incarnation* (ed. Stephen T. Davis, Daniel Kendall, SJ, and Gerald O'Collins; New York: Oxford University Press, 2002), 143-63. Coakley's argument makes a similar point in regards to the goal of the early formulas, namely, their boundary-establishing role. My thanks to S. Poe for pointing out this essay. She writes: "Schleiermacher is indicating the boundaries of orthodoxy by setting out the edges of thought beyond which Christians cannot go. In this way, his theological method here is similar to what Sarah Coakley, an influential reader of the Chalcedonian Formula, takes as that Formula's function" (*Essential Trinitarianism*, 106).
11. "Understanding God as Triune," *Cambridge Companion to Friedrich Schleiermacher*, 174. Cambridge University Press, 2005.
12. CF §172.1, 1032.
13. CF §154.2, 956.
14. Schleiermacher does not approve of separating the divine attributes and essence, writing, "[I]n God no distinction can exist between essence and attributes, and precisely on this account the concept 'attribute' is not really suitable for presentation of the divine being" (CF §167.1, 1007). However, I have retained this more traditional language throughout and in what follows for the sake of clarity. Schleiermacher uses it as well but always in this qualified sense.
15. "Schleiermacher and the Names of God," *Schleiermacher as Contemporary* (ed. Robert Funk), 188-9. New York: Herder & Herder, 1970.
16. See James 2:19.

SIDEBAR: SABELLIUS RECONSIDERED

Schleiermacher's essay on Sabellius was published the same year Part Two of the first edition of *Christian Faith* appeared (1822), and it has been called an unofficial postscript to his dogmatics.[1] It examines the Sabellian doctrine of the Trinity in contrast with the Athanasian. He argues that the Early Church fundamentally misunderstood Sabellius. But as Schleiermacher investigates the true impulses behind Sabellius' theory, he discovers a level of creativity unparalleled by the Athanasian Trinity.

As we have seen, Schleiermacher thinks the doctrine of the Trinity is long overdue for revision. While he does not adopt Sabellius' theory wholesale, he does think Sabellius has much to offer to future Trinitarian theology. He explains, "My present design is to exhibit only such points as may serve to communicate, if possible, some new impetus to the spirit of investigation."[2] Ultimately, Schleiermacher's goal is to move beyond both the Athanasian and Sabellian theories.

Sabellius' "Heresy"

Very little is known about Sabellius directly. We know he was a third-century priest and theologian who probably came from northern Africa, most likely Libya. He also may have been a teacher in Rome for a time. And we know he was excommunicated as a heretic in 220. But the only real insight we have into his life and teachings comes from the polemic writings against him. That is, we only have access to him through the harsh eyes of his critics. None of his original manuscripts have survived.

Sabellius' critics gave his Trinitarian theory many names, from subordinationism, patripassianism, monarchianism, modalism, nominalism, to outright unitarianism (denying the Trinity). The basic premise of their interpretation is succinctly summarized by William Rusch: "Sabellius taught that God was a monad, expressing itself in three operations."[3]

By conflating the Triune persons, it is commonly said that, for Sabellius, Jesus Christ was not the *Son* incarnate but actually the Father (thus, patripassianism). Father, Son, and Spirit were only names God used to represent Godself, and accordingly, they are not distinct persons in God but the three modes of one person. Thus, modalism is the most common charge against him, so much so that the very term "Sabellianism" has become interchangeable with modalism.

This is how Epiphanius described Sabellius and his followers in the fourth century:

> Their tenet is as follows: that one and the same Being is Father, Son and Holy Spirit, in such sense that to one substance belong three names, much as in a man [we find] body, soul and spirit. The body, so to say, is the Father; the soul, so to say, the Son; and the Spirit in the Godhead is what the spirit is in a man. Or as in the sun: it is one substance but has three activities; I mean light, heat and orb. The heat, whether warmth or fervour, is the Spirit; the light is the Son; and the Father Himself is the form of the whole substance. Once on a time the Son was sent forth, like a ray; and, after accomplishing in the world all that had to do with the dispensation of the Gospel and human salvation, was then received back again into heaven; just as a ray is emitted by the sun and is then withdrawn into the sun again. The Holy Spirit is still being sent forth into the world; and, successively and severally, into every one of those who are worthy to receive it. The Spirit re-creates him; fills him with fresh fervour; and supplies him, so to say, with heat and warmth, infusing fresh power and influence into his spirit. Such are the tenets they inculcate.[4]

If all this is true about Sabellius, then he was rightly deemed a heretic by the Early Church and should be ignored. But Schleiermacher suspects the Nicene theologians[5] misunderstood him because of their own presuppositions regarding the Trinity. Therefore, it is his task to rightly understand Sabellius and to see whether or not his theory could offer some help to Trinitarian theology today.

Sabellius According to Schleiermacher

Schleiermacher's interpretation of Sabellius centers around the *God hidden* and *God revealed*. The One God in unity is God hidden, and the Triune God in threeness is God revealed. In other words, *God hidden* is God in God's undivided essence, the unapproachable and unknowable divine monad, but *God revealed* is God in relation to the world, the "economic" Trinity. Schleiermacher claims that, for Sabellius, the "Trinity was not essential to Godhead as in itself considered, but only in reference to created beings and on their account."[6] Sabellius restricted the doctrine of the Trinity to the relationship God has with created beings.

The Father is God revealed in the works of creation and providence. The Son is God revealed in relation to human sin, the Redeemer. The Holy Spirit is God in relation to the Church, God revealed in the gifts of the Spirit and the sanctification of the faithful.

Moss Stuart helpfully summarizes Schleiermacher's reading of Sabellius:

> The sum of Schleiermacher's opinion [...] is, that the Unity is *God concealed,* and the Trinity is *God revealed.* The Unity or [monad], as he supposes, is God [itself], i.e. simply and in and by himself considered, immutable, self-existent, eternal, and possessed of all possible perfection and excellence. But as to the Trinity; the Father is God as revealed in the works of creation, providence, and legislation; the Son is God in human flesh, the divine Logos incarnate; the Holy Ghost is God the Sanctifier, who renovates the hearts of sinners, and dwells in the hearts of believers. The *personality* of the Godhead consists in these *developments,* made in time, and made to intelligent and rational beings.[7]

A vital point in Schleiermacher's reading is Sabellius' use of the divine monad (μονάς or *monas*). He criticized the Nicene theologians for equating the divine monad with the Father, which meant assigning divinity to the Father *alone*. The Son and Spirit were considered God only in a derivative sense, as the Son is "begotten of" and the Spirit "proceeds from" the Father. The Father alone was deemed the *source* of the Godhead. So, in Irenaeus' terms, the Son and Spirit were called the "two hands" of the Father.[8] This is why Schleiermacher argues that the Nicene theologians retained a somewhat subordinationist vision of the Trinity. To these points, he writes:

> Here Sabellius might come in and with as good a right say, that the assertions of his opponents are blasphemy against the Son and Spirit: yea, against the Trinity itself; inasmuch as they make two members of

the Trinity have a part in the divine Unity, only through the causality of the other member.[9]

In contrast, Sabellius constructed a doctrine of the Trinity on the basis of true equality in the Godhead. He did this by first separating the Father from the divine monad. The divine monad—the hidden God—is the source of the Father, Son, and Spirit equally. This is reminiscent of the "God above God" concept in modern theology.[10] The God above God is God in undivided unity, God in Godself, the hidden God. Yet God in relation to finite being is the Triune God. This is what drove Sabellius to criticize the Athanasian Trinity and to be criticized by its proponents in return.[11] Yet Schleiermacher thinks Sabellius' approach is noteworthy since it resolves many of the Christological issues that later developed as a result of the Church's subordinationist tendencies.

Sabellius' Trinitarian theory, according to Schleiermacher, can be summarized like this: God is one and undivided, the ineffable divine monad, but God developed Godself in relation to created beings so that we might know God. If God did not become Triune, then the hidden monad of God's essence "would be altogether unknown to other beings."[12] God in love and grace freely related Godself to that which is not God, and therefore, revealed Godself to finite being.

God developed Godself by acting in and upon the world to become the "first person" of the Trinity, the Father. Thus, "Before the creation of the world [...] he was not Father, strictly speaking, but the pure divine Unity, not yet developed, but existing in and by himself."[13] Likewise, "The self same one Godhead, then, when developed in the person of the Redeemer, is according to him the second [person] in the Trinity; but still without undergoing any change of its own proper nature by this union."[14] The Son did not exist before the incarnation. God developed Godself in the act of redemption to become the "second person" of the Trinity. Finally, the Spirit is God "when the one and the same God unites himself with the church."[15] God developed Godself in the act of sanctification in the Church to become the "third person" of the Trinity, the Holy Spirit. God is one divine monadic being, but God freely became Triune in relation to finite being. All three persons of the Godhead share equally in one, undivided being. No person is above another or the source of the others. Sabellius strove to achieve true equality in the Godhead.

It is important to point out that, for Sabellius, "[T]he one God remains in this case unchanged and undivided."[16] In other words, God is Triune in relation to the world but remains undivided in Godself. This raises the issue of how the persons are not confused or conflated. But the issue is not a question of whether Sabellius failed to distinguish between the three persons (he did not[17]) but of what constitutes a person in the Godhead. Is what we call a "person" eternally in God or is it a development of God in relation to creation? In other words, is divine personality original, substantial, and essential to divinity itself? Or is it a development of divinity for the sake of created being? Sabellius denies that personality is the essence of divinity,[18] and therefore, the three persons must be a development of God in relation to human persons. Accordingly, the one God remains unchanged even in self-development and self-differentiation. The one, monadic Godhead is the same source of all three persons, even in their distinction from each other. They are not the same person, but the same Godhead is in each person. They cannot be conflated simply because their roles are distinctly their own.[19] God remains one and undivided yet God's relation to created being is Triune.

Modalism

But the question remains whether or not the Early Church was right about Sabellius. How does his doctrine of God not result in modalism, as they supposed? Answering this is the critical point of Schleiermacher's argument.

For Sabellius, God is Triune in relation to created beings. But does this mean God will one day cease to be Triune? Schleiermacher argues no: "Sabellius did not hold the Trinity to be only a *transitory* development."[20] In other words, once God creates the world, God is eternally Father; once God becomes incarnate, God is eternally Son; and once God sanctifies and dwells with humanity by the Spirit, God is eternally Spirit. God's relation to the world persists, and therefore, God is irrevocably Triune. While before the world it may be said the Trinity was not essential to God, after creating, redeeming, and sanctifying finite being, God becomes Triune; the Trinity is essential to God's innermost Self.

Sabellius' sun analogy, to which Epiphanius alluded above, was misunderstood by his critics to imply that God's relation to the world is revokable. Yet the very opposite is meant: "Sabellius did *not* regard the personality of the Godhead as a *transitory* phenomenon."[21] Just as the sun cannot cease to shine and produce heat, so God cannot cease to be Triune. Because creation continues, the Father cannot cease to be Father; because redemption persists, the Son cannot cease to be Son; because the Church goes on, the Holy Spirit cannot cease to be the Holy Spirit. God's triunity may not have been essential before creation, but it is now and forever a vital part of God's being.

Sabellius is essentially arguing that 1) God in Godself before creation is one and unknowable (the divine monad). It is only by engaging in empty speculation that we might imagine God's Triunity in Godself before the creation of the world. Therefore, to speak of an antecedent Trinity would be to engage in a kind of mythology. But 2) what we *do* know about God has been revealed in the history of God's relation to humanity. In this history, God reveals Godself as Father, Son, and Holy Spirit. In time and in relation to the world, God *is* Triune. This was not denied by Sabellius. It is only an antecedent, mythologically speculative Trinity that he refuses. Sabellius does not reject the doctrine of the Trinity itself (unitarianism), nor does he conflate the persons of the Trinity as mere names or activities of one person (modalism). The critical difference between his doctrine of the Trinity and that of the Early Church is merely this: Sabellius denied the antecedent Trinity, while they affirmed it.

As an example, consider how theologians typically deal with the incarnation. Few would say God the Son has *always* been a human being. The Word *became* flesh and was not antecedently flesh. At the same time, we could not deny that God the Son became a human being in time. So theologians *already* admit that God developed Godself in relation to the world. And furthermore, some theologians have argued (such as T. F. Torrance) that because the Son became flesh in time, the Son is now and forever bound to our humanity, at once God and man. In other words, what developed in time persists eternally.

Similarly, Sabellius argues that God developed Godself in relation to the world as Father, Son, and Holy Spirit. And because God refuses to give up on humanity, God's relation to humankind *remains eternal.* Therefore, God remains eternally Triune. In Godself before creation, God is one in undivided unity, the hidden God. We do not know if God was Triune before the world, and perhaps we should avoid speculating about what God was doing before creation. But what we do know and can assert with certainty is that in relation to humanity and in time, God is Triune, the revealed God. That is what we have to keep in mind to understand Sabellius' point. Most importantly, it is also why he cannot be called a modalist, if Schleiermacher's reading is correct.

As we can see, the end result of both Sabellius and the Nicene theologian's doctrine of the Trinity is exactly the same. Both theories affirm that God is eternally Father, Son, and Holy Spirit. The only practical difference seems to be Sabellius' refusal to speculate about an antecedent Trinity.[22]

Sabellius' approach is noteworthy because of how it solves the issue of subordinationism. He excludes the possibility of any member of the Trinity being the source of the whole Godhead, or that the remaining members are God only in a derivative sense. All three persons are equal developments of the same divine monad, not merely the "two arms" of the Father.

Sabellius' Appeal

There are a few reasons why I think Schleiermacher was drawn to Sabellius' theory (though he did not adopt it fully). First, it is non-speculative, as we have noted. This is a major impulse of Schleiermacher's own dogmatics, and it is only natural that he would emphasize this aspect of Sabellius' thought. By pointing to Sabellius' theory, Schleiermacher is saying that if the Trinity is revised, it should be along non-speculative lines.

Second, Sabellius returned dogmatic reflection on the Trinity to a concrete basis, the history of salvation. It is only from the Christian self-consciousness of redemption in and through Christ that the Trinity should be developed, and this guideline is followed by Sabellius' theory as he restricted the doctrine to God's relation with the world. As Williams notes, Schleiermacher "is attracted to Sabellianism as a more historical, less speculative account of Christian faith."[23]

And finally, Schleiermacher is drawn to the originality of Sabellius' theory, in contrast with the Athanasian Trinity, which he thinks arose only negatively, in reaction to conflicting theories.[24]

While it could be said that all of this is simply Schleiermacher misreading Sabellius to serve his own ends, it still remains a contribution worth considering for its originality and systematic merit. But such a judgment should be left with patristic scholars.[25] For our part, we have no reason to suspect Schleiermacher intentionally misreads Sabellius, and so we should give him the benefit of the doubt.

Sabellius deserves to be reconsidered. If Schleiermacher is even partially correct in his analysis, then there are indeed many creative insights worth thinking through more carefully. This does not mean we should fully adopt Sabellius'—or even Schleiermacher's—conclusions.[26] But it does mean his proposal is well worth exploring further, especially if we take Schleiermacher's challenge seriously that the Trinity needs to be reformed.

---

1. It was translated into English by Moss Stuart in 1835 and reprinted by Beloved Publishing in 2018. The translation is rough and needs updating, but even in its present form, it is a brilliant essay. It is often referred to as an unofficial postscript because it continues the arguments outlined in the Conclusion of *Christian Faith* (§§170-172).
2. *An Essay on the Trinity*, 65. Columbus: Beloved Publishing, 2018.
3. *The Trinitarian Controversy*, 9. Philadelphia: Fortress Press, 1980.
4. *Adversus Haereses (Panarion)*, 63.1.2. Public domain.
5. Sabellius predates the Council of Nicaea (325), but I refer to his critics as "Nicene" to indicate more broadly the early period of Church history that lead up to Nicaea. It was during this period that the doctrine of the Trinity was being developed. Nicaea normalized and solidified the doctrine, and so it is the epitome of orthodox Trinitarian theology.
6. *An Essay on the Trinity*, 142. Columbus: Beloved Publishing, 2018.
7. Ibid., 53.
8. *Against Heresies*, 5.6.1. Public domain.

9. *An Essay on the Trinity*, 161. Columbus: Beloved Publishing, 2018.
10. Paul Tillich is known for coining the "God above God" phrase, but he uses it in an apologetic sense, while Schleiermacher does not. Robert Streetman notes the similarity, "Schleiermacher's concept of the *monas* is an anticipation of the concept of 'the God above God'" (*Barth and Schleiermacher*, 128; Philadelphia: Fortress Press, 1988).

    It is also interesting to note that Tillich's other famous concept of God as the "ground of being-itself" finds similarities with Schleiermacher. He writes, "God is designated as the one grounding this interconnected being in all its diverse parts" (CF §30.1, 183).
11. The main point of disagreement is over the *source* of the Godhead. For Sabellius, the divine monad, God in undivided unity and hiddenness, is the source of the Father, Son, and Spirit equally. For the Nicene theologians, the *Father* is the source of the Godhead. Schleiermacher shows how this is the root cause of why Sabellius was misunderstood.
12. *An Essay on the Trinity*, 151. Columbus: Beloved Publishing, 2018.
13. Ibid., 150.
14. Ibid., 149.
15. Ibid.
16. Ibid.
17. According to Stuart, Sabellius excommunicated anyone who denied the distinct nature of Father, Son, and Holy Spirit. Ibid., 127.
18. This is a point Schleiermacher agrees with, since he consistently denied the "personal" God, and preferred instead to speak about the "living" God. He also thinks "personality" cannot be attributed to God's essential being. See supplementary note 19 from chapter two of *On Religion*, third edition.
19. For example, the Father is not the Son (nor the Son the Father) because the Son is God in the act of redemption while the Father is God in the act of creation. God is fully manifest in each person yet each person is distinct in their personality. As we will soon see, because creation and redemption persist eternally, God remains eternally Father and Son—these are not transitory persons. Admittedly, this is an issue that would need to be developed further if Sabellius' theory were to become the basis for a future Trinitarian theory, and perhaps that is one of the reasons why Schleiermacher does not adopt it fully.
20. *An Essay on the Trinity*, 143. Columbus: Beloved Publishing, 2018.
21. Ibid., 144.
22. Schleiermacher makes a similar point with reference to Beryll, stating rhetorically, "And why should we rather lay stress, in respect to true Christian belief, upon an *eternal* plurality in the Godhead, which has no relation to any thing without, than content ourselves with such a distinction in it as is connected with Christian revelation? For this is the only difference that existed between Beryll and his opponents" (ibid., 110). In other words, the only difference between the two theories is that one speculates God's eternal plurality while the other is content with God's revelation in history.
23. *Schleiermacher the Theologian*, 145. Philadelphia: Fortress Press, 1978.
24. Schleiermacher concludes his essay with this: "All this shews that the Athanasian form of doctrine arose much less from any definite and positive basis, than from the effort to avoid the force of other assertions made by an opposing party, and to wind one's way through them. To the Sabellian views we cannot refute at least to yield our testimony, that they are the result of originality of thought and independence of mind" (*An Essay on the Trinity*, 170; Columbus: Beloved Publishing, 2018).
25. Robert F. Streetman, for his part, thinks Schleiermacher's "reinterpretation of Sabellius's view of the Trinity was essentially correct (and was largely accepted by Schleiermacher's major critics)" (*Barth and Schleiermacher*, 116; Philadelphia: Fortress Press, 1988). See further, Streetman: "Friedrich Schleiermacher's Doctrine of the Trinity and Its Significance for Theology Today" (PhD. Dissertation, Drew University, 1975).
26. I want to be clear: I have my doubts about the value of Sabellius' theory and the accuracy of his critique of Nicene theology. But I have presented Schleiermacher's reading here without much personal comment so that his point can be understood. It is, indeed, an interesting study, but not one to be taken without a grain of salt.

SIDEBAR: GOD HIDDEN AND REVEALED

> No theologian in the modern age can compare with Schleiermacher in his attempt to refashion the doctrine of God. He subjected the dubious aspects of its traditional formulation to a penetrating criticism, but thought through the abiding elements of the doctrine of divine attributes with a systematic power which puts all previous models in the shade.[1]
>
> — Gerhard Ebeling

One of the most fascinating books on Schleiermacher's doctrine of God is Robert R. Williams' *Schleiermacher the Theologian*. We are now at a point where his argument can be fully appreciated.

Williams' thesis is that Schleiermacher "has put the entire doctrine of God—including divine attributes and trinity—on a single, nonspeculative, phenomenological footing."[2] In other words, Schleiermacher is no speculative theologian, as his critics have argued, but explicitly non-speculative because phenomenologically based. Williams thinks a phenomenological reading is far more faithful to Schleiermacher's intentions and can be used as a helpful interpretive tool. The feeling of absolute dependence does not indicate a speculative self-projection, "speaking of God in a loud voice," but the non-speculative, empirical explication of a given phenomenon, namely, God's self-disclosure in Jesus Christ.

Phenomenology is a complex subject, but its basic premise is to study the phenomenon of being, or lived experience. A phenomenon is that which manifests itself, an experience of direct consciousness. Edmund Husserl is often considered its modern founder, and he explains that "pure phenomenology is the science of pure consciousness."[3] While Schleiermacher predates phenomenology, it may be shown that his work bears striking similarities to its modern proponents.

In theological terms, phenomenological thinking presupposes the unity of God's being and act. So Williams further argues that Schleiermacher's doctrine of God centers around the complete coincidence of God hidden and revealed, God in Godself and God-for-us. Williams explains:

> The task of phenomenological theology is to describe the actual correlation between God and world as immediately given in religious consciousness. This distinguishes the *Glaubenslehre* [CF] from speculative natural theology; for the latter, owing to the universalizing formalism inherent in conceptualization, involves an abstract separation between God's being (abstractly conceived in universal terms) and God's acts (concretely experienced). It is precisely this abstract formalism and separation which Schleiermacher is determined to avoid, and whose pernicious influence in theology he seeks to overcome.[4]

Theology must continually refer to redemption in and through Jesus Christ, not an abstract theory about God's being in Godself but God in relation to the world, which means theology involves reflection on the lived experience of the Christian Church. Schleiermacher's goal is to remove all speculation regarding the being of God apart from the acts of God towards us in Jesus Christ.[5] Schleiermacher writes, "[W]e have no formulation for the being of God as such distinct from the being of God in the world" (CF §172.1, 1032). By focusing on Christian religious self-consciousness, Schleiermacher presupposes the unity of God's being and act, the phenomenon of God's self-disclosure.

Central to Schleiermacher's doctrine of God is the complete coincidence of God hidden and revealed. As such, Williams sees parallels between Schleiermacher and the work of Nicholas of Cusa.

Nicholas of Cusa was a fifteenth-century forerunner to Luther's famous concept of God hidden and revealed, *Deus absconditus et Deus revelatus*. Nicholas of Cusa's thesis was that theology is "learned ignorance," and that God is the coincidence of opposites. Williams finds a similar contrast in Schleiermacher's doctrine of God, but Schleiermacher goes further than Nicholas of Cusa by asserting the *complete* coincidence of God hidden and revealed. Williams writes:

> It is no exaggeration to say that Schleiermacher's doctrine of God and divine attributes is structured by the fundamental contrast between God hidden and revealed. [...] If the terminology is not new or original with Schleiermacher, what is novel and original is his making it the central operative concept in the entire doctrine of God. Further, it is the central structuring theological principle because hiddenness and revealedness are the general phenomenological features of divine self-disclosure constitutive of actual religious experience. [...] God is one with his self-disclosure.[6]

God's being and act coincide completely. God corresponds to Godself.[7] But God's being is never *given* in God's act, it remains a *giving*. That is, God does not become an object subject to human control but remains the living God.

The hidden God is not in conflict with the revealed God, but the two, by definition, coincide. They are the phenomenological features God's self-disclosure. The hidden God is the *terminus a quo,* the "limit from which" theology develops, and the revealed God is the *terminus ad quem,* the "limit to which" it forms its propositions.[8] In other words, God hidden and revealed establishes the boundary for what we can and cannot say about God as finite beings. Hiddenness is an essential component of revealedness and vice versa. Revelation does not mean a full unveiling or complete de-mystifying of God, in the sense that we objectify God or directly apprehend God's essence. Revelation is the self-disclosure of God for whom nothing greater can be conceived. Since finite being cannot know infinite being, God remains hidden even in God's self-revelation.

The complete coincidence of the hidden and revealed God is a brilliant formula for safeguarding theology's limitations as a human discipline, reminding us that we are limited in what we can and cannot say. We dare to claim only one truth about God's essence, according to Schleiermacher: God is love. The doctrine that God is love is the highest reflection for not only Schleiermacher's theology but *all* theology. It establishes the outermost boundary of what we can say about God's being, and anything beyond this point lapses into empty speculation.

Where Schleiermacher departs from Cusa is precisely in the assertion "God is love." God is not merely *a* coincidence of opposites, but *the* coincidence of opposites. According to Williams, the proposition that God is love

> represents a significant departure from negative theology and learned ignorance. [...] What is disclosed through incarnation and redemption is not merely *a* coincidence of opposites, or a relative coincidence [...], but rather *the complete* coincidence of opposites;

God hidden is *homoousios* [same in being] with God revealed. There is nothing held back in incarnation: God and Redeemer are one and the same.[9]

In other words, phenomenological theology results neither in a purely negative theology (apophatic) or a positive theology but the coincidence of both.[10] Both God's hiddenness and revealedness are essential to the doctrine of God, and Schleiermacher's innovation is the systematic consistency with which he worked out this distinction and the centrality he placed on the concept.

So while Schleiermacher "does not teach an immanent Trinity in the traditional sense,"[11] he also does not teach *only* an economic Trinity. Rather, he is aptly called an "essential Trinitarian."[12] Schleiermacher's nuanced approach to the mystery of God in Godself, together with his disdain for all speculative content in dogmatics, allows him to avoid the "fallacy of misplaced concreteness" that immanent Trinitarians have fallen into.[13] His doctrine of God is one of his most significant—yet most often overlooked (because misunderstood)—contributions to the history of theology. By stressing the unity of God's being and act, Schleiermacher's doctrine of God presents a revolutionary vision of divine ontology. The hidden God *is* the revealed God. God in Godself and God-for-us completely coincide. While God is not given *over* to human control (and thus remains hidden), there is complete harmony between God's being and act.

Similarities with Dialectical Theology (Barth)

It is here that Schleiermacher's theology bears a striking resemblance to Karl Barth and twentieth-century dialectical theology. One of the primary impulses of dialectical theology is the "non-objectifiability" of God. Barth writes, "Who God is and what it is to be divine is something we have to learn where God has revealed Himself and His nature."[14] God's non-objectifiability stresses that God is not an object we can control. God is always the God above God, or the "wholly other" God—God above every human conceptualization of God. God's being is revealed to us not through rationalized concepts (natural theology) but according to the acts of God towards us, the event of divine revelation. There are still irreconcilable differences between Barth and Schleiermacher, but fundamentally they agree: God is beyond objectification. Barth and Schleiermacher refused to separate God's being from God's act.[15]

George Hunsinger, in his now-classic text, *How to Read Karl Barth*, identifies an essential motif in Barth's theology: actualism. This motif bears a striking resemblance to Schleiermacher's phenomenological theology, though differences undoubtedly persist. Hunsinger offers this definition:

> Actualism is the most distinctive and perhaps the most difficult of the motifs. It is present whenever Barth speaks, as he constantly does, in the language of occurrence, happening, event, history, decisions, and act. At the most general level it means that he thinks primarily in terms of events and relationship rather than monadic or self-contained substances. So pervasive is this motif that Barth's whole theology might well be described as a theology of active relations. God and humanity are both defined in fundamentally actualistic terms.[16]

The same could be said of Schleiermacher's work. If we correctly understand what he means by the "feeling of absolute dependence" and Christian religious self-consciousness, then we will see he is quite close to what Barth means by "event." These terms indicate the relationship God establishes with us by grace, and it is thus God's act towards us, the "event" or phenomenon of divine self-disclosure, which is central to Schleiermacher's theology. As I have stressed since chapter one, Schleiermacher is preeminently a theologian of grace. Divine revelation is never a "given" but a "giving." It is an event, and theology is merely the explication of this revelatory phenomenon as it affects our consciousness. His theology may, too, be called "actualistic."

Further similarities come to light as Hunsinger continues. In describing the motif of "objectivism," he writes, "There is no hidden God beyond the revealed God. The hidden God and the revealed God are essentially one and the same."[17] We would do just as well to say that the hidden and revealed God completely coincide. So Barth and Schleiermacher stand in relative agreement about the coincidence, or unity, of God's being and act.

These points establish a sharp contrast between non-speculative theology and the tendencies of natural theology, which *both* Barth and Schleiermacher rejected. Natural theology constructs a doctrine of God from a logical basis in nature and reason, but we cannot know God through speculation. Only where God has revealed Godself can God be known.

I do not mean to say that Barth and Schleiermacher are fully united in this, but they are remarkably similar. The result of their approach is the same: Both end up with a doctrine of God where God alone determines Godself— either through God's self-revelation mediated through Scripture and preaching (Barth) or God's revelation in the modification of self-consciousness in and through the redemption of Christ (Schleiermacher). Their methods may differ, but the result is still a doctrine of God that refuses to objectify God's essence. Only love, for Schleiermacher, may be identified with

God's essence, and everything else we say remains a human reflection on God's relation to the world, the revealed God.

Williams emphasizes how Schleiermacher's bipolar theology (the coincidence of opposites) is a decisive break from classical theology. This same impulse bears a strong resemblance to dialectical theology. In fact, when I first read the following description of Schleiermacher, it sounded like something that could have come from Barth's hand. Williams writes:

> Consequently, this bipolar concept of God represents an alternative to classical theology. Instead of static substance, God is free, self-moving, dynamic, and living. Such a deity is able to be immanent in and related to the world without loss of being or perfection. To be related is not to be dependent, because God remains free even in relation. [...] God is both absolute and related.[18]

For Barth, God is the "One who loves in freedom."[19] This indicates at once God's freedom and God's determination to be our God, to be bound to humanity. God is both "wholly other" and God-for-us. While Williams does not directly make this comparison, he describes Schleiermacher's doctrine of God in remarkably similar terms:

> The best, least speculative formula for God's being, which structures Schleiermacher's discussion of divine attributes, is that God is absolute inwardness and absolute vitality. The concept of God is bipolar: absolute inwardness is the inner or freedom pole; absolute vitality is outer or necessity pole. God is the perfect coincidence of both. Thus God is both immanent in the world as world-ordering omnipotence, and at the same time transcendent to the world in his freedom. God is both absolute and related, both hidden and revealed.[20]

While Barth and Schleiermacher will work out each of these insights differently, they have nevertheless committed to the coincidence of God's hiddenness and revealedness.[21] God is the One who loves in freedom, absolute inwardness and absolute vitality. This results in doing theology on God's terms, in the unity of God's being and act, without lapsing into empty speculation. God is not objectified by their respective approaches.

Schleiermacher's complete coincidence of opposites is quite close, then, to Barth's idea that there is no God "behind the back" of Jesus Christ.[22] Because God's will, act, and essence all seamlessly coincide, then what God does God is, and vice versa. While the hidden God remains un-objectified, God freely objectified Godself in Jesus Christ so that we might know and be united with the God of love. Both Barth *and* Schleiermacher can say that the act of God in Jesus Christ for our redemption *is* God's self-revelation because God's being and act coincide.[23]

Conclusion

While it is not always the best practice to read a past thinker in the light of modern trends, Williams' reading of Schleiermacher as a phenomenologically based theologian is a helpful interpretive tool. At the very least, it is a far better reading of Schleiermacher than the superficial misreadings that turn him into a subjectivist. The feeling of absolute dependence is a grace-infused concept. God remains the determinant even in our consciousness of God. Revelation is a phenomenon of *grace,* of God's desire to be with humanity and to be known by us.

It is also in the light of this reading that we can reckon with the radical nature of Schleiermacher's doctrine of God. The common notion that Schleiermacher has little to offer either Trinitarian theology or the doctrine of God is proven false. In one of his most striking departures from traditional dogmatics, Ebeling has argued that Schleiermacher's *Christian faith* "as a whole" is "one single exposition of the doctrine of God. The old twofold division into *theologia* and *oikonomia* [God's being and act] [...] must be overcome."[24] Rather than separately examining God in Godself and God's acts towards us, Schleiermacher entire dogmatics is an exposition of God in the unity of God's being and act. The innovation and systematic merit of his approach are not recognized often enough.

Furthermore, regarding the doctrine of the Trinity, Schleiermacher not only placed it at the high-point or conclusion to his dogmatics, but he helped initiate its revival. He is rightly called an "essential" Trinitarian, as both Williams and the recent efforts of Shelli Poe have shown.[25] In the future, theologians should take his criticisms regarding the Trinity more seriously and engage his thought with the care it deserves.

Finally, I hope to have sparked some interest in the possibility that Barth and the dialectical theologians are closer to Schleiermacher than often thought. At the very least, Schleiermacher's doctrine of God seems to stress the non-objectifiability of God with equal force because of his usage of God hidden and revealed. Ultimately, Gerhard Eberling was right: Schleiermacher's doctrine of God is unmatched in its creativity and systematic construction.

---

1. "Schleiermacher's Doctrine of the Divine Attributes," *Schleiermacher as Contemporary* (ed. Robert Funk), 127. New York: Herder and Herder, 1970.
2. *Schleiermacher the Theologian*, 156; Philadelphia: Fortress Press, 1978.

3. *The Phenomenology Reader,* 129. New York: Routledge, 2002.
4. *Schleiermacher the Theologian,* 10. Philadelphia: Fortress Press, 1978.
5. As Ebeling notes: "What Schleiermacher has in view in all this is unquestionably the central biblical description of God as the living God. [...] In living things, however, all is action. The activity of God is not to be separated from the being of God in such a way that the latter could somehow be treated alone" ("Schleiermacher's Doctrine of the Divine Attributes," *Schleiermacher as Contemporary* [ed. Robert Funk], 142. New York: Herder and Herder, 1970).

    Ebeling further identifies a number of polarities that Schleiermacher will not accept as a result: There is no division, for God, between what is real/actual and what is possible, between what God wills and does, between divine necessity and freedom, and between an effectual or ineffectual divine will (ibid., 143). This explains why Schleiermacher found it impossible to say that God creates, wills for creation to be redeemed, yet redeems only in part. What God wills God does.
6. *Schleiermacher the Theologian,* 147-8; Philadelphia: Fortress Press, 1978.
7. Eberhard Jüngel used this phrase—"God corresponds to Himself"—to summarize Barth's doctrine of God. He writes, "Barth's *Dogmatics* is in reality basically a thorough exegesis of this statement" (*God's Being is in Becoming,* 36; Grand Rapids: Wm. B. Eerdmans, 2001). It is not by mistake that I have used the same phrase here. This is where I find the harmony between Barth and Schleiermacher most apparent, both in their rejection of speculative theology and their phenomenological (actualist) method. See the discussion below.
8. See R. Williams: *Schleiermacher the Theologian,* 83, 151. (Philadelphia: Fortress Press, 1978.) Williams writes: "God hidden does not mean God in his abstract eternity and aseity, utterly transcendent to and absence from the world. Rather, 'God hidden' is meant as the phenomenological limiting feature of God's self-disclosure or self-manifestation. [...] That is, even in his revealedness God does not cease to be hidden" (ibid., 83-4).
9. *Schleiermacher the Theologian,* 152. Philadelphia: Fortress Press, 1987.
10. Williams writes, "Schleiermacher's pairing of negative and positive attributes reflects his attempt to construct the doctrine of God on the fundamental phenomenological contrast between God hidden and God revealed" (ibid., 70-1).
11. Ibid., 153.
12. See S. Poe: *Essential Trinitarianism.* Bloomsbury T&T Clark, 2017.
13. *Schleiermacher the Theologian,* 154. Philadelphia: Fortress Press, 1987.
14. *Church Dogmatics* IV/1, 186. Peabody: Hendrickson Publishers, 2010.
15. Barth writes about his doctrine of God: "Therefore our first and decisive transcription of the statement that God is, must be that God is who He is in the act of His revelation" (*Church Dogmatics* II/1, 262; Peabody: Hendrickson Publishers, 2010).
16. *How to Read Karl Barth,* 30. New York: Oxford University Press, 1991.
17. Ibid., 37.
18. *Schleiermacher the Theologian,* 68. Philadelphia: Fortress Press, 1987.
19. See *Church Dogmatics* II/1. Peabody: Hendrickson Publishers, 2010.
20. *Schleiermacher the Theologian,* 87. Philadelphia: Fortress Press, 1987.
21. See Barth's unique usage of God's hiddenness in *Church Dogmatics* II/1 §27.1, contrasted with the "Veracity" or accuracy of the knowledge of God in §27.2, which is strikingly similar to Schleiermacher's coincidence of opposites. Furthermore, see Barth's important section on "The Being of God as the One Who Loves in Freedom" in *Church Dogmatics* II/1 §28. A comparison of these sections would be fruitful for future studies of Barth and Schleiermacher.

    Here we might point to a key example from Barth regarding both the coincidence of hiddenness and revealedness as well as his "actualized" ontology:

    "A true doctrine of the divine attributes must in all circumstances attest and take into account both factors—God's self-disclosure and His self-concealment. The knowledge of God must not be swallowed up in the ignorance. Nor, again, must the ignorance be swallowed up by the knowledge. Both demands are laid upon us by God Himself in His revelation: the obedience of knowledge and the humility of ignorance. And in laying down both requirements God is equally the one true God. The one grace of His self-revelation is at the root of both, and, because His self-revelation is His truth, we must add: He Himself, His own most proper reality. And in both ways, through His self-disclosure and His

concealment, He is at one and the same time knowable and unknowable to us" (*Church Dogmatics* II/1, 342; Peabody: Hendrickson Publishers, 2010).
22. James Gordon writes, "There is, then, for Schleiermacher, no 'other' God that exists behind the back of Jesus Christ, as Barth worried" ("A Glaring Misunderstanding?", 324; *International Journal of Systematic Theology*, Vol. 16, number 3, July 2014).

    The removal of a God behind the back of Jesus Christ is certainly a concern of Barth's theology. But the exact phrase finds more traction in T. F. Torrance, who writes, "There is thus no God behind the back of Jesus Christ, but only this God whose face we see in the face of our Lord Jesus" (*The Christian Doctrine of God*, 243; T&T Clark, 1996). Torrance's phrase goes a long way in articulating the major concern of Barth's anti-speculative doctrine of God, but as we have discovered, it also aptly summarizes Schleiermacher's.
23. Accordingly, Schleiermacher writes: "[T]here is only *one* source from which all Christian doctrine is derived, namely, Christ's self-proclamation" (CF §19.PS, 138).
24. "Schleiermacher's Doctrine of the Divine Attributes," *Schleiermacher as Contemporary* (ed. Robert Funk), 152-3. New York: Herder and Herder, 1970.

    Theologia and *oikonomia* do not literally mean God's being and act, but I have translated these accordingly to highlight the importance of Ebeling's claim and Williams' reading. *Theologia* is "God-knowledge," and *oikonomia* means the divine "economy" (lit. "housekeeping"), such as the acts of creation and redemption. They may also indicate the hidden and revealed God. So it is not improper to translate these as God's being and act.
25. Poe's project is different from Williams', and she is critical of him on some points. But their work shares similar goals, specifically, revitalizing Schleiermacher's Trinitarian theology.

3

CHRIST OUR REDEEMER

SUMMARY: The true "heart" of Schleiermacher's theology is Jesus Christ our Redeemer. It is the basis from which everything is constructed and the end to which everything points. While his Christology has been criticized as unorthodox, Schleiermacher saw himself in basic harmony with the Chalcedonian Definition by rejecting the same heresies. But he was also critical of its propositions, particularly the two-nature doctrine of Christ, and offers a revised formula. His Christology hinges on the being of God in Christ, expressed by Christ's "absolutely strong" (or perfect) God-consciousness. Christ is the completion of creation, the ideal human being in unhindered fellowship with God.

IN SCHLEIERMACHER'S OWN WORDS:

> Christianity is a monotheistic mode of faith belonging to the teleological bent of religion. It is distinguished essentially from other such modes of faith in that within Christianity everything is referred to the redemption accomplished through Jesus of Nazareth.[1]

> [F]or all times [Christ] is the most complete mediator between God and every single part of the human race.[2]

> The common element of all Christian doctrine is that the fact of redemption

is acknowledged through Christ, and without this there is no Christian doctrine.[3]

SECONDARY QUOTES:

Schleiermacher is profoundly aware of the difficulties the modern Christian has in making sense out of the language of classical Christology. Thus, if the church's faith in the Redeemer is to be sustained, it must subject itself to continual criticism, the aim of which is to rediscover the religious intentions behind the Christological creeds and then to reconstruct dogma so as to express these inner intentions effectively for a new day.[4]

— C. W. CHRISTIAN

One of the most important things Schleiermacher does in his theology is to change our focus back to relationships. Christian faith is not about what we believe; Christian faith is about our relationship with God. This relationship is patterned after the example of Christ.[5]

— CATHERINE L. KELSEY

Introduction

For Schleiermacher, everything in the Christian faith is related to or determined by Jesus Christ, the Redeemer. This is why Richard Niebuhr aptly called Schleiermacher's theology "Christomorphic." This expresses how, for Schleiermacher, everything is founded upon the redemption Christians experience in and through Jesus Christ. It is the heartbeat of his entire theology, the center from which everything derives and to which everything points.

To rightly understand Schleiermacher, we must now turn our attention to his doctrine of Christ and redemption. But this is also one of the most criticized aspects of his theology. I hope to navigate through Schleiermacher's complex argument and understand the reasons why he developed his Christology in such a controversial way. I do not intend to defend his work from every attack, but I do hope to show the logic behind his conclusions. My goal is to appreciate his proposal for what it has to offer, but then leave it up to you to form your own judgments regarding the success of his ideas.

Schleiermacher's doctrine of Christ is paradigm-breaking, and it is impossible to adequately comprehend him if we expect his work to fit within traditional categories. In some respects, Schleiermacher presents his Christology in classical terms, but he alters those concepts so drastically that they are no longer recognizably the same. As Dawn DeVries notes, it was to retain a systematic consistency with traditional Christology that Schleiermacher presented his radically altered Christology in a more conventional *form*. However, she writes, "This kind of Christological language is not Schleiermacher's, and he has to strain to fit his doctrine into a structure not of his choosing."[6] To sort through this problem, we will first examine how Schleiermacher agrees with yet is critical of traditional Christology.

The Problem with Chalcedon

Schleiermacher's doctrine of Christ begins by reflecting on the given experience presupposed in Christian self-consciousness, namely, the experience of redemption in and through Jesus Christ. The "basic consciousness of all Christians regarding their pardoned status" is that we "have communion with God only in the community of life with the Redeemer" (CF §91.1, 559). Schleiermacher argues that this experience must be the starting point for Christological reflection. He then asks: What are the conditions that made redemption possible? Who or what must Christ be to establish redemption as His work?

Schleiermacher identifies four heresies that *cannot* be true about Christ if the Church's experience of redemption is also true. These are the "natural heresies" of the Christian faith. If we allow any of these to creep into our thinking and teaching, then it would undermine the Church's collective experience of redemption in and through Christ. Christianity from the Early Church onwards has combated these heresies and it always will. Schleiermacher writes:

> In Christianity the natural heresies are the Docetic and Nazarean, the Manichean and the Pelagian.[7]

These heresies establish the boundary for who Christ must be if He is our Redeemer and what conditions must be met if redemption in Him is secured.

The first pair—the Docetic and Nazarean—have to do with Christ's nature. If Jesus is indeed the Redeemer, then two conditions must be met. First, Jesus must be like us in every way. That is, He must be a human being fully sharing in our essential nature. This counters the Docetic heresy, which placed Jesus *above* humanity, giving Him no share in our actual existence. For Christ to be our Redeemer means Christ must be one of us, a real human being. The Docetic heresy must be avoided at all costs. Yet, on the other hand, the Nazarean heresy goes in the opposite direction by asserting that Jesus' humanity leaves no room for the being of God in Him, that is, it denies His absolutely strong God-consciousness. In that case, Jesus would be just as in need of redemption as we are. Therefore, if Jesus truly is our

Redeemer, then He must be like us in every way—*except* for sharing in our need for redemption, that is, except for sin.

The second pair—the Manichean and Pelagian—have to do with the possibility of and conditions for redemption. The Manichean heresy presupposes that human nature *cannot* be redeemed at all, and the Pelagian heresy thinks it is up to human beings to redeem themselves. Both positions nullify the need for and the possibility of redemption. In the former, the impossibility of redemption leaves no fault in humanity to remain unredeemed, and in the latter, the possibility of self-redemption makes the redemption of God equally unnecessary, since we could just as well redeem ourselves without God's help.

In short, for Schleiermacher, Christ must be a true human being like us in every way except for sin. His soteriology then asserts that humanity must be redeemable, in need of redemption, and unable to redeem itself. These are the boundaries within which Schleiermacher works out his doctrine of Christ and redemption.

By rejecting the Docetic and Nazarean heresies, Schleiermacher *agrees* with traditional Christology. Schleiermacher's Christology *is* orthodox to the extent that it is situated within the same limitations established by those early theologians. He has not trespassed beyond the reaches of orthodoxy. As Mariña writes:

> It is clear from Schleiermacher's discussion that he is in complete agreement with Chalcedon in regard to the positions it *rejects*. The humanity of Jesus [...] cannot be done away with, yet we must affirm a veritable existence of God in him.[8]

But Schleiermacher differs drastically with the early theologians over their propositions regarding Christ. That is, he agrees with the limitations set by orthodoxy—their reflections on what Christ *cannot* be—but he thinks there is a better way to contemplate who Christ is from within that limit. It is important to stress that in what they are *against*, Schleiermacher and the Chalcedonian theologians agree, but not in how they define Christ and the being of God in Him.

Schleiermacher takes particular issue with ascribing "two natures" to Christ. A large part of this has to do with his refusal to anthropomorphize or objectify God. Schleiermacher writes, "God is to be placed above all being and nature" (CF §96.1, 585). God cannot be conceived of as if God were an object of human control, as if God were a being like us. To say Christ possessed a human nature and a divine nature implies that both "natures" are on the same plane. But God's "nature" is categorically unfit to be compared with human "nature."

Accordingly, it is inappropriate to speak of God having a nature or as a person in the everyday use of these terms. If we must use these terms, they have to be carefully qualified. Schleiermacher writes, "The word 'nature' is especially ill suited," and we "cannot attribute a 'nature' to God" (CF §96.1, 584). It is unhelpful and confusing to use this kind of language in Christology, and thus Schleiermacher thinks applying two natures to Christ is severely problematic.

Schleiermacher refers to the "total fruitlessness of this mode of presentation." It can only lead to incoherence. For example, questions will naturally arise as to whether or not Christ had two wills alongside two natures, which threatens the unity of Christ's person, as Schleiermacher shows:

> [I]f Christ has only *one* will, then his divine nature is incomplete if this will is human, and his human nature is incomplete if this will is divine. However, if Christ has two wills, then the unity of the person is really always simply fictitious, even if one intends to protect that unity by Christ's always willing the same thing with both wills.[9]

The essential unity of Christ is at risk with two-nature Christology. If we follow it to its logical conclusion, then we either have a false or limited humanity or a false or limited divinity in Christ. Schleiermacher aims to treat the doctrine of Christ so that these two expressions "most troublesome, to put it mildly—namely, 'divine nature' and 'duality of natures in the same person,' are avoided entirely" (CF §96.1, 589). His proposed alternative aims to capture the original *intent* of the Early Church—to defend the faith against its natural heresies—while moving past these problematic formulas. In this sense, Schleiermacher is not going *against* the tradition, but rather, he is seeking to reform it.

Schleiermacher is not alone in pointing out the flaws of this doctrine, and he should not be seen as wholly unorthodox for thinking there is a better way to understand the person of Christ. Wolfhart Pannenberg, for his part, calls the two-nature formula "problematic" and mostly agrees with Schleiermacher's critique. Pannenberg writes, "Thus in the interest of God's otherness over against everything creaturely, Schleiermacher rejects using any expression uniformly or in the same way for God and for man." And he says this argument "scores a direct hit: one cannot speak of divine being and human being as though they were on the same plane."[10] He praises Schleiermacher's "penetrating insight" into "the weakness of the two-natures doctrine."[11] Furthermore, Pannenberg notes that the dialectical theologians—Brunner, Gogarten, and even Barth—often expressed similar reservations about applying "nature" in a uniform way to both God and man.[12] So Schleiermacher has blazed a trail upon which modern theology is still traversing.

Finally, Schleiermacher's argument is not merely negative, as Mariña succinctly puts it:

> His crucial move to avoid [the pitfalls of Chalcedon] lies not so much with his rejection of the language of the two natures, however, as with his understanding of the ideal of human nature becoming real in Jesus Christ. Two moves are crucial for his resolution of the Christological enigma. First, the essential character of perfect human nature is just to express the divine. Second, human nature only achieves its perfection in Jesus Christ; in fact the creation of human beings is ordered to perfection in and through Jesus Christ.[13]

This seamlessly leads us to consider the unity of Christ's person and work, the fact that, for Schleiermacher, all that is necessary for redemption is the being of God in Christ.

God was in Christ

The essential component of redemption is the nature of the relationship Jesus Christ has with God. As Schleiermacher reflects on the experience of redemption in the Christian community, this is what he discovered to be its vital condition. That is, Christ's unbroken communion with the Father is central to His existence as our Redeemer. Christ is the ideal human being in whom perfect God-consciousness is realized. All creation has been wisely ordered by God for the sake of Christ's appearance and the perfection of all creation in Him. "Christ is [...] the completion of human nature" (CF §89).[14]

Schleiermacher's Christology is summarized best by the Pauline and Johannine expressions *God was in Christ, the Word became flesh.*[15] He writes:

> [T]he being of God in the Redeemer is posited as his innermost primary strength, from which all his activity proceeds and which links all the elements of his life together. [...] Thus, if this expression departs greatly from former scholastic language, nonetheless, it rests in equal measure on the Pauline expression 'God was in Christ' and on the Johannine expression 'The Word became flesh,' for 'word' is the activity of God expressed in the form of consciousness and 'flesh' is the general designation for what is organic.[16]

Accordingly, Schleiermacher places more significance on the *life* of Christ than on any work He performed. Terrence Tice notes:

> [T]he most important thing to say about Jesus of Nazareth, in Schleiermacher's view, is that he lived. In itself his death may bear redemptive

overtones, as it were, but it is not a necessary component of redemption for the religious consciousness of Christians.[17]

So far, Schleiermacher's Christology may seem simple enough: Christ must be like us in every way (against the Docetic heresy) except for sharing in our sin (against the Nazarean heresy). All that is necessary for redemption is that Jesus lived in unbroken fellowship with God from within our humanity, that God was in Christ. But things become more complicated when we dive further into what exactly this means.

Schleiermacher argues that Christ did not have a divine nature, only a human nature.[18] But He *did* possess what he calls a perfect, absolutely strong "God-consciousness," and thus, He was sinless. We should not jump to the conclusion that Schleiermacher denies the being of God in Christ because that is exactly what he is affirming. Schleiermacher argues that "to attribute an absolutely strong God-consciousness to Christ and to ascribe to him a being of God in him are entirely one and the same thing" (CF §94.2, 576). Christ's absolutely strong God-consciousness *is*, for Schleiermacher, the same as saying "God was in Christ." But this phrase more precisely stresses Christ's *dynamic* relationship with God, in contrast with a *static* state of having a divine nature. It is a dynamic (or living) Christology that Schleiermacher is proposing, against a static one.

Schleiermacher writes, "God's being can be conceived only as *pure activity*" (CF §94.2, 576).[19] This is why Schleiermacher strove after a more dynamic Christology. One of the primary features of his doctrine of God is its emphasis on God's livingness. In the previous chapter, we saw that God's essence can be equated only with love, but God's essential livingness merely says the same thing in a different way. Because what is love if not an activity? For God to be the living God is the same as saying that God is love. God is not some lifeless, abstract deity in an immobile state of being called "love" but the living God whose essential being is love actively seeking fellowship. To say Christ "possessed" a divine nature is problematic because it implies the divine nature is something capable of being possessed, as if it were a "thing" and not the living God that was in Christ. So it was to protect the livingness of God that Schleiermacher refused to accept the Chalcedonian Definition completely.

These two points guide Schleiermacher's doctrine of Christ: the rejection of a personalized, objectified God, and the conviction that God is the living God. A proper doctrine of Christ can only be conceived of *dynamically*, or we might say *relationally*, through Christ's absolutely strong God-consciousness.

Schleiermacher strived to retain the *spirit* of traditional Christology without feeling bound to the *letter* of its formula. He admitted as much himself: "The purpose of this procedure is to show successively the extent to which the intent of these propositions agrees with what is set forth in that [Chalcedonian] formulation" (CF §96.3, 590). Accordingly, Schleiermacher did not think he had set forth an unorthodox Christology. Instead, he felt he had continued in the spirit and mission of the original councils while offering an improved solution to the problems they faced.

We should not hastily judge Schleiermacher as a heretic with his revision to Christology, but aim to see him through his own perception, namely, as a theologian striving to serve the Church and continue the mission of the Reformation: *Ecclesia semper reformanda est*—"The Church must always be reformed."[20]

Absolutely Strong God-Consciousness

The key phrase in Schleiermacher's Christology is Christ's "absolutely strong God-consciousness."[21] It stresses the real activity of God in Christ, resists all four of the natural heresies, and protects the livingness of God from objectification. But what does it mean to have an absolutely strong God-consciousness?

It does not mean Christ was merely aware of God, thinking about God, or merely conscious of God's existence, as if God were some being "out there" separate from Christ. Likewise, Schleiermacher's concept of "self-consciousness" does not mean an awareness of one's self. Instead, it is more properly that consciousness which arises *from out of the self*, the self-in-relation to an "other" (i.e., that which is not the self). Similarly, Christ's God-consciousness originates *from God*. It is not a subjective awareness of God grounded in the self, but God's relation to the self by grace. Therefore, it is the immediate presence of God in Christ. Schleiermacher's use of "consciousness"—self-, world-, or God-consciousness—always implies a being-in-relation with another, an I and a Thou (in Buber's terms).[22] Christ's absolutely strong God-consciousness indicates unhindered communion with God, His absolute dependence upon and surrender to God. It is a fundamentally *relational* term.

The influence of God in Christ, Christ's God-consciousness, determined *every* thought and action throughout His life. Kelsey explains: "When saying that Christ has a sinless perfection, Schleiermacher is referring to the complete and utter openness to God that Christ has in every single moment, his God-consciousness."[23] God-consciousness itself is pre-cognitive, but it always *produces* thoughts and actions. We often ignore the influence of God in our lives, leading neither to thought nor action, but for Christ, *every* thought and action derived from His God-consciousness. He lived in utter dependence upon God. This does not mean Christ was God's puppet, but that Christ perfectly exemplified ideal humanity in relation to God. Schleiermacher considered Christ the ideal human being, the completion of human nature. In Him, the divine is perfectly expressed. To be fully human *is* to be in unhindered communion with God. So there is no contradiction between Christ's dependence on God and His ideal humanity.

Furthermore, Christ's relation to God is unmediated, while humanity's relation to God is mediated through Him. Christ's God-consciousness is wholly unique and original. So while it is possible to compare our God-consciousness with Christ's, in an effort to understand it, we must remember that Christ is the sole mediator between God and humankind because of His "absolutely strong," unmediated God-consciousness.

This is where Schleiermacher's doctrine of sin becomes helpful. For Schleiermacher, saying Christ possessed an absolutely strong God-consciousness is the same as referring to His "sinless perfection." Sin is a "turning away from God" that "exists in the situations of our lives" whenever our thoughts and actions originate from ourselves rather than God. In contrast, whenever we are conscious of communion with God through the Redeemer, this is grace (CF §63, 385). Christ's absolutely strong God-consciousness is His unmediated fellowship with God. Christ's life was wholly Godly, entirely dependent on God.

Schleiermacher's theology remains one of *grace*. This is especially true at the theological "heart" of his dogmatics, the doctrine of Christ. Jacqueline Mariña rightly calls Schleiermacher's Christology a Christology "from above." It is not a low-Christology, but a high-Christology. She writes, "[I]t is in Christ that the completion of human nature has been ordained, and in this fundamental sense Christ is related to the past and future of humanity. In Christ the fullness of human nature is perfected."[24] Even Schleiermacher's Christology is permeated with divine grace. Far too many of his critics settle for a shallow reading of his doctrine of Christ and fail to see its grace-infused logic. Christ is not merely *a* perfect human before God, but *the* ideal human being, graciously sent by God to redeem all creation.

Redemption to New Life

A fundamental presupposition of Schleiermacher's soteriology is that the person and work of Christ are inseparable. In a sense, the person of Christ *is* the work of Christ. It is not necessarily what Christ *did* that matters, but who Christ was (and is still today). It is not that Christ's death was meaningless, but it is no longer *the* essential element in redemption. That Jesus *lived,* and how He lived, is what matters most of all.

How, then, does Christ's life redeem? It is by the influence of Christ and the communication of his sinless perfection. Communion with God in the Christian community is the result of being taken up, in and through Christ, to share in the strength of His God-consciousness. Reconciliation means participating in the fellowship of Christ's "unclouded blessedness." It is by grace alone. It is only by partaking in *Christ's* unhindered fellowship with God, and the blessedness that ensues as a result, that we are redeemed, which is the same as saying we are set free from sin. We are a new creation in Christ Jesus. Schleiermacher presents our union with Christ, our being "in Christ," as that which is essential for redemption.

But how does this work, exactly? Schleiermacher writes, "In this collective life, a life extending back to the efficacious action of Jesus, redemption is wrought by him by virtue of the communication of his sinless perfection" (*CF* §88, 547). It is on account of Christ's direct influence in the community He established. Here Schleiermacher describes a crucial presupposition. He writes:

> [I]t must be possible to have the same experience today too if the faith of later generations, consequently our own faith as well, is to be the same as the original faith and not, as it were, another faith.[25]

Christ's mediation is the same in the Church today as it was in Christ's first community, His disciples. Redemption is wrought in and through Christ as He communicates His sinless perfection, the strength of His God-consciousness, to the Church. Because it is through the gracious communication of Christ's sinless perfection that we share in His new life, its communication must also be the work of Christ.

But how does Christ communicate His sinless perfection to us today? Following the arguments put forth by Lessing's famous "ugly ditch," in which the truths of history and the truths of faith are separated by an unbridgeable chasm, this is a challenge that haunts modern theology still to this day. Schleiermacher's response is unique and noteworthy. He essentially argues that it is through the "efficacious action of his community" that Christ communicates His sinless perfection, and this efficacious action bridges Lessing's famous chasm. For Schleiermacher, "[T]his working of the community to bring forth the same faith is also simply the working of that personal perfection of Jesus himself" (CF §88.2, 550). In the collective life of the Church, Christ communicates the strength of His God-consciousness to us today. Schleiermacher draws an important conclusion:

> We have communion with God *only* in a community of life with the Redeemer. Within this community of life, the Redeemer's absolutely sinless perfection and blessedness manifests a free activity proceeding directly from himself.[26]

This explains why Schleiermacher thought if the Christian community were to die out, if the Church were to be no more, then redemption would be impossible. Redemption depends on the communication of Christ in and through the community of the faithful. In the Christian community, Christ is present in its proclamation and collective life. Christ communicates His sinless perfection by the common spirit of the Church—which is the presence and activity of God in our midst—and thus we are taken up into the strength of His absolutely strong God-consciousness and share in His unclouded blessedness. In this sense, the Church continues the incarnation.

Schleiermacher's doctrine of redemption culminates in the new creation, the "world-forming" activity of Christ to establish God-consciousness as a "new principle of life." Yet this is also "the continuation of God's creative activity" (CF §100.1, 625). Christ's redemptive activity is the process through which God *completes* creation. Creation was oriented towards Christ from the very beginning. Its goal has always been for the totality of all created things to be brought under the influence of Christ's absolutely strong God-consciousness and thus to share in His unclouded blessedness, that is, to be in communion with God in and through Him. Christ is *the* catalyst for the new creation of all things. It is only by "being united with Christ" that we are in "actual possession of blessedness in consciousness that Christ is the focus of our life" (CF §101.1, 631). Therefore, Schleiermacher does not think of Christ merely as an important figure in history alongside others, but Christ is the one true mediator between God and all creation. Furthermore, redemption is inseparable from the Redeemer so that one cannot be obtained without the other. Schleiermacher writes that "this possession of blessedness always exists only as his gift" (CF §101.1, 631).

Here Schleiermacher has moved further away from a *transactional* understanding of redemption to Irenaeus' *relational* understanding. Irenaeus famously wrote, "He [Christ] became what we are so that we might become what He is."[27] Schleiermacher even puts a clever spin on Irenaeus' phrase when he writes, "[I]n order to take us up into community with his life, Christ would first have to have entered into our community" (CF §104.4, 659). This highlights the community-centric logic of Schleiermacher's theology and his conviction that redemption is primarily relational. By coming among us as one of us, Christ displayed what it means to be genuinely human. He was the ideal human being by virtue of His absolutely strong God-consciousness, His unbroken fellowship with God. By grace, we are taken up into the strength of His fellowship with God and are, therefore, partakers of His unclouded blessedness. Redemption is *relational*.

Finally, Schleiermacher considers how redemption is expressed in an individual life. Here he considers regeneration and sanctification. Note that the primary emphasis of his doctrine of redemption is on the redeemed community and only then on the individual as a part of the community.

For Schleiermacher, God-consciousness has always been a possibility because of our "original perfection," but before Christ's influence, it was only an occasional spark. What must happen in the individual life, first and foremost, is regeneration: new life in Christ. This new life, however, is "life in the process of becoming" (CF §106.1, 683-4). Therefore, the turning point from old to new is regeneration, but the process of becoming new is sanctification. Regeneration is the starting out, whereas sanctification is the movement towards unclouded blessedness.

Schleiermacher writes:

> At the outset, individuals were seized by Christ; and today, as well, it is still always a working of Christ himself, mediated by his spiritual presence in the Word, whereby individuals are taken up into the community of the new life.[28]

Just as the first disciples were seized by Christ's influence, so today Christ is at work, mediated through the Scriptures and in the community, to influence the individual. Both processes—regeneration and sanctification—are the direct work of Christ. It is entirely by grace that we are redeemed.

Schleiermacher then considers justification and conversion. Conversion is the beginning of a new life in communion with Christ. It is "manifested through repentance," which includes contrition and a change of heart, and through faith, "which consists of a person's taking the perfection and blessedness of Christ into oneself" (CF §108, 690). Justification is God's work on the converted person, in which God forgives their sins and recognizes them as a child of God. Schleiermacher notes that "we participate in Christ's relationship of Son to the Father, which by the impression Christ makes on us empowers us to be children of God" (CF §109.2, 714). Christ in us and our union with Christ is *the* essential aspect of our justification, through which we participate in *Christ's* Sonship as if it were our own.

Another unique aspect of justification is Schleiermacher's concept of Christ's person-forming activity. For God, Schleiermacher argues, an individual is not yet regarded as a person before regeneration but are merely a part of the mass of humanity. It is only when a person is justified by faith that they first become a person "through the ongoing work of God's creative act from which the Redeemer himself has come" (CF §109.4, 721). But Schleiermacher is quick to say that "faith arises only through the efficacious action of Christ" (CF §109.4, 721). Therefore, we share in Christ's unclouded blessedness by grace through faith. Schleiermacher connects the communication of Christ's unclouded blessedness with justification and the communication of Christ's sinless perfection with conversion. Christ is the cause of our fellowship with God, and through His person-forming work, we are a new creation.

Sanctification is the process in which "a life is built that is conformed to Christ's perfection and blessedness" (CF §110, 723). Schleiermacher characterizes the life of sin as a life lived through self-initiation, and in contrast, the life of grace is in the process towards "a steadfast willing-to-be-determined-by-Christ" (CF §110.2, 727). From this, he concludes that "sin itself cannot be completely extirpated in anyone but ever remains in the process of disappearing." But "sin can win no new ground" in the new life of grace (CF §110.2, 728). Sin has no power to annul God's grace. Regeneration is never threatened by sin. The life of grace is one of becoming more fully under Christ's influence, more gradually free from sin.

Three Presuppositions in Summary

In her published dissertation, Catherine L. Kelsey identified three presuppositions that characterize Schleiermacher's doctrine of Christ and redemption. These summarize well the major points we have discussed. She writes:

1. It is apparent to all who come into the sphere of Jesus' influence that he is the Redeemer.
2. Redemption is available through the Redeemer prior to his death and resurrection.
3. Redemption is directly associated with incorporation into a community of Christians.[29]

These guide much of Schleiermacher's theology and preaching, but they are also directly related to his Christology. The first articulates the communication of Christ's sinless perfection as the influence that brings about redemption. The second emphasizes the fact that it is Christ's life, not merely his death or resurrection, that is the essential element in redemption. And finally, the third expresses the vital role of the Christian community in redemption. Altogether, these three presuppositions explain, in part, the unique shape of Schleiermacher's doctrine of Christ.

Evaluation

It may be tempting to evaluate Schleiermacher's proposal concerning redemption as a kind of moral influence theory, in which Christ merely sets the standard for how we are supposed to live. But we have to keep in mind what I have tried to stress since chapter one: Schleiermacher is a theologian of grace. It is by being taken up into Christ's fellowship with God in and through His absolutely strong God-consciousness that we are redeemed, *not* through our own attempts at mimicking Christ's life. Of course, the natural result of grace is to produce fruit, good works, but even this is the result of Christ's gracious activity and influence. A real change in our nature takes place: The "old man" is dead and gone, and the "new man" has appeared.

Only when we rightly understand Schleiermacher can the strength of his proposal be appreciated for what it is. Although weaknesses may be found, I will leave it up to you to make any such critical judgments. My task here is only to celebrate and understand Schleiermacher on his own terms. So we will conclude this chapter by evaluating the merits of Schleiermacher's Christology and soteriology.

One such strength is Schleiermacher's emphasis on the *goal* of redemption, namely, *fellowship with God*. He has no tolerance for the idea that Jesus saves us from an "angry God." Redemption was not a legal *transaction,* but the loving act of *reconciliation* to new life in communion with God. In fact, Schleiermacher once said:

> We must consider this concept of God's wrath to be altogether fruitless and out of place in a Christian knowledge of God. [...] There is nothing in the word 'wrath' that could correspond to anything in God's essential nature.[30]

It is problematic to think of salvation in such a way that we are saved *from God*. We do not flee fearfully from the wrath of God or the threat of hell but are lifted up into a loving fellowship. Schleiermacher's doctrine of redemption rightly emphasizes what we are saved *for* and forgoes what we are saved *from*.

Schleiermacher challenges us to rethink the very nature of salvation. And this is the second benefit of his work. Rather than imagining redemption in terms of an abstract, legalistic *transaction* between God and humanity—such as in the prevailing Protestant atonement theory, penal substitution—we are forced, instead, to use only *relational* terms to understand Christ. Schleiermacher consistently argued that Christ's life and work are directed towards one simple goal: communion with God. That goal is overlooked whenever we force legalistic, transactional concepts onto redemption. By stressing that not only the *goal* of redemption is relational, but that the very *means* of redemption are also relational, Schleiermacher places the Gospel in its proper context. Christ redeems *relationally* as we are united to Him and share in His unbroken communion with the Father. The relational means of redemption correspond perfectly with its proper end. Traditional atonement models are forced to change metaphors, from transactional to relational, to rightly express the goal of the Gospel. But Schleiermacher is consistent in his vision of a relational doctrine of redemption.

Another helpful contribution is Schleiermacher's unique emphasis on the community of Christ as the essential place for Christ's self-communication. Western Christianity has become far too individual-centric, especially in the American, Protestant Church. Many have this false notion that "all I need is the Bible," as if they might discover for themselves all the truths of our faith. But this is nothing less than the sin of pride. The truth is we depend on the Christian community. The life of faith cannot be lived alone.

Finally, Schleiermacher's Christology may have its issues, but it is thoroughly original. This is the final point worth celebrating. His creativity is on full display as he reconstructs a modern yet faithful vision of Christ and the being of God in Him. He sought to retain the spirit and intentions of the Early Church's formula while correcting some of their misleading images. His criticism of traditional Christology is thus worth considering, and his proposed solution is unique, even if both have been judged as problematic. When we soberly assess his contribution, however, we cannot help but be impressed by his solution's originality. Reading him charitably is vital. By his own admission, he is not stepping into an unorthodox position, but merely attempting to bring theology into the modern era so that it may hold up against the criticisms of historical and scientific inquiry. In this sense, even if we disagree with his results, his goal remains admirable.

---

1. CF §11, 79.
2. CF §104.6, 669.
3. iCE, 51.
4. *Friedrich Schleiermacher (Makers of the Modern Theological Mind)*, 118. Waco: Word Books, 1979.
5. Ibid., 71.
6. "Introduction," *Servant of the Word*, 15. Philadelphia: Fortress Press, 1987.
7. CF §22, 144.
8. "Christology and Anthropology," *The Cambridge Companion to Friedrich Schleiermacher*, 155. Cambridge University Press, 2005.
9. CF §96.1, 586.
10. *Jesus—God and Man*, 285. Philadelphia: The Westminster Press, 1968 and 1977, second edition.
11. Ibid., 286-7.
12. Ibid., 286.
13. "Christology and Anthropology," *The Cambridge Companion to Friedrich Schleiermacher*, 156. Cambridge University Press, 2005.
14. Mackintosh and Stewart translation, 366. T&T Clark, 2008 (reprint). Used for stylistic reasons. All other citations refer to the new translation (see abbreviations page).
15. 2 Corinthians 5:19, John 1:14.
16. CF §96.3, 590.
17. *Schleiermacher (Abingdon Pillars of Theology)*, 37. Nashville: Abingdon Press, 2006.
18. Terrence Tice writes: "First, contrary to much traditional doctrine, Christ is not God, as such, and therefore has only a human nature, not a divine nature. However, he does have a completely formed God-consciousness, and this alongside his sinlessness is sufficient for redemption, the central purpose of his existence" (*Schleiermacher (Abingdon Pillars of Theology)*, 37; Nashville: Abingdon Press, 2006).
19. Emphasis mine.
20. This is a variation of a phrase from Augustine, popularized by Karl Barth in 1947.

21. "Perfect" God-consciousness is more common in Schleiermacher-scholarship. I have opted for this version to conform to its usage in the new critical edition of *Christian Faith*. The same meaning is implied, but "absolutely strong" is preferred because of its *active* connotations (vs. a passive state of being implied by "perfection").
22. The young Martin Buber was influenced by Schleiermacher significantly. Schleiermacher's theology is closer to, and better understood in connection with, Buber's personalism than subjectivism.
23. *Thinking about Christ with Schleiermacher*, 59. Louisville: Westminster John Knox Press, 2003.
24. "Christology and Anthropology," *The Cambridge Companion to Friedrich Schleiermacher*, 168. Cambridge University Press, 2005.
25. CF §88.2, 550.
26. CF §91, 559; emphasis mine.
27. *Against Heresies,* preface to book V. Public domain.
28. CF §106.1, 685.
29. *Schleiermacher's Preaching, Dogmatics, and Biblical Criticism*, 67-70. Eugene: Pickwick Publications, 2007.
30. *Servant of the Word,* 156-7. Philadelphia: Fortress Press, 1987.

SIDEBAR: DEATH AND RESURRECTION

[Christ's] absolutely self-denying love is indeed manifested to us in his suffering unto death—itself evoked by his unfailing perseverance. Moreover, in this love we come to realize in utmost clarity how it was that God was in him reconciling the world to Godself, just as we most fully come to share a feeling of how unshakable his blessedness was in his suffering. This is why one can say that the conviction of his holiness as well as of his blessedness always becomes clear to us above all from our being engulfed in his suffering.[1]

— SCHLEIERMACHER

On his deathbed, Schleiermacher spoke warmly about the reconciling blood of Christ as he took communion for the last time. But the death and resurrection of Christ is less essential to his theology than it often is to traditional dogmatics. For most theologians, the death and resurrection of Christ is *the* essential fact about Christ's life. But Schleiermacher shifted the emphasis away from Christ's death onto His life, so much so that it is conceivable for Schleiermacher to say that even if Christ did not die, He would still be our Redeemer.[2] The task of this sidebar will be to assess why and how Schleiermacher makes this shift and what role the death and resurrection of Christ play in his theology.

The Death of Christ "For Us"

The primary cause of this shift is simple. Because redemption was available to the disciples *before* Christ's death, Schleiermacher argues that redemption must not depend upon that death itself. The influence of Christ's unbroken fellowship with God was the decisive factor. We see the effect of redemption on His disciples before Golgotha. The disciples were not left waiting for Christ to die so that they might be redeemed, and Christ regularly forgave sins and healed the sick—signs of the new creation and reign of God—before the cross. The conditions for redemption are fulfilled by Christ's *life*, not His death. We are not redeemed because Christ satisfied the wrath of God and appeased God's blood-lust, but because Christ lived in unbroken communion with God as a human being like us in every way except for sin. That is, Christ's absolutely strong God-consciousness is the vital element in redemption. The only condition, for Schleiermacher, that must be true about Christ for Him to be our Redeemer is that He lived.

In the Protestant Church today, we often overemphasize Christ's death for our salvation to the extent that Christ's life has little to no redemptive significance. When God is thanked for redemption, it is for sending Jesus to die for our sins. We talk about Jesus in such a way that He might as well have been born and died the very next day, and the Gospel would remain the same. Schleiermacher's refocusing of redemption back onto the life of the Redeemer is a helpful step forward beyond this reductionistic presentation.

Schleiermacher once confessed a "bad habit" of intentionally moving to the other side of the theological "boat" so the whole ship will not capsize. He purposely worked to counter-balance some of those areas that he thought needed correcting. He writes:

> When one-sided tendency becomes as strong as it has in this case, it is my custom—or should I say my bad habit?—to shift my weight, for what it is worth, to the other side, lest the little boat in which we all travel should capsize.[3]

Schleiermacher's shift from emphasizing the death of Christ to His life may be seen in this context. The truth is not that Schleiermacher finds Christ's death irrelevant—as we will soon see, Christ's death does have a vital role to play—but that overemphasizing His death to such a degree that His life is overlooked almost entirely is something Schleiermacher cannot accept.

What then is the significance of Christ's death in Schleiermacher's theology?

First, Schleiermacher considered Christ's death the culmination of His life. Therefore, it confirms the significance of His life. Namely, because of the nature of Christ's death, Schleiermacher concluded that His absolutely strong God-consciousness was confirmed and secured, Christ's communion with God was unbroken. Because Christ remained sinless even up to His death—that is, His absolutely strong God-consciousness did not falter—Christ is our Redeemer. Christ's death offers proof that He truly was the "Son of God," as the Roman soldiers that crucified Him realized.[4] What was behind their confession? It could have been nothing other than the influence of Christ's unbroken fellowship with God that remained absolutely strong even in the face of darkness and death. In other words, Christ remained obedient even unto death.

Pastorally, this means there is no despair Christ has not met and overcome, no darkness He has not endured and yet remained faithful to God. Not only in Christ's death but also throughout the trials of His life, this communion remained unbroken. The strength of Christ's God-consciousness is vital because redemption means sharing in Christ's fellowship with God. And on the cross, He proved His faithfulness to God, and thus redemption is secure in Him.

The death of Christ *does* have significance for Schleiermacher, but only as it relates to the life of Christ in unbroken fellowship with God. What is explicitly denied, then, is the possibility that Christ's death appeased God's wrath, as if it were some kind of sacrificial, legal atonement for sin. Christ may be deemed a sacrifice and His death may be called "atoning," but not in the traditional sense. Christ's death *is* significant because He bore the effects of evil as a human being, and therefore, he died for the human community while remaining in perfect communion with God. For Schleiermacher, evil is the effect of communal sin. To be part of the community, therefore, necessitates that we suffer the evils of our community's sins. If Christ was indeed like us in every single way except for sin, then Christ must be susceptible to suffering the evils of His community. He did not *contribute* to its sins, but He nevertheless suffered the evils that resulted from its sin. It is in *this* sense that Schleiermacher can say Christ's death was atoning and that He died "for us." And because His absolutely strong God-consciousness was undisturbed, Christ is our Redeemer even in the face of death. *Because* He suffered and died without breaking or faltering even the slightest from communion with God, His God-consciousness is proven to be the source of our redemption.

In a Good Friday sermon, Schleiermacher begins with a prayer that highlights just how vital Christ's death is for the Christian life:

> Heavenly Father! On all who are assembling to day to commemorate the death of the Holy One, in whom Thou wast well pleased, look graciously down! Let not one go away from the cross of Thy Wellbeloved without exclaiming, with new, living faith, Truly this was the

Son of God! Let not one wipe away his tears of emotion until the heartfelt desire has taken possession of him that his end may be like that of this righteous One! Let not the feeling of holy reverence and admiration, that must lay hold on every one at the remembrance of the dying Christ, be left behind within these walls and bear no fruit; let it go forth with us all into our life, so that it may be more and more consecrated to Thee, and become more like to His, until at last we follow Him, in departing with good courage to Thee. Amen.[5]

While, in theory, redemption could have been possible even without Christ's death, it would be a mistake to assume Schleiermacher did not consider the crucifixion vital to the Gospel. The death of Christ is essential to our faith because we recognize Christ is the "Son of God" in the triumph of Christ's absolutely strong God-consciousness, unbroken even in the face of death. Christ is our true mediator, who shares in our humanity and yet lived in uninterrupted fellowship with God. He is truly our high priest, the one who understands our struggles and has overcome them.

Resurrection

Schleiermacher himself did not deny the resurrection. In fact, he thought there were many good reasons why we should believe in its historical accuracy. But he did not consider it essential to faith. Schleiermacher thinks if we force individuals to base their faith on historical proof of the resurrection, then we would be asking too much from them. Ultimately, it would also distract from the inner substance of faith by focusing too much on its external conditions. Demanding that our faith must conform to historical research, which is ever-changing, would be the same as depending on a scientific investigation to prove God exists. Both are problematic foundations—sand—upon which Schleiermacher does not think we should build the house of faith. While affirming the resurrection himself, Schleiermacher did not consider its historicity essential to faith.

While many consider belief in the historical resurrection to be the litmus test for orthodox theology, Schleiermacher is more gracious towards those who doubt. Ultimately, whether we think it was historically factual or not, it is not an essential component of redemption. We are therefore free to doubt the resurrection and still remain faithful to the original teachings of the Apostles. Schleiermacher aims to secure the *spirit* of the doctrine—its original meaning and significance for faith—without forcing anyone to subscribe to its external *letter,* namely, its historicity.

This approach is similar to how Schleiermacher deals with the doctrine of the virgin birth. In contrast with the resurrection, he denied its historical basis, but he sought to retain the doctrinal importance the virgin birth held for the first Christians. It was their way of proclaiming Christ's sinless perfection. Schleiermacher sees this as its essential component while denying its factual history. Demanding every Christian to believe that Christ was born a virgin would be asking too much of them, but the doctrine it proclaims regarding Christ's sinless perfection must be retained.

Likewise, the essential fact of the resurrection is the new creation in Christ, which does not depend upon its historical accuracy. Those who deny it can remain faithful to its essential meaning. The vital element of our faith is that Christ is the first and last in the new creation, its source and sustainer. Whether or not a specific historical event took place in which Christ was raised from the dead is irrelevant, for Schleiermacher. What matters is Christ is the firstborn of the new creation. As Dawn DeVries notes:

> The significance of Easter is not to be found, according to Schleiermacher, in the physical, historical event of Christ's raising. It has less to do with an empty tomb or a resuscitated corpse than with the living presence of the Redeemer in the lives of his own.[6]

Again, it is crucial to remember Schleiermacher *did* believe in the historical resurrection of Jesus Christ.[7] He merely argues that as a historical event it is not faith's foundation, even though its meaning remains essential. The resurrection is a matter of historical research, not faith.

This confession will likely place Schleiermacher sharply at odds with the defenders of orthodox Christianity. But it is important to recognize his motivations. One of the strengths of Schleiermacher's dogmatics is how inclusively he presents Christian faith. He embraced those who doubt into the community of Christ by focusing on the inner elements of our faith that unite us rather than forcing agreement with its non-essential outer husk. We might not agree with where he has drawn the line between what is essential and superfluous, but his goal is a more inclusive understanding of Christian faith.

---

1. CF §104.4, 661.
2. Schleiermacher never says this directly, but it is conceivable in theory. Although, as we will soon see, the death of Christ *is* important for Schleiermacher's interpretation of His life, and so it should not be treated as if this were the case.
3. OG, 68.
4. Matthew 27:54; Mark 15:39; Luke 23:47.
5. *Servant of the Word*, 52. Philadelphia: Fortress Press, 1987.
6. *Servant of the Word*, 79n1. Philadelphia: Fortress Press, 1987.
7. It is worth noting that this is still a matter of debate. Gary Dorrien aptly describes Schleiermacher as being "carefully vague" regarding the resurrection (*Kantian Reason and*

Hegelian Spirit, 107). Schleiermacher was not as clear as I am making him seem. Although, Catherine Kelsey succinctly confirms my point:

"Belief in resurrection is a historical judgment based on the historical evidence, not a test of faith. Schleiermacher himself thinks good historical reason exists to believe the resurrection occurred [...] [Namely,] if those first witnesses, who were reliable when it came to redemption, all agree that Christ was resurrected, Schleiermacher trusts their account" (*Thinking about Christ with Schleiermacher,* 91).

Another issue should be clarified. Albert Schweitzer thought Schleiermacher denied Christ's death and thus thought the resurrection was only an illusion. But this has been disproven by Verheyden (*The Life of Jesus,* 456n60). In spite of what his critics have often said, Schleiermacher believed Christ died and was raised again.

SERMON: ETERNAL LIFE

Will eternal blessedness persist after death? Schleiermacher's soteriology placed such a strong emphasis on the now-ness of redemption that some have wondered if he did not deny eternal life entirely—or at least considered it nonessential to faith in Christ. Schleiermacher also considered the consummation of the Church a "prophetic" doctrine of faith, which has led to further confusion.[1] So what exactly was Schleiermacher's understanding of the afterlife? Three points from CF §158 provide helpful insight.

First, God-consciousness neither concludes in nor necessitates belief in eternal life. This is somewhat misleading, however, because it does not mean such a conclusion can or should be deemed invalid. Instead, Schleiermacher means that an imperfect God-consciousness can have no *direct* connection with a doctrine of the afterlife. In other words, that we persist after death cannot be explicated from a *feeble* religious consciousness. We cannot know for sure whether or not we will persist after death. Since we have not yet died, we have no consciousness of that state of being, and thus, the afterlife is excluded from our religious self-consciousness. Therefore, there is no dogmatic connection between God-consciousness and the doctrine of eternal life.

Second, although no direct connection exists, Schleiermacher insists that eternal life is vital to faith in Christ on account of *Christ's* immortality. Indeed, eternal life is a *certainty* established by Christ's own God-consciousness in us. Because we share in Christ's unclouded blessedness by grace, we are partakers of His immortality. While this reality cannot be explicated from our (imperfect) religious consciousness directly, it is a necessary implication of faith in Christ. Schleiermacher explains:

> It may be claimed, however, that belief in the continuation of personal existence after death coheres with our faith in the Redeemer. That is to say, if he ascribes such a continuation to himself in all that he says regarding his return or reunion with his own, and given that he can say this of himself only as a human person, since only as such could he also share in community with his followers, so, by implication, the same must be true of us as well. This is the case, by virtue of the selfsameness of human nature in him and in us.[2]

The question of life after death is not an anthropological question but a Christological one: "Hence, if the Redeemer's soul were imperishable but ours were perishable, then it could not rightly be said that as a human being he was like us in all things except sin" (CF §158.2, 971). Only when we hold to a heretical image of a docetic Christ—a Christ not fully human in every way except for sin—will we conclude that His immortality is unshared with all humanity. Life after death is assured because of faith in Christ. It is not rooted in *our* self-consciousness, but *Christ's*.

Furthermore, even though this reality is known by faith, it is not exclusive to people who have faith but a hope for all humanity. Schleiermacher writes:

> [A]ll members of the human race have that continuation to look forward to. In this way, however, the Redeemer certainly also remains the mediator of immortality, only not alone for those who have already had faith in him here but for everyone without exception.[3]

In ourselves, we are plagued with doubt and uncertainty. Death remains an existential terror that will never cease to haunt us. But in Christ, sharing in His unclouded blessedness and absolutely strong God-consciousness, we possess the assurance that we will be with God after death. Belief in the resurrection of all flesh, the final judgment, and eternal life are all necessary conclusions to Schleiermacher's dogmatics, Without these doctrines, his system would be incomplete. As we saw in chapter one, that we live on after death is a presupposition supporting the doctrines of election and universalism. Arguments that impose either annihilationism or the denial of an afterlife altogether onto Schleiermacher are misleading and false, they force inconsistencies onto Schleiermacher that would ultimately disrupt his entire theological system.[4]

Third, even though we have this hope in Christ, we may *not* take any steps towards speculating specific, graphic content as to what eternal life might be like. Schleiermacher admits that we will inevitably try to form images of life after death, but "we cannot make even the least claim that up to a certain point we would succeed in such a venture" (CF §158.3, 972). Since it is not established by our religious self-consciousness directly, we find rest only in an imageless hope. The foundation of this hope is not ourselves but Christ alone. If we attempt to say more than what is permitted, we step into vain speculation.

Sermon at Nathanael's Grave

Schleiermacher's son, Nathanael, died suddenly at the age of nine. Standing before his grave, Schleiermacher preached a moving sermon about life and death. The premature demise of his son had, in Schleiermacher's words, "shaken my life to the core." This sermon is undoubtedly Schleiermacher's most personal, and it offers a lucid presentation of his thoughts on the afterlife.

Schleiermacher first expresses skepticism regarding the prevailing images of "heaven" that are so often used to comfort the grieving:

> Still others who grieve generate their consolation in another way, out of an abundance of attractive images in which they represent the everlasting community of those who have gone on before and those who as yet remain behind; and the more these images fill the soul, the more all the pains connected with death are stilled. But for the man who is too greatly accustomed to the rigors and cutting edges of thinking, these images leave behind a thousand unanswered questions and thereby lose much, much of their consoling power.[5]

But even if we find ourselves doubting these images of "heaven," we can still find solace in an imageless hope, namely, that we will be with Christ. Schleiermacher writes:

> Thus I stand here, then, with my comfort and my hope alone in the Word of Scripture, modest and yet so rich, 'It does not yet appear what we shall be, but we know that when he appears we shall be like him, for we shall see him as he is' (1 John 3:2), and in the powerful prayer of the Lord: 'Father, I would that where I am, they also may be whom thous hast given me' (John 17:24).[6]

We will be with Christ. This is our only solace. Anything we imagine beyond this simple confession is vain speculation into that great unknown. Against the Church's tendency today to place so much hope in "going to heaven," Schleiermacher reminds us that we simply do not know what will happen to us when we die. But we *do* know the only thing we *need* to know: We will be with Jesus. That promise, "modest yet so rich," is more than enough.

---

1. See CF §159 and §163.PS.2. Schleiermacher is clear in these sections that it is only the graphic content of an afterlife (which is included in the Church's consummation) that is excluded from faith-doctrine, while eternal life is a necessary presupposition for his entire dogmatics, as I will argue here. By calling a doctrine "prophetic," Schleiermacher distinguishes it from other doctrines because it is not explicated from direct consciousness, but it is nevertheless essential.
2. CF §158.2, 970.
3. CF §158.2, 972.
4. For a more in-depth argument regarding life after death and its essentiality to Schleiermacher's system, see Daniel Pedersen, "Eternal Life in Schleiermacher's *The Christian Faith*." *International Journal of Systematic Theology*, Vol. 13, number 3, July 2011.
5. *Servant of the Word*, 212. Philadelphia: Fortress Press, 1987.
6. Ibid.

4

THE ENTRANCE HALL AND BOUNDARY LINE

SUMMARY: The feeling of absolute dependence, an essential term in Schleiermacher's controversial methodology, denotes an immediate existential relationship with God. All theology presupposes the relationship God establishes with us by grace, or it has given into the illusion of false objectivism. Theology is faith seeking understanding. So Schleiermacher's method is far more orthodox and conventional than it is often portrayed. In its arrangement, the Introduction to and Part One of *Christian Faith* are *preliminary* orientations to the heart of his dogmatics in Part Two.

IN SCHLEIERMACHER'S OWN WORDS:

> [V]indication of the method used here cannot be provided other than through the actual execution of it.[1]

> [W]hat I understand as pious feeling is not derived from a representation, but is the original expression of an immediate existential relationship.[2]

> In our proposition all genuine doctrines of faith have to be based on Christian religious self-consciousness or, in other words, taken from the experience of Christians.[3]

SECONDARY QUOTES:

> Like a word, the meaning of Schleiermacher's introduction is its use. I am convinced that we understand the controversial claims of his introduction to *The Christian Faith* best by looking to the particulars he took those remarks to authorize, rather than by focusing most on his putative definitions.[4]
>
> — Daniel J. Pedersen

> Here, while Schleiermacher speaks of the religious feeling as a self-consciousness, it is clear that this cannot mean simply a 'consciousness of oneself' without reference to any reality other than oneself. The self-consciousness of which Schleiermacher speaks is a consciousness of the self as determined by, or acted upon by, what is other than the self, as well as its own inwardly motivated actions. It is the self-in-relation which is the object of consciousness. This must be stated in view of the frequency with which, especially under the neo-orthodox attack, Schleiermacher has been accused of indulging in a concentration on the self's own feelings and emotions, resulting in an entirely subjectivist, individualist occupation with 'religion' instead of attending to the true 'object' of faith, namely God himself. This is to ignore the depth and subtlety of Schleiermacher's analysis, which sets forth not the self *per se,* but the self in relationship. It is the self grounded in a realm of what is other than the self, of other persons, the realm of nature and society, the whole finite realm grounded in the Infinite, which Schleiermacher is concerned with. The human consciousness is thus never entirely *self-* awareness, for the self can never be extracted from the realm of otherness.[5]
>
> — Keith W. Clements

Introduction

When Karl Barth lectured on Schleiermacher's *Christian Faith,* he only examined the first fourteen propositions (because time would not permit a full study). But at the end of these lectures, he speculated that the first *twelve* propositions alone were necessary for understanding Schleiermacher and that his students could "stop here in the confidence that in these twelve sections we have perhaps in some sense come to know the whole of this version of the Christian faith."[6] His interpretation of Schleiermacher hinged on this extremely limited portrait of his dogmatics, alongside a study of his sermons. It is likely Barth thought that in these first propositions he had discovered the true heart and foundation of Schleiermacher's dogmatics, upon which its whole system rests, and thus, he felt no need to progress any further into the work.[7] But Schleiermacher clearly warns about such a hasty procedure when he writes, "[T]he method of a work and its arrangement are best justified by their outcome" (CF §1.2, 2). In other words, the proof of the pudding is in the eating.

One of the major causes behind misreading Schleiermacher is an overemphasis on the Introduction to and Part One of *Christian Faith*. Theology students are commonly introduced to Schleiermacher by reading the second speech of *On Religion* and these early sections from *Christian Faith*, but this presupposes that the most essential elements of Schleiermacher's theology are contained in these sections. That is just not true, and in Schleiermacher's own day, he regularly argued against such a reading.

Previous chapters have established that 1) Schleiermacher is chiefly a theologian of grace, 2) he is a Trinitarian theologian whose essential conviction about God is that God is love, and 3) everything in his dogmatics is determined by Christ and the redemption wrought in and through Him. We must admit that Schleiermacher is, indeed, far more "orthodox" than he is often portrayed. This chapter will continue that argument by recognizing a simple truth, namely, that Schleiermacher's methodological focus on the concrete experience of the Christian community is a consistent and honest reflection on what *every* theologian must do (and what most *already* do, including Barth) if they are not resigned to vain speculation. His controversial method is more common to Christian theology than his critics are willing to admit, and Schleiermacher's brilliance is he brings it forward, out into the open, and develops it into a consistent, systematic principle. So we will examine the method as well as the structure of his dogmatics.

We have to learn a new way of thinking about these two sections of Schleiermacher's *Christian Faith*. The Introduction and Part One deserve to be understood in their rightful place, not as the foundation of his dogmatics, but as its entrance hall (Introduction) and boundary line (Part One).

The Introduction: Locating and Describing

The first thirty-one propositions of *Christian Faith* make up its Introduction. These function as the portal through which we enter into the proper work of dogmatic theology. They do not provide any dogmatic content but merely arrange the preliminary outlines that will be filled in later. What exactly does the introduction accomplish?

The arrangement of *Christian Faith* was just as controversial in Schleiermacher's own time as it is today. He wrote two open letters to his friend and colleague, Dr. Lücke, which answered some of his critics' concerns ahead of publishing a revised, second edition. In these letters, he offers valuable insight into the thought processes behind his dogmatics. Schleiermacher writes:

> I had stated clearly enough that the first part, though truly part of the structure itself, was only a portal and entrance hall and the propositions there, insofar as they could be set forth in an Introduction, could be no more than outlines that would be filled in with their true content from the ensuing discussion.[8]

Schleiermacher further states that the Introduction "was intended only as a preliminary orientation, which, strictly speaking, lies outside of the discipline of dogmatics itself" (OG, 56). We have to take these kinds of statements with utter seriousness, or else we will misread Schleiermacher's work. There is a particular goal Schleiermacher has in mind for each section.

Schleiermacher uses the mathematical image of "lemmas" to explain his goal for the Introduction (CF §2.3, 6). Lemmas are preliminary propositions (assumptions) borrowed from one discipline to demonstrate the propositions of another discipline. In other words, lemmas do not contain truth in themselves but borrow the truth of other propositions to establish a preliminary orientation. So they may be used to establish a discipline's place within the whole territory of scientific disciplines. Therefore, the propositions of the Introduction are often "borrowed" from those found in philosophy, ethics, or apologetics. This is what Schleiermacher means when calling the introduction an "entrance hall" and "portal."

You cannot visit a new restaurant without having its address. But consider the very nature of an "address." What is it? An address is nothing more than its placement-in-relation-to other addresses. Those numbers and that street name are irrelevant if they are not placed in relation to other numbers and other streets. A street address serves a similar function as lemmas do in dogmatics by indicating theology's relation to other scientific disciplines such as philosophy. The very first task is to establish *where* dogmatics fits within the whole field of scientific disciplines. We have to have its address before we can enter into the discipline itself. That is what the Introduction seeks to accomplish.

So we will follow Schleiermacher's own outline and ask two preliminary questions. First, what is dogmatics? And second, what is its method? Schleiermacher answers these questions by borrowing propositions from other scientific disciplines to carve out the proper placement and method of Christian dogmatics, to *contrast* dogmatics with philosophy, ethics, psychology, and apologetics. This is worth stressing. It is not to *ground* theology on philosophy that philosophical "lemmas" are implemented, but it is actually to *contrast* theology with philosophy.

What is Dogmatics?

For Schleiermacher, dogmatics is a reflection on the highest stage of human self-consciousness. But if we recall from the previous chapter, self-consciousness is not a consciousness of the self but that consciousness which arises out of the self, the self-in-relation to another. Then what is the *highest* stage of self-consciousness? It is the feeling of absolute dependence. Ultimately, this means the very same thing as being-in-relation with God,[9] and it merely describes this relation with more precision. Schleiermacher writes:

> [W]e are conscious of ourselves as absolutely dependent or, which intends the same meaning, as being in relation with God.[10]

The feeling of absolute dependence is not an emotion or some kind of subjective "feeling" (in the ordinary sense of the term). Instead, it is a specialized term used with intention: to indicate our being existentially grounded and dependent upon God absolutely as the Whence of our existence. It is Schleiermacher's way of suggesting that to be human is to be dependent upon God, to be God's creature. Essential to our very existence as human beings is this precognitive, intuitive perception or feeling that we did not determine our own existence and thus we depend absolutely on God as the Whence of our being. Schleiermacher explains:

> So, present in every instance of self-consciousness are two features: a being positioned-as-a-self and a not-having-been-positioned-as-such, so to speak, or a being and a somehow-having-come-to-be. Thus, for every instance of self-consciousness, something other than one's 'I' is presupposed, something whence its determinate nature exists and without which a given self-consciousness would not be precisely what it is.[11]

The feeling of absolute dependence, or God-consciousness, is defined clearly in contrast with self-consciousness and world-consciousness. In these other relations, we feel at once *relatively free* and *relatively dependent*. For example, we can have an effect on the world just as we can be affected by it. We are dependent upon the world, but we are also free in relation to it. So we can now recognize why our being-in-relation with God, our God-consciousness, is a feeling of *absolute* dependence. We have no feeling of freedom, partial or otherwise, in relation to God. We are affected absolutely by God as the Whence of our being, and we cannot affect God or cease to be dependent upon God. We did not establish this relation, and we cannot escape it. We have no feeling of freedom in relation to God, and this is what contrasts God-consciousness with self- and world-consciousness.

Dogmatics is a scientific reflection on the feeling of absolute dependence, or simply, on our existential being-in-relation with God. In other words, theology is faith seeking understanding, a particular kind of knowledge that arises from the existential relationship of faith, namely, communion with God in and through Jesus Christ. It is an empirical science with a historical basis in the life of the Church, and so theology is bound to the collective experience of redemption in the Church of Jesus Christ.

With this, Schleiermacher establishes his conviction that proper dogmatics belongs within the limits of piety alone. Dogmatics is not empty, abstract speculation, but a reflection on that highest state of self-consciousness, the feeling of absolute dependence. If we remove the density of this expression, then his proposal is actually quite simple: *Dogmatics is a reflection on our being-in-relation with God, faith seeking understanding.*

Our being-in-relation with God is presumed in every kind of dogmatic reflection. It would be nonsense if we attempted to speak about God without first presupposing some sort of relation to God. *This* observation is the purest form of the point that Schleiermacher is making. Note: *Every theologian already does this.* No theological system can escape this presupposed conviction. To do theology, to engage in the task of dogmatics, is simply to reflect on the fact that we are related to God and that we are not the authors of this relation, which is the very same thing as saying that dogmatics reflects on the feeling of absolute dependence. It is an unavoidable methodological limit. Anyone who imagines they could do theology without first recognizing and presupposing an existential relation to God would be deceiving themselves. Since we cannot imagine dogmatics without this relation, Schleiermacher is correct to argue that dogmatics must be done within the confines of piety alone. This is not something new for dogmatics but what it has *always* done. Schleiermacher's genius is that he not only recognizes this fact but implements it as a systematic principle.

Furthermore, those who try to downplay the necessity of this presupposition will end in self-contradiction. They will attempt to ground theology on something more "objective," whether that is the Bible, the tradition, logic, or natural revelation. But an objectivist dogmatics is an impossibility, and so they will end up, ironically, with a more completely subjectivist dogmatics than the one they attempted to overcome. Yes, all these things are vital for dogmatics, but they are not *the* proper foundation. All theological propositions derive from our being-in-relation with God. It is not our relation to the Bible (although the Scriptures do have a mediating role), nor is it our relation to logic (even though logic is also a necessary aid). No, what is vital for dogmatics is that God is first, the One to whom we depend absolutely for our very breath. In other words, that God is gracious and relates Godself to us. Theology must operate within the existential relation that God has already established by grace. To begin anywhere else would be to build upon an unrealistic foundation. It is this relation that is being indicated with the feeling of absolute dependence, and its importance for Schleiermacher's dogmatics is nothing less than a desire to do theology by grace alone. If we know God, it is because God has related Godself to us, not because we have discovered God in a book or through logic. It is therefore improper to base dogmatics on anything else but this existential relationship, the feeling of absolute dependence.

So whenever Schleiermacher discusses either the feeling of absolute dependence, immediate Christian religious self-consciousness, or God-consciousness, we can translate each of these difficult phrases to mean the relationship God establishes with us by grace. When we do, we will be in a place to rightly understand Schleiermacher's intentions. From there we may be able to perceive and appreciate the subtleties implied by each term. Rather than stumbling over these first and missing the larger goal, it is helpful if we keep the general sense Schleiermacher has in mind, namely, that these are *relational* terms denoting an immediate existential being-in-relation with God.

WHAT METHOD IS PROPER TO DOGMATICS?

Schleiermacher's dogmatic method is *descriptive*. In his mind, he was not attempting anything revolutionary but merely wanted to describe the faith-doctrines already present in the Evangelical Church. Because dogmatics is a reflection on our being-in-relation with God, then the method of dogmatics is to *describe* the immediate religious self-consciousness of the Church in its normative form.[12] For example, why is Christ the Redeemer? It is because in the Christian community we collectively experience Christ's influence, which results in redemption. The feeling of absolute dependence as a methodological limit means every doctrine must correspond to its appearance and development in the Church.

B. A. Gerrish explains:

> [Schleiermacher] began neither with ancient dogmas nor with ancient history, but with what every Christian experiences, and he sought to give an honest account of it that would not run away from the intellectual problems of the modern world.[13]

The shared experience of Christians is the basis of Schleiermacher's work

—not because theology is subjective but that God has, in grace, initiated a relationship with us. It is not our word but God's that we experience in immediate self-consciousness. Theology reflects on the relationship God has already formed with us by grace.

Each section of Schleiermacher's dogmatics includes critical reflections on self-consciousness, world-consciousness, and God-consciousness. Ultimately, all three forms of consciousness refer to one relationship, namely, the relationship God has with finite being by grace. In Schleiermacher's theology, even his references to self-consciousness and world-consciousness indicate that relatedness essential to the self and the world, our being-in-relation with God. The three forms of dogmatic proposition are thus arranged in this way for convenience alone.

The clearest example of how Schleiermacher uses this threefold pattern comes in Part Two. The second section is arranged first according to the doctrine of Christ and redemption, second the doctrine of the Church and the Holy Spirit, and third the doctrine of God. First, he explicates our immediate religious self-consciousness, our experience of redemption in and through Christ. Second, world-consciousness recognizes the constitution of Church and non-Church according to God's gracious election. And third, God is explicated from the consciousness of redemption, namely, that God is love.

To understand this more fully, think about the very concept of divine revelation. If God reveals Godself, then *to whom* does God reveal Godself? In other words, when God reveals God, is it into a vacuum of empty space? Or is not God's self-revelation *for us?* It would be nonsense to say God reveals Godself to empty space. Therefore, the very concept of revelation presupposes that it is in the self among the world that God reveals Godself. The basis and foundation of God's revelation remains God, but the location of God's self-revelation is our consciousness—plainly because God does not speak into the void but to us. The divine Logos became human flesh, which means revelation is always directed towards human beings. The very notion of God's self-revelation implies that in the feeling of absolute dependence, in our "God-consciousness," God reveals Godself. God remains God over and against God-consciousness, that is, God never becomes an object of human control. By grace alone, we know God's self-proclamation in Christ.

With this in mind, we are capable of appreciating Schleiermacher's vital claim regarding the true basis and source of his dogmatics:

> [T]here is only *one* source from which all Christian doctrine is derived, namely, Christ's self-proclamation, and there is only *one* way in which Christian doctrine if pursued, whether it is more complete or less complete,

namely, based on religious consciousness itself and on the immediate expression of it.[14]

Schleiermacher explicitly denies that his method results in a subjectivist dogmatics, as if it were nothing more than an individual's opinions about God. Theology is not a reflection on our subjective state but on the *effect* of Christ's self-proclamation. It is a reflection on our being-in-relation with God, as God proclaims Godself in Christ. In the end, Schleiermacher's method is the absolute denial of all theological speculation. We can only speak of God as God has spoken of Godself to us. We cannot remove the fact that is *to us* God speaks, that it is only through religious God-consciousness that we *hear* God's self-proclamation. When stated in these terms, Schleiermacher's "controversial" method is, in fact, nothing less than an honest reflection on how God proclaims Godself to us.

It is this very same method that every theologian must admit is their own.[15] Dogmatics is a reflection on the relationship God forms with us by grace, and its method must begin with religious self-consciousness, the self in absolute dependence on God, which hears and receives God's self-proclamation in Jesus Christ. Dogmatics cannot define who God is in Godself, but only describe who God is for us. God in Godself is the "hidden God," and God for us is the "revealed" God, as we saw in chapter two. Yet, the hidden and revealed God completely coincide, so that God-for-us is at once a real revelation of God's Self in and through Christ. This is why Schleiermacher can aptly claim that his dogmatics has its basis on Christ's self-proclamation. A finite being cannot know divinity. Theology is a human possibility by grace alone.

A Theologian of the Word

Is Schleiermacher a theologian of the Word of God? It is often denied, but in the light of what we have said, the truth is evident: God's Word is *central* to Schleiermacher's theology. Think about it like this: Is it any less a theology of the Word if it focuses on the effect of God's Word (Christian self-consciousness) instead of pretending to hold onto an objective apprehension of that Word? In other words, can a theology of the Word exist that does not also reflect on our encounter with that Word? This is Schleiermacher's point. He presupposes a seamless continuity between Christian self-consciousness and God's Word, writing, "The Lord cannot be different in his effects in believers' souls than he reveals himself to be in his Word."[16]

By grace, God communicates Godself in Christ, and we feel absolutely dependent upon God in the modification of our self-consciousness. Our

God-consciousness is further developed by the influence of Christ in the common spirit of the Church, which is God's presence in the community. God's Word remains non-objectified, that is, God does not become an object of our control. Barth claims Schleiermacher only speaks of God by speaking of man in a loud voice, but this is not the case. The very notion of "absolute dependence" negates the possibility of God's Word becoming *our* words about God.

Schleiermacher writes:

> [A]ny sort of givenness of God's being remains completely excluded. This is so, because everything that is externally given must also always be given as an object to which some counteraction is directed, to whatever small degree that may occur. The rendering of that notion to any sort of sense-perceptible object is always a corruption[.][17]

God's being remains hidden even in self-revelation. The feeling of absolute dependence excludes every possibility of God becoming an object of human control.[18] Schleiermacher is, in his own way, quite close to apophatic (negative) theology. Hilary of Poitiers, for example, offers a strikingly similar reflection on our inability, as finite beings, to conceive of the infinite essence of God. He writes:

> Finite minds cannot conceive the Infinite; a being dependent for its existence upon another cannot attain to perfect knowledge either of its Creator or of itself, for its consciousness of self is coloured by its circumstances, and bounds are set which its perception cannot pass.[19]

Hillary further writes that "the best combination of words we can devise cannot indicate the reality and the greatness of God,"[20] and therefore, "Let us confess by our silence that words cannot describe" God.[21] Negative theology shares similar convictions with Schleiermacher's dogmatics, namely, that human beings, absolutely dependent on God, cannot define God in Godself but may only describe God-for-us, the God who is the Whence of our very existence. We are the recipients of God's gracious Word in Jesus Christ, and this Word never becomes our word, a word we control. Schleiermacher is arguably the most significant modern theologian to continue in the apophatic tradition because of how consistently and thoroughly he implemented its core convictions.

Yet it is worth stressing that Schleiermacher is not *only* doing negative theology. Instead, he seamlessly combines negative and positive theology with his usage of the God hidden and revealed.[22] God-for-us *is* a real revelation of God's being in Godself, even while God remains a mystery beyond our grasp.

Schleiermacher can say the essence of God is love but also stress that we cannot define what love is ourselves, but only in connection with Christ and redemption. The harmony of negative and positive theology, of the God hidden and revealed, is the genius of Schleiermacher's doctrine of God. He harmonizes the traditional refusal to "conceive of the Infinite" with a phenomenological approach that stresses the unity of God's being and act, highlighting the inability of humans to speak of God but, at once, the reality of God's speech about Godself, God's Word, Jesus Christ.

Part One: Establishing the Boundary

Now that we have come to terms with the controversial propositions of the Introduction, it will also be essential we understand Part One in its proper context. Part One should not be considered the true "heart" of Schleiermacher's dogmatics. The propositions of Part One *establish the boundary* for what dogmatics can say about God, the world, and the self. It establishes the "frame," in other words, that will only be filled out when the complete picture is unveiled. The doctrines of Part One are those already *presupposed* in Christian religious self-consciousness and are necessarily treated before those extrapolated from the consciousness of redemption.

Julia Lamm explains the boundary-establishing, presuppositional task of Part One and the reasons why Schleiermacher arranged his dogmatics in the way he did, writing:

> In the order of experience, the affections described in part 2 are prior, since it is only through our experience of redemption that we come to view the world as created. In the order of logic, however, the world as a nature system, created and preserved by God, is prior, for otherwise there could be no experience of redemption. Although part 2 is indeed the heart of his dogmatics, part 1 sets the limits to what can be said theologically: metaphysics and speculation must be excluded as alien; science, morality, and piety cannot be compromised; religious language and images must be demythologized and made intelligible in the context of the dogmatics system.[23]

Schleiermacher's dogmatics is arranged logically, not experientially. We first experience redemption in and through Jesus Christ and only then come to recognize that the world was created by this same God and preserved for the sake of redemption. Part Two of *Christian Faith* is the most *immediate* presentation of religious self-consciousness, while Part One follows after the experience of redemption and is presupposed by Part Two. But it is crucial to recognize that Part One and Part Two are tightly interconnected, even if Part

Two alone offers the fullest expression of Christian faith. Part One serves its purpose by establishing a boundary for what can and cannot be said in dogmatics.

With all this in mind, we will now turn to explore a few of the critical doctrines Schleiermacher works through in Part One, paying particular attention to how they help establish a dogmatic limit.

Creation and Preservation

The fullest expression of Schleiermacher's doctrine of creation is that God, in loving wisdom, has ordained all things for the sake of redemption in and through Jesus Christ. Therefore, creation itself is the "artwork" of God that expresses the revelation of God's love. To be a creature of God is one and the same as to be God's elect because creation, from the beginning, is ordained towards the completion of creation in redemption, the new creation. This is articulated in Part Two.

But in Part One, the doctrine of creation takes on a boundary-forming role. The doctrine of creation is treated on an entirely *negative* basis. That is, Schleiermacher is far less concerned about what creation *is* than with what it is *not*. There is a strong preference for the doctrine of preservation since in it the feeling of absolute dependence is fully presented. Schleiermacher explains:

> The doctrine of creation is to be explicated, first and foremost, with a view to warding off anything of an alien sort, so that nothing of the way in which the question of how the world has emerged is answered elsewhere will slip into our domain and stand in contradiction to the pure expression of the feeling of absolute dependence. In contrast, the doctrine of preservation is to be explicated, first and foremost, so as fully to present that basic feeling itself.[24]

The purpose of the doctrine of creation is to clear away any foreign elements that might contradict the feeling of absolute dependence. The doctrine of preservation more fully reflects the positive implications of the feeling of absolute dependence and the world's relation to God. In other words, the doctrine of preservation is immediately present in the feeling of absolute dependence, while the doctrine of creation is only a secondary—but necessary—conclusion.

Nothing in the world emerged by itself. God alone is the source of all things (CF §40). The world, therefore, is not responsible for itself but is absolutely dependent upon God. Everything that is is because God wills it. Furthermore, God is not the world. God cannot be conceived of within the limits of what is worldly, that is, God cannot be thought of as being just another part of the world-system. Any definition of God limited by the confines of the world is unacceptable. Even though Schleiermacher has sometimes been called a pantheist (mostly because of *On Religion*), his doctrine of creation clearly sets him apart from any kind of pantheistic outlook.

A few other common interpretations are subsequently rejected. First, Schleiermacher does not think the Scriptures offer a literal account of creation. He consistently denied the historical Adam. The only conviction required for faith is that the world is absolutely dependent on God, that it does not owe its origin to itself. Whatever scientific theories we use to explain *how* this is so are irrelevant to religious self-consciousness. That the world is and is absolutely dependent on God is all we have to say. The historical Adam is an unnecessary stumbling block because it trespasses into the field of science. It is not required that we believe this story corresponds to a literal event in history, or that creation only took six days. The only proposition that concerns faith is that the world is absolutely dependent on God.

An interesting caveat to this is Schleiermacher's acceptance of the theory of evolution. He was likely the first theologian, or among the first, to take the theory seriously enough to consider it viable.[25] This involves his conviction regarding an "eternal covenant" between faith and science, in which science and faith do not have proper grounds to contradict each other. Schleiermacher offered such a broad definition of the doctrine of creation that any number of scientific theories, including evolution, may very well be true without contradicting religious self-consciousness. Science may guide our understanding of the world, but it cannot tell us what is essential to faith. Likewise, faith cannot trespass into science any more than science can trespass into faith. Schleiermacher would disapprove of anyone who argues that the doctrine of creation is incompatible with the theory of evolution.[26]

Finally, Schleiermacher considers three further doctrines unnecessary: angels, demons, and the devil. These are wholly irrelevant and have no place in dogmatics. The fact that the Bible seems to point to the existence of these beings should not be taken literally as if these are, in fact, real entities. These images may be useful still in Christian rhetoric, such as preaching, but we are not obligated to take them seriously as something real. Especially in regards to the devil, Schleiermacher has strong words of disapproval, calling the doctrine "so unsupportable that a conviction of its truth cannot be expected of anyone" (CF §44, 235).

As this brief summary has shown, Schleiermacher's doctrine of creation establishes the boundary for what can and, perhaps more importantly, cannot be said about creation in connection with the religious self-consciousness. What is essential, however, is the doctrine of preservation, which includes Schleiermacher's vital concept of the "interconnected process of nature." He writes:

> Religious self-consciousness—by virtue of which we locate all that bestirs us and influences us within our absolute dependence on God—wholly coincides with our discernment that precisely all of this is conditioned and determined by the interconnected process of nature.[27]

> Being-conscious-of-oneself-as-part-of-the-world is one and the same thing as finding-oneself-placed-in-a-general-interconnectedness-of-nature.[28]

There is a close connection between the preservation of God and the interconnectedness of the natural order. In fact, these concepts are inseparable, even though they must be distinguished from each other. God's preservation *is* expressed through the interconnected process of nature. Preservation, then, is not a "supernatural" event in which God interferes with the natural order. No, because the world is dependent upon God, the nature-system itself is an expression of God's preservation. The interconnected process of nature brings to fruition God's preserving will. The feeling of absolute dependence always includes this sense of being part of an interconnected system of nature. The editors to the new critical edition of *Christian Faith* offer a helpful summary:

> God's 'absolute causality' as activity to which the feeling of absolute dependence refers, [is] a causality equal in scope to the whole interconnected process of nature but to be distinguished from it.[29]

This is why Schleiermacher considered God's will to elect, create, and redeem humanity singular, it is *one* decree. In the beginning, God said the world is "good." It is good because it has been ordered and preserved for the sake of redemption in and through Jesus Christ. To be created is at once to be elected for redemption, and all creation is preserved and ordained for that end.

The Doctrine of God in Part One

The doctrine of God in Part One is also best understood within its larger boundary-forming context. It establishes what we cannot say about God and what we must say about God by reflecting upon religious self-consciousness.

Arguably one of the most crucial statements regarding Schleiermacher's method, especially as it affects his doctrine of God, is expressed here in Part One. He writes:

> None of the attributes that we ascribe to God is to designate something particular in God; rather, they are to designate only something particular in

the way in which the feeling of absolute dependence is to be referred to God.[30]

Only divine love, as we have seen, can be equated with the essence of God. The only valid "God is…" statement ends with "love." Robert F. Streetman points out that "for Schleiermacher *every* action of the divine causality is an inconceivable expression of the divine love."[31] The divine omni-causality, which is chiefly expressed in the four attributes of God outlined in Part One, is therefore rooted in the divine love and wisdom.

This does not mean that the attributes explained in Part One are false. Instead, Schleiermacher is echoing a conviction long held in the Christian tradition: the inability of human beings to speak of God.[32] Take, for example, the claim that God is omnipotent. This tells us almost nothing about God's essential being. The only thing it tells us about God is that God is *not* limited. Likewise, God's eternity and omniscience tell us that God is not limited by time or ignorance. The essential nature of God is not indicated by any of these attributes, but they are nevertheless true statements about God's *relation to the world*. Schleiermacher's "proposition disclaims the speculative contents of all divine attributes" (CF §50.1, 282).

Schleiermacher describes four attributes of God in Part One: God is eternal, omnipresent, omnipotent, and omniscient. In other words, God is *not* limited by time, space, inability, or ignorance.

These attributes are placed under the overarching concept of God's "causality," which is simply God's "livingness." Schleiermacher explains:

> [S]ince all divine attributes to be discussed in a presentation of Christian faith-doctrine are meant simply to explicate [i.e.: declare, define, clarify, and explain] the feeling of absolute dependence, all of them must somehow be traced back to divine causality.[33]

This significantly effects how each attribute is described. Each attribute articulates divine causality in relation to space and time. And since no attribute can "signify something different in God," that is, no attribute can be set apart from the others, then "'omnipresence,' in being attributed to divine causality, is itself already omnipotence as well, and 'omniscience' is itself already 'eternity' as well" (CF §51.1, 292). In other words, all of God's attributes coincide. In God's relation to space and time, these attributes may be summarized by simply asserting God's "livingness" because this is "an exhaustive way to put the matter" (ibid.).

God's eternity is God's "absolute timeless causality" (CF §52, 292). God's omnipresence is God's "absolutely spaceless causality" (CF §53, 297). That is, God is unconditioned by time (eternal) and space (all-present). God's omnipotence receives a longer definition from Schleiermacher. He makes two important claims. First, the "entire interconnected process of nature" is "grounded in divine causality." And second, the divine causality "is completely presented in the totality of finite being," which means that "everything for which there is a causality in God also comes to be realized and does occur" (CF §54, 305). God's power is effective and always achieves its proper end. What God wills God does. If anything occurs in time or space, then it is rooted in the divine causality. And therefore, God works through the "interconnected process of nature." God does not go outside of the natural process to act, to display God's power, but the very process of nature itself *is* the work of God's omnipotence. This explains why Schleiermacher rejected supernatural miracles (except for Jesus Christ, the Word made flesh, whose appearance was the "only one" miracle).[34] It also explains why he stressed the *one* decree of election, which unites creation and redemption into the same decree (so that all creation is ordained towards redemption and no individual is excluded).

Finally, the divine omniscient is called the "absolute spirituality of divine omnipotence" (CF §55, 316). This attribute indicates that the divine causality is "living." It opposes any fatalistic understanding of God's causality. That is, it denies the possibility of equating the divine causality with lifeless necessity, such as the idea that divine causality is merely blind "fate." For Schleiermacher, there is no difference between God's thinking and willing, between God's foreknowledge and causality. But God's knowledge is all-pervading, as he explains, "God knows everything that exists, and everything that God knows exists" (CF §55.1, 321). God is not a lifeless force causing all things, but the living God in whom will and thought coincide seamlessly. Because God is the living God, this fact qualifies each of the divine attributes.[35] Omniscience is rightly called the "absolute spirituality" of God's omnipotence. The divine wisdom—which is the actualization of God's love—fills out this concept best. God ordains all things in a *loving* and therefore *wise* causality for the sake of redemption in and through Jesus Christ.

As I hope it is now clear, the propositions of Part One are still only preparatory. If we were to stop here (as so many seem to), we would misread Schleiermacher. Yes, Schleiermacher has offered us a large (nearly four-hundred-page) appetizer with the sixty-one propositions of Part One, but the main course is found in those doctrines we have already discussed, namely, the doctrines of an explicitly Christian self-consciousness from Part Two, such as God's love, redemption in Christ, and the Church.

Reading Backwards: The Arrangement of *Christian Faith*

Schleiermacher's *Christian Faith* is best understood backwards. He had his reasons for retaining the book's (somewhat misleading) arrangement from the first edition to its second, but he consistently claimed that the most essential components of the work are in Part Two. In fact, the final forty-five pages (on love, wisdom, and the Trinity) are undoubtedly among the richest theological texts I have ever read.

Schleiermacher's *Christian Faith* is arranged so that its *form* is first presented before its actual *content*. This has led many to base their reading on the frame of Schleiermacher's theology rather than its complete presentation. The organization of this study, however, has tried to show that only after we recognize the content of Schleiermacher's dogmatics—namely, his doctrines of redemption, divine love, and divine threeness—can we understand its form. In other words, Schleiermacher's method is best interpreted *in the light of his conclusions*, not in spite of them. As Pedersen succinctly puts it, "Like a word, the meaning of Schleiermacher's introduction is its use."[36]

But why did Schleiermacher organize his dogmatics in such a confusing way? He offers two reasons. First, and most simply, because of Schleiermacher's distaste for anti-climatic writing. So it was a formal, stylistic decision. He purposefully wanted to end the book at its highest point, at its climax, with the doctrine of the divine love and threeness, rather than beginning there only to go "downhill" with what followed.

The second reason is materially based and thus more complex. It is because of his conviction that theology must maintain an "eternal covenant" between "the living Christian faith and completely free, independent scientific inquiry, so that faith does not hinder science and science does not exclude faith" (OG, 64). It was in the hopes of presenting faith-doctrine within the confines of this "eternal covenant" that he arranged the work. He begins by establishing the limit and boundary of dogmatics before presenting those doctrines immediately conveyed through the Christian consciousness of redemption in Christ. Establishing this limit is necessary to maintain a covenant with natural science. Schleiermacher indicates just how important this was for him, writing to Lücke:

> But in my opinion a textbook that deals with Christian faith as a whole has enough to do if it fulfills the essential duty of defining the limits within which a representation can move without losing its relation to the principles of the church.[37]

In other words, dogmatics must first define its territory and then strive to remain within its own limitations. This explains quite a lot about Schleiermacher's theology. Elsewhere, he argues that "if we wish to be theologians, the scientific and the Christian faith must be compatible."[38] We can and should "borrow" propositions, or "lemmas," from other scientific disciplines, but we must not lose sight of our own limitations. Defining the field of dogmatic theology and remaining within that boundary is one of Schleiermacher's primary goals, not only in *Christian Faith* but also in his important work, *Brief Outline*.

Furthermore, this explains Schleiermacher's expressed desire to "extend orthodoxy" and demonstrate

> at every point how much distance there is between the theses of the church and those of heresy and that within this open area how much friendly agreement is still possible on points common to both the heterodox and orthodox.[39]

Least we think this boundary is small, Schleiermacher consistently reminds us how wide and deep our faith truly is, how much freedom exists for a variety of expressions.

There is a mathematical precision to how Schleiermacher draws the boundary lines for what can and cannot be stated in doctrines of faith. Schleiermacher's doctrine of the Trinity and of God's love express this well. We cannot say more than what is given to us in Christian religious self-consciousness, that is, we cannot speculate beyond our actual situation in the community of faith. This limitation actual *frees* Christian theology to be what it is supposed to be by no longer striving to be what it is not. For example, when theology attempts to be science, to say scientists are wrong about this or that idea, then it is theology in chains, enslaved to defending an ideological point by trying to be something it cannot be. Theology is faith seeking understanding, and thus it takes place within the limits of piety. The propositions of the Introduction, which limit theology to piety alone, liberate Christian theology by defining its limitations.

Schleiermacher's dogmatics is one of the most inclusive ever written. He establishes the outer limits for what can be said and then gives space for a wide variety of possibilities within that boundary. He clearly distinguishes between what propositions are absolutely essential to the faith and what ones are more flexible and open. Whereas most systematic theologies trap their readers into a narrow perspective, Schleiermacher's goal is to open up his readers to reflect on their faith freely. His doctrine of creation is a good example of this. It is non-essential for us to think of creation as a literal six-day event—and, in fact, we trespass into the field of science whenever we attempt to make such a claim. But what *is* essential is the feeling of being absolutely dependent upon God.

Ultimately, it is vital for us to recognize the distinct purpose Schleiermacher had in mind for the Introduction and Part One. The doctrines that bear the fullest weigh are those in Part Two, the true heart and foundation of his theology. Therefore, to properly read Schleiermacher's dogmatics, we have to pay attention to its unique organization.

Conclusion

It was not by mistake that Schleiermacher placed two quotes from Anselm on the epigram of *Christian Faith*:

> For I do not seek to understand so that I may believe; but I believe so that I may understand.[40]

> For those who have not believed will not find by experience, and those who have not found by experience will not know.[41]

Anselm's famous maxim, "credo ut intelligam"—"I believe so that I may understand"—has long been accepted as a classic definition of theology. Schleiermacher's proposal to refer all theological propositions to the concrete reality of religious consciousness, to refer every dogmatic statement back to our being-in-relation with God, is best understood within this definition. Is he not saying, with more precision, what Anselm has already said here? Schleiermacher himself seemed to think this was the case.

Two further points might be made in this regard. In his open letters to Dr. Lücke, Schleiermacher alluded to the fact that his dogmatics essentially follows the structure of the Heidelberg Catechism, which takes basic Christian feeling as its starting point. Likewise, what Schleiermacher admired most about Calvin's *Institutes* was that it never lost its connection with religious affections. That is, it was just as devotional as it was systematic. B. A. Gerrish writes:

> [W]hat Schleiermacher admired most in Calvin's *Institutes* was exactly what he himself strove to achieve in his own *Glaubenslehre*: a dogmatics that has at once a churchly character, given by its consistent reference to the Christian affections, and a scientific character, given by the exactness and mutual coherence of its concepts.[42]

Likewise, Shelli Poe concludes that Schleiermacher "stands in a line of Protestant theologians who are committed to understanding God in relation to the world rather than apart from it."[43] And Ebeling agrees, "For myself, the more I study Schleiermacher, the more I see the deep interconnection between Schleiermacher and the Reformers."[44] As I have stressed in this chapter, Schleiermacher "controversial" methodology has far more in common with the Protestant tradition than his critics like to admit.

These comparisons highlight the fact that if Schleiermacher's method is in error, then he is, at the very least, in good company. He should be understood in terms of these great traditions—Anselm, Calvin, and Heidelberg—and less in terms of the standard, subjectivist misreading of his work.

My goal has been to show that Schleiermacher's controversial method is perhaps not as far-fetched as it seems. Anselm wrote most of his theology in the form of prayer. He kept central the fact that we cannot speak of God as an object "out there" somewhere, but as the God who loves us and encounters us through Jesus Christ and in the Church of His Spirit. Theology within the limits of piety alone is not an original idea. In fact, it is how the Church has always done theology and always will. Anyone who attempts to strip theology free from its religious character will end up with a God of their own making, not the God to whom we depend absolutely, the gracious God who meets us in Jesus.

---

1. CF §31.PS, 186.
2. OG, 40.
3. CF §64.1, 389.
4. *The Eternal Covenant*, 18. Berlin: Walter de Gruyter, 2017.
5. *Friedrich Schleiermacher: Pioneer of Modern Theology*, 37. London: Collins Liturgical Publications, 1987.
6. *Theology of Schleiermacher*, 243. Grand Rapids: William B. Eerdmans Publishing Company, 1982.
7. This is not to imply that Barth failed to read beyond §14. To his credit, Barth was a lifelong student of Schleiermacher's dogmatics and read him diligently and frequently.
8. OG, 57.
9. I use the phrase "being-in-relation with God" throughout this text to indicate a few ideas: First, that our relation to God is irrevocable. It is a *being-in*-relation, not merely a relation, because it is graciously established by God in Christ. It is not a self-established relation but a grace-infused one; because it is a relation of *absolute* dependence, it is by grace. Second, it connotes the essential interconnectedness of our nature. We are *always* beings in relation. Schleiermacher's insight is that the core relation of our being is our being-in-relation with God, the feeling of absolute dependence. Finally, I use this phrase repeatedly to drive my primary point home: The feeling of absolute dependence is a *relational* concept, not a subjective one.
10. CF §4, 18.
11. CF §4.1, 19.
12. Furthermore, Schleiermacher wanted to describe those normative beliefs often left unspoken. For example, when discussing the Old Testament (see the sidebar to this chapter), Schleiermacher argues that it is not canonical in the same way that the New Testament is. He backs up this claim by asserting the *normality* of this belief in Christian self-consciousness—that the average believer does not base their faith on the Old Testament but the New—even if it is not explicitly stated. A description of our unspoken beliefs is just as necessary in dogmatic reflection as a description of our stated confessions.
13. *A Prince of the Church*, 49. Philadelphia: Fortress Press, 1984.
14. CF §19.PS, 138.

15. For example, it is interesting to compare Schleiermacher's argument with a quote from T. F. Torrance, a Barthian critic of his work. Torrance's point is akin to Schleiermacher's:
"By the Word of God is meant not man's word about God but quite definitely God's own Word as God Himself lives and speaks it—Word as personal mode and activity of God's being. Yet we have to do with the Word of God only as it has been addressed to us and has actually reached us, Word that has called forth and found response in our hearing and understanding and living—otherwise we could not speak of it. We do not begin, then, with God alone or with man alone, nor even with God speaking on the one hand and man hearing on the other hand, but with God and man as they are posited together in a movement of creative self-communication by the Word of God" (*God and Rationality*, 137; Edinburgh: T&T Clark, 1971).
For Torrance, God's Word and its human response are included in Christ's hypostatic nature. God speaks as God and receives revelation as a man simultaneously in Christ, and as we participate in Christ, we take part in Christ's knowledge of the Father. (See chapter six in my book *T. F. Torrance in Plain English*; Columbus: Beloved Publishing, 2017).
Schleiermacher does not have this understanding in mind, but his method is more complicated than his critics assume. It is not a man alone speaking of God with a loud voice, as Torrance alludes (though without naming Schleiermacher directly). It is God in grace meeting human beings and communicating Godself in a way we might understand, in religious self-consciousness. Torrance's concept of revelation is certainly more Christological, but Schleiermacher's is not as one-sided as it is often said to be. God does not speak into a vacuum but *to human beings*. Even in Torrance's concept of revelation, there must still be a subject who hears God's gracious Word. As much as he has tried to remove the self and place the focus on Christ—perhaps rightly—there remains an inescapable limitation: We are bound to ourselves and will never know the otherness of others objectively but only in and through self-consciousness.
16. *Servant of the Word*, 112. Philadelphia: Fortress Press, 1987.
17. CF §4.4, 27. The editors of CF note regarding this passage: "That is, any claim of knowing God's being in God's self, as it were, apart from God's distinct work of creation and preservation, redemption, and reconciliation in history, is strictly a matter of speculation, not of faith-doctrine" (ibid. n28).
18. This once again shows Barth's congruency with Schleiermacher. Bruce McCormack examines Barth's effort to conceptualize divine revelation as a *dandum*, a giving, instead of a *datum*, a given. And he notes the harmony of their perspectives, "For Schleiermacher, too, revelation was a 'giving,' not a 'given'" ("What has Basel to do With Berlin?, 165; *The Princeton Seminary Bulletin*, 2002). Schleiermacher makes the same point with the feeling of absolute dependence because this concept highlights the primacy of God over God's self-revealing, and denies any such givenness in revelation. The non-objectifiability of God is central for Barth, dialectical theology, *and* Schleiermacher.
19. *On the Trinity*, book 3.24. Public domain.
20. Ibid., book 2.7.
21. Ibid., book 2.6.
22. See S. Poe, *Essential Trinitarianism*, chapter 6. Bloomsbury T&T Clark, 2018.
23. *The Living God*, 130. The Pennsylvania State University Press, 1996.
24. CF §39, 215.
25. Of course, Schleiermacher died before Charles Darwin published *On the Origin of Species*, but the notion of evolution predates Darwin. Schleiermacher's account of creation is, indeed, an "evolutionary" account. For a details study, see Daniel J. Pedersen, *The Eternal Covenant*, chapter two. Pedersen notes, "Even though Schleiermacher died twenty five years before *The Origin of Species*, the major requisite scientific notions needed to form a genuinely modern account of evolution were [...] in the air before Charles Darwin proposed natural and sexual selection as the mechanisms of biological evolution" (36).
26. Another example of just how fruitful the eternal covenant can be is the possibility of constructing an eco-theology from Schleiermacher's thought. The pursuit of an environmentally conscious way of life is not only compatible with the religious life, but it is arguably a necessary conclusion of religious self-consciousness, according to Schleiermacher's concept of world-consciousness and the interconnected process of nature. Schleiermacher's this-worldly theology makes care for the earth a religious duty. See *Schleiermacher and Sustainability*, ed. by Shelli M. Poe. (Louisville: Westminster John Knox Press, 2018.)

27. CF §46, 247-8.
28. CF §34.1, 198.
29. CF §46.PSn4, 258.
30. CF §50, 279. Petersen notes: "This quotation has been a source of much misunderstanding." But with this Schleiermacher is simply reaffirming a tradition long held by Reformed theologians, namely, the ineffability of God, that finite cannot know the infinite. So the divine attributes *describe* God even though they do not *define* (or limit) God, just as the finite cannot comprehend the infinite. (Pedersen: "Schleiermacher and Reformed Scholastics on the Divine Attributes," *International Journal of Systematic Theology*, vol. 17, no. 4, Oct. 2015.)
31. *Barth and Schleiermacher*, 131. Philadelphia: Fortress Press, 1988.
32. As Pedersen argues, we cannot *define* God in Godself but only *describe* God's relation to the world, God's self-revelation. This places Schleiermacher in the tradition of Reformed Scholastics as he shares an almost identical approach to the divine attributes. Pedersen writes: "Because there is no proportion between the finite and the infinite, the divine essence can never be exhaustively comprehended. It will only ever be open to partial, and thus inadequate, description. Any description of the divine essence, though certainly a description *of that essence*, will be attributed by human inquirers and adequate only to God's effects, not to the divine essence in itself." ("Schleiermacher and Reformed Scholastics on the Divine Attributes," *International Journal of Systematic Theology*, vol. 17, no. 4, Oct. 2015.)
33. CF §50.3, 285.
34. An absolutely supernatural miracle must go outside the natural order, while the appearance of Christ takes place within nature, even though it is beyond the capabilities of individuals. Schleiermacher calls "the sending of Christ" the "Only one miracle" (CF §47.1, 260). He stressed that the "supernatural becomes natural" within the interconnected process of nature and not apart from it.
35. Williams notes: "In other words, unqualified omnipotence, or omnipotence conceived as sheer efficient causality, is equivalent to atheism, because it denies that God is living and free, and this is to deny God" (*Schleiermacher the Theologian*, 95; Philadelphia: Fortress Press, 1978).
36. *The Eternal Covenant*, 18. Berlin: Walter de Gruyter, 2017.
37. OG, 76.
38. *The Life of Jesus*, 24. Philadelphia: Fortress Press, 1975.
39. OG, 68.
40. *Proslogion* 1, in *Anselm of Canterbury: The Major Works*, 87. New York: Oxford University Press, 1998.
41. *De fide trinitatis* 2 in *Anselm of Canterbury: The Major Works*, 236. New York: Oxford University Press, 1998.
42. *Continuing the Reformation*, 185. Chicago: The University of Chicago Press, 1993.
43. *Essential Trinitarianism*, 30. Bloomsbury T&T Clark, 2018.
44. "Schleiermacher's Doctrine of the Divine Attributes," *Schleiermacher as Contemporary* (ed. Robert Funk), 173. New York: Herder and Herder, 1970. Ebeling points to Luther as an example: "When we think about the way in which Luther interpreted the First Commandment, we come very near to the phenomenon which Schleiermacher had in mind when he spoke of absolute dependence" (ibid).

SIDEBAR: ON SCRIPTURE

[T]he Word-centered character of Schleiermacher's theology has been almost universally ignored or misinterpreted. [...] Schleiermacher's doctrine of the Word of God is not only at the center of his own dogmatic system, but also can be seen as a faithful development from Calvin's doctrine of the Word.[1]

Schleiermacher, in the tradition of his Reformed forebears, puts the Word of God at the center of his whole system of theology.[2]

— Dawn DeVries

Schleiermacher's passion for and devotion to the Word of God in Holy Scripture is not often given the recognition it deserves. But upon further investigation, it is difficult to imagine how Schleiermacher's devotion to the Scriptures could be overlooked. The vast majority of Schleiermacher's lectures at the University of Berlin were on the New Testament, especially on Paul, he was an early proponent of the historical-critical method of Biblical interpretation, and finally, but also most importantly, he was a devoted preacher of the Word every single week for over forty years. This explains why Terrence Tice claimed:

> Thus, the record would show that his continual exegetical studies of Scriptures (also in yearly university courses) and allied sermonic

presentations influenced his doctrinal theology more than anything else.[3]

The fact that the Scriptures are Schleiermacher's greatest doctrinal influence is not evident upon first reading his dogmatics, but there are significant Biblical undertones all throughout *Christian Faith* if we pay attention to them. Julia Lamm argued that Schleiermacher's doctrine of God, while being "rooted in the Christian self-consciousness," is, "at its core, biblical. Its key proposition is taken from 1 John 4: 'God is love.'"[4] Schleiermacher's theology is deeply indebted to his careful reading of the New Testament and his passion for preaching.

Accordingly, in this sidebar, we will examine Schleiermacher's understanding of the Bible and its relation to dogmatics. The overall point I want to make is that Schleiermacher's theology *is* Biblical, even if it is only implicitly and rarely explicitly so. But to do this, we must reckon with precisely how he understood the Scriptures.

Dogmatics and the Bible

When Schleiermacher placed dogmatics and Biblical interpretation apart from one another as separate tasks, it was not to downplay the significance of either. The opposite is true. Separating these fields of inquiry means giving them their proper space to flourish and accomplish their respective goals. It is *because* Biblical exegesis was so crucial to Schleiermacher that it must be separated from dogmatics. And he stressed that we should not confuse the two, dogmatics is not exegesis and exegesis is not dogmatics. They follow different methods and have different goals.

Schleiermacher's understanding of dogmatics results in what might appear to us today to be a strange preference for Evangelical confessions over the texts of Scripture. In the Introduction he writes, "Evangelical doctrine must gain warranty, in part, by appeal to Evangelical confessional documents and, where these are found wanting, to Scriptures of the New Testament" (CF §27, 166). This preference is proven by Schleiermacher's use of confessional creeds and documents more frequently than any Biblical text. He never used Scripture as a "proof text." But this should not be taken to imply that the Bible has no place in his dogmatics. Instead, Schleiermacher's use of Church confessions accomplishes two critical tasks.

First, for Schleiermacher, confessions must be derived from the Bible. There is no antithesis between Scripture and tradition, they are inseparable. So this preference for confessional documents is at once a dedication to the *living* Word of God in the Scriptures, as it has been reflected upon in the historical life of the Church.

Second, the primary reason for this preference has to do with the task of dogmatics itself. Dogmatics, for Schleiermacher, is a positive science that arises from the Christian religious self-consciousness of redemption. It is therefore bound to the Church as the community of Christ's body, through which He communicates His sinless perfection and His absolutely strong God-consciousness. Schleiermacher never set out to produce an entirely *original* dogmatics, in the sense that he wished to create something new out of nothing. Instead, he was convinced his task was merely to *describe* the faith of the Christian community. In its descriptive role, dogmatics is not concerned with studying the Biblical texts themselves. So the confessions of the Evangelical Church are preferred.

The Doctrine of Scripture

Schleiermacher's doctrine of Scripture is a part of his ecclesiology (doctrine of the Church). Here he makes a series of significant claims about the nature and purpose of the Bible. In short, for Schleiermacher, the Bible is presuppositionally authoritative, it is the norm for Christian faith, and it was inspired by God. Thus:

> The Scriptures of the New Testament are authentic in their origination and sufficient as norm for Christian doctrine.[5]

This may seem surprising to read coming from the "father of modern liberal theology," but that is precisely our mistake: We think about Schleiermacher wrongly whenever we apply false labels to his work. As I have said before, he would have disapproved of the "liberal" label entirely. This is an example of Schleiermacher the *centrist,* not the liberal. With these sections, he situates himself between the liberal enlightenment scholars and conservative Biblical literalists (or supernaturalists) of his own time. The "liberal" and "conservative" labels are meaningless, however, when applied to past figures because these are time-conditioned, cultural terms and are improperly used when assessing past figures of significance.

With that said, there are five parts to Schleiermacher's doctrine of Scripture that we will consider.[6]

First, if the Scriptures are authoritative, then this fact itself is a presupposition of faith. That is, it is not *proven* by faith, nor does faith *rely* upon the authority of Scripture, it is presupposed. Dogmatics gives special authority to the Bible because of this presupposition. It is Christian faith that gives the Bible its authority, not the reverse.[7]

Piety, for Schleiermacher, is neither knowing or doing but feeling (an immediate existential relationship). Faith is an internal phenomenon bound to an external cause. The *source* of faith is God's grace. Faith is a gift. As such, faith is not based on the Bible, but the Bible is presupposed to have authority because of faith. This follows Schleiermacher's conviction that "the ground of faith must be the same among us as among the first Christians" (CF §128.2, 835).

Christianity does not belong to the Bible, that is, the Bible does not determine what is and is not Christian. Rather, what is Christian determines what is and is not in the Bible. The truth of this is clear whenever we examine Church history, particularly the Reformation, which removed books from the Bible on these same grounds. Any Protestant who takes issue with Schleiermacher over this claim has failed to recognize that the Reformers did exactly the same thing by excluding the Apocrypha. And Luther would have excluded even more texts if he had his way. ("Luther's canon" removed Hebrews, James, Jude, and Revelation.) So it should not be a surprise to discover the same Reformation principle in Schleiermacher's doctrine of Scripture.

Second, Schleiermacher excluded the Old Testament from the Christian canon. Because of the rule established above, the Old Testament may still be useful, but, for Schleiermacher, it does not determine what is Christian. Its basis is different from what founded the Christian faith. The Old Testament deserves a place in the Bible, but it does not earn the same normative and authoritative status as the New Testament. It offers a historical connection with the Jewish origins of Christian faith, but it is not a reliable foundation.

Ultimately, Schleiermacher argues that this understanding of the Old Testament is the same one the majority of Christians already presuppose, often without vocalizing it. Very few believers would claim their faith depends on the Old Testament. Who would be willing to place equal weigh on the laws of Leviticus as the words of Christ? In theory, perhaps some might assert this is the case, but in practice, very few believers actually consider the Old Testament normative. That is Schleiermacher's point. He merely articulates a presupposition most Christians already have about the Bible.

Third, because the New Testament represents the first presentation of the Christian faith, it is the *norm* for all future presentations. The self-proclamation of Jesus Christ is the heart and foundation of Christianity, and its first record was presented in the New Testament. So whatever future doctrines or interpretations may arise about the faith, they must fall under the norm of the Biblical testimony.

Fourth, the books of the New Testament are "inspired by the Holy Spirit" (*CF* §130, 840). Schleiermacher contrasts "inspired" with "learned." Inspiration depends on something being internally communicated, through grace, while learning depends on outward communication. Therefore, he writes:

[T]he speaking and writing of the apostles, moved as they were by the Spirit, was also a communicating of the divine revelation that existed in Christ.[8]

This is why Schleiermacher stressed that "everything must be referred to the conception of Christ that comes from Scripture" (CF §133.1, 858). But Schleiermacher is fervently opposed to an individualistic interpretation. He has not fallen into relativism, as if we can interpret the Bible however we see fit. Instead, all this is bound up with his understanding of the Church (which is why the doctrine is placed in his ecclesiology). Only in the community of faith does Christ's self-communication persist, and therefore, only in the community, as it stands on the shoulders of the Christian tradition, can the Scriptures be rightly interpreted. The individual is never without the community just as the community depends upon the individual.

As such, the Scriptures are *reliable*. This is our fifth and final point. Schleiermacher writes:

Moreover, if Sacred Scripture is described as sufficient in this respect, this means that the Holy Spirit can guide us into all truth through its use, just as the Holy Spirit did the apostles themselves and all others who were gladdened by the direct instructions of Christ.[9]

To demand anything else from the Scriptures would be to turn the Bible into something it is not. Those who strive to prove its inerrancy or infallibility are missing the point. The Biblical texts may not be perfect in every way, but they are inspired by the Holy Spirit, normative for the Church, authoritative, and therefore, they are *enough*. We can rely on the Bible for everything essential to our faith. Clearly, then, the Bible takes up a central place in Schleiermacher's thought. While he resisted the temptation of providing empty "proof texts" for his dogmatic propositions, his theology has its foundation firmly fixed on the Bible.

---

1. *Jesus Christ in the Preaching of Calvin and Schleiermacher*, 4-5. Louisville: Westminster John Knox Press, 1996.
2. Ibid., 98.
3. *Schleiermacher: The Psychology of Christian Faith and Life*, 13n11. Lanham: Lexington Books, 2018.
4. *The Living God*, 219. The Pennsylvania State University Press, 1996.
5. CF §131, 848.
6. Schleiermacher presented these points in a different order than I present them here. I have re-arranged them for clarity.
7. Barth makes a similar claim. With some essential differences, he is following Schleiermacher when he describes the Word of God in Holy Scripture as a "miracle" of grace: "To say

'the Word of God' is to say the miracle of God" (*Church Dogmatics* I/2, 528; Peabody: Hendrickson Publishers, 2010), and this miracle is "the foundation of the dignity and authority of the Bible" (ibid., 530). The result of both approaches is the same: the Bible is not grounded on itself but on God. Its authority is not its own. Thus, we can only presuppose the authority of the Bible and cannot ground it on anything other than the grace of God. See further, *Church Dogmatics* I/2 §19.2.

8. CF §130.1, 842.
9. CF §131.2, 851.

5

CONCLUSION TO PART I

REEVALUATING SCHLEIERMACHER'S SIGNIFICANCE

SUMMARY: Two stumbling blocks stand between us and a better appreciation of Schleiermacher's theology: First, his use of philosophy in theology, and second, his placement and explication of the doctrine of the Trinity. A reevaluation of Schleiermacher requires clarity on these issues.

IN SCHLEIERMACHER'S OWN WORDS:

> [B]ut what draws on reason and philosophy cannot be Christian theology. It is surely a great gain, here and elsewhere, to banish all materials of this kind from the domain of Christian faith-doctrine.[1]

> The last thing I ever expected was that I would be associated at so many points with the speculative dogmaticians [...] for I am not at all inclined to philosophize in dogmatics.[2]

> The fundamental thought of the inquiry before us is that the philosophical and the dogmatic are not to be mixed.[3]

SECONDARY QUOTES:

> Christian doctrine must be presented in total independence of any philosophical system whatever. In [Schleiermacher's] account of God [...], he has not looked to any philosopher, either on the right or the left, but has

quite simply interrogated the feeling common to all devout Christians and only sought to describe it without one-sidedness. [...] Anyone who thinks of the doctrine of God in the *Glaubenslehre* in terms of some philosophy or other must therefore be confused.[4]

— B. A. Gerrish

All, therefore, is sham and false religion that the theologian have adduced from philosophy as to what God is.[5]

— Ulrich Zwingli

Introduction

Ask a theology student or pastor their opinion of Schleiermacher and, if they are even aware of him at all, most will express disdain for his theology. They may call him a heretic or say because of him theology turned sour, but unless they have spent a great deal of time studying him (or even if they have), it is unlikely they will see him favorably. And this is because, perhaps more than anyone else in modern theological history, his work has been poorly caricatured. But examining him with a more charitable lens, as I have attempted here, results in a drastically different portrait. If we read Schleiermacher expecting the worst, then we will wrongfully pass judgment on him as our enemy. We will marginalize his significance and overlook the many helpful things he can teach us still today. I hope to have shown in the first part of this book that there are still many things we can learn from Schleiermacher. If we ignore his multi-faceted contribution, it is only to our own detriment. We may not agree with each and every one of his conclusions, but we owe Schleiermacher, at the very least, a reassessment that goes beyond his caricatures.

This book began with a brief assessment of the relationship between Barth and Schleiermacher. I want to conclude Part I by returning to that discussion and, in the light of all that we've discovered so far, reevaluate Schleiermacher's significance from the Barthian perspective. This will require the recognition and removal of the two most common stumbling blocks standing in the way of appreciating him rightly, which were briefly mentioned in the introduction.

The Usefulness of Philosophy

Implicit to much of the debate regarding Barth and Schleiermacher is the proper use of philosophy in theology. What kind of relationship exists between these two disciplines? Surprisingly, the way Barth and Schleiermacher answer this question is remarkably similar, though not without some disagreement. A common misconception is that Schleiermacher placed theology under the control of a philosophical framework, but this is not an altogether new misreading, he combated it in his own time. We will examine more closely this misconception and recognize similarities in the relationship of theology to philosophy for both Barth and Schleiermacher.

For Barth, philosophy may offer some help to theology, but ultimately, theology must never become *dependent* upon philosophical presuppositions. Barth writes, "In one way or another the very thing theology seeks (because in fact it needs it) would be lost whenever theology attempted to rely upon such an arbitrary presupposition."[6] For theology to try and support itself by using presuppositions from other sources (such as philosophy), would be, according to Barth, the same as selling its birthright for a mess of pottage (Gen. 25: 29-34). God alone is the proof of (and foundation for) theological accuracy. Barth then concludes, "In its total poverty evangelical theology is rich, sustained, and upheld by its total lack of *presuppositions.*"[7]

To say that Barth has no use for philosophy, however, would be misleading. There are significant philosophical undertones throughout his *Church Dogmatics*. A quick glance at the index will reveal just how often Barth engages with philosophers and philosophical systems.[8] But he was adamant that philosophy can never become the foundation of theology. Theology must stand on its own two feet, so to speak.

Barth charged Schleiermacher with doing precisely that, of subjecting theology to a foundation of philosophy.[9] But this is a misreading of Schleiermacher's work. Schleiermacher's approach was actually not all that different from Barth's.[10] Schleiermacher summarized his relationship to philosophy with an expression: "*timeo Danaos et dona ferentes*," which translates, "I fear the Greeks even when they bring gifts" (OG, 87). Philosophy may have "gifts" to offer theology, but we must maintain a healthy skepticism regarding its influence. He further explains:

> Even if I had referred more often to the domain of philosophy, I would still follow the rule of not allowing philosophy to influence the content of the *Glaubenslehre* [faith-doctrine, CF].[11]

Schleiermacher refused to let the content of his dogmatics be determined by philosophy. He was willing to borrow propositions from philosophy to help establish the proper place of dogmatics. But when we rightly understand Schleiermacher's goals for the Introduction to and Part One of *Christian Faith*, then we will not make the same mistake of thinking these sections are the true foundation of Schleiermacher's dogmatics. It is only those doctrines immediately present in the Christian self-consciousness of redemption that make up the heart and foundation of his theology. Everything before Part Two is preliminary or serves a boundary-forming function.

Schleiermacher explicitly states in the Introduction that his dogmatics stands on its own two feet and does not depend on philosophy. He writes:

> The Evangelical church, in particular, is of one mind in bearing within itself the consciousness that the shaping of dogmatic propositions that is distinctive to it does not depend on any philosophical form or school, or has not proceeded from any speculative interest in any respect. Rather, it has proceeded only from the interest of satisfying immediate self-consciousness, which is mediated by the genuine and unadulterated foundation endowed by Christ alone.[12]

And elsewhere, Schleiermacher writes, "[T]here is only *one* source from which all Christian doctrine is derived, namely, Christ's self-proclamation" (CF §19.PS, 138). Jesus Christ alone is the true foundation of Schleiermacher's dogmatics. One of the reasons why we have so much difficulty believing this is true is that we are poor readers. We might easily pick up *Christian Faith*, read the first hundred pages of the Introduction, and conclude that philosophy, not Christ, is the foundation of this work. Schleiermacher has not made it easy for us to understand him rightly, but when he declares the true heart and foundation of his work to be Jesus Christ, we have to take him seriously enough to withhold judgment until we have adequately examined his entire dogmatics. Schleiermacher's dogmatics, perhaps unlike any other modern work, requires an incredible amount of patience and trust.

So it should be clear that both Barth and Schleiermacher are in relative agreement. Philosophy cannot provide a foundation for theology. Christian theology must stand on its own two feet, on God's self-proclamation in Jesus Christ. Schleiermacher's Introduction is not an attempt to provide a philosophical foundation for dogmatics but to *contrast* theology against philosophy. He borrows from other fields to set apart Christian theology as its own *independent* field of study. In other words, "I fear the Greeks even when they bring gifts."

Why the Misreadings?

The Barthian critique of Schleiermacher as a subjectivist whose theology centers around human emotions without any real content is not new. In fact, it is likely the oldest misreading of his work since it first appeared. What is the root cause of this misreading? According to B. A. Gerrish, Georg Wobbermin was the first to recognize the common thread behind all such misreadings: approaching Schleiermacher's theology from the perspective of his philosophy. Gerrish writes:

> Writing in 1933, Wobbermin identified as the fundamental error [...] of Schleiermacher criticism that his theology must be approached from the perspective of his philosophy; and he found this tradition of interpretation going back to the influential work of Wilhelm Bender (1845-1901), written under Ritschlian auspices, and even beyond—to Schleiermacher's first Hegelian critics. 'One can bluntly describe Brunner's Schleiermacher book,' he remarked, 'as a modernized new edition of Bender's work'.[13]

By reading Schleiermacher in a speculative lens, it makes sense why his critics would *mis*read him as a subjectivist. Beginning in error can only lead to erroneous conclusions. But, as we have seen, the very opposite is true: Schleiermacher's theology is thoroughly anti-speculative. Understanding his relationship with philosophy, therefore, is crucial to reading his work accurately. As I have tried to show since the beginning of this book, Schleiermacher did not ground his theology on philosophy but on Jesus Christ and redemption, and we must read him accordingly. In fact, he went so far as to state, in the first edition of *Christian Faith,* that "the philosophical and the dogmatic are not to be mixed."[14] This is why it was vital for us to begin in reverse, not with the feeling of absolute dependence but with the doctrines of God, Christ, and election.

This does not mean philosophy and theology are *opposed* to one another, but merely that they are different.[15] They share common themes, and thus inevitably overlap and borrow from each other, but they cannot be mixed. So we must avoid the temptation of reading Schleiermacher as a speculative theologian. It was the root error behind Barth and Brunner's misreadings.

The Trinity

Schleiermacher's placement of the doctrine of the Trinity in the Conclusion of his dogmatics actually *heightens* the importance of the doctrine rather than diminishing it. But Barth criticizes Schleiermacher for this move. He argued that Schleiermacher does not give the Trinity a *determinative* role in his dogmatics, that it was only a secondary consideration. But, as we have seen, this is not an accurate reading of his work.

By concluding with the Trinity, Schleiermacher restates the whole of his dogmatics with a single point. The doctrine of the Trinity has been *the* implicit doctrine pervading the whole work. Because the doctrine of the Trinity is, at its core, a defense of Christ and redemption, then this is indeed the case. He writes that "precisely these features"—meaning those essential to his dogmatics, namely, the uniting of divine nature and human nature "both through the individual person of Christ and through the common spirit of the church"—"are also the essential features in the doctrine of God's tri-unity" (CF §170.1, 1020). The heart of Schleiermacher's theology is that Christ is our Redeemer, and this is defended by and concluded in the doctrine of God's threeness.

Fiorenza offers a helpful summary:

> Schleiermacher grounds the Trinity neither through speculation nor through direct immediate experience, but rather in terms of the Christian community's historical experience of the presence of God's being as 'person forming' in Christ and as 'community-forming' in the Christian community. The Trinity is not based upon a Hegelian concept of God as Spirit that grounds the Trinitarian differentiation of God in God's self-consciousness. Instead, it is the Christian consciousness of the deity of the Son and the Spirit that necessitates the threeness of God as Father, Son, and Spirit.[16]

Consider how the Trinity is traditionally conceived. Now, imagine how we might go about constructing the doctrine if we rejected every speculative impulse. How would we proceed? The result would, perhaps, be nothing less than Schleiermacher's own proposal.

We would be forbidden to begin with some abstract "substance" of God who is self-differentiated. Instead, we could only begin with the shared Christian experience of redemption in and through Jesus Christ. This would be further developed as we come to terms with the community formed by Christ's Spirit, the Church, the medium through which Christ communicates His sinless perfection. We would then have before us the undeniable threeness of God. It would not be through speculation that we discovered this but the result of reflecting on the experience of redemption shared by all believers in the Christian church. God's Tri-unity is not directly given in this experience, but it is a necessary *conclusion* of it. The redemption wrought in and through Jesus Christ leads us towards this end. So it is entirely fitting for Schleiermacher to conclude his dogmatics with the doctrine of the Trinity because it is what his entire system has been building towards.

If Schleiermacher began with the Trinity, like Barth, then it would disrupt his entire method. But is Barth's method really all that different? His approach shares the same convictions that drive Schleiermacher's, namely, to refer everything concretely to the person of Jesus Christ. So, like Schleiermacher, does Barth not *also* presuppose the redemption of Christ when he places the doctrine of the Trinity in the Prolegomena of his *Church Dogmatics*? For Barth, revelation and reconciliation go hand in hand.[17] So the revelation of God's Tri-unity presupposes the reconciling work of Christ, and therefore,

Barth's doctrine of the Trinity also has its foundation in redemption.[18] Is it really such a stretch to say that their approach is more congruent than it seems?

Barth was just as dedicated to non-speculative theology as Schleiermacher.[19] Therefore, it cannot be said that Barth begins the entirety of his work with the Trinity, in the sense that it is a speculative doctrine without concrete grounding in the person and work of Christ. Barth's own method seems quite similar (with several essential differences) to Schleiermacher,[20] though his presentation is merely reversed. Beginning with the doctrine of the Trinity does not guarantee that the Trinity has a controlling and determinative place in theology. Any theologian could just as easily begin there and proceed to develop unitarian doctrines of faith. The proof is not in the order itself but in the inner logic of a system. So it could be argued that the Trinity is just as essential to Schleiermacher's dogmatics as it is to Barth's. With this, we can clearly see the core conviction shared by Barth and Schleiermacher: a non-speculative approach. They are not united in everything, but perhaps they are closer than commonly thought.

Appreciating Schleiermacher Rightly

Schleiermacher's place within the Christian tradition is secure. But the question remains: What will history make of his significance? There is no doubt that he should stand shoulder to shoulder with the great dogmatic thinkers of our faith, yet theologians tend to pass over his work as something heretical or dangerous. But there is still so much we can learn from him, as Emanuel Hirsch recognized, "Theology to this day has not learned from him what it should."[21] Whatever problems we may find in his theology, they are far outweighed by its benefits. May we move past the caricatures and learn to appreciate Schleiermacher rightly.

Barth, for his part, believed he deserved at least that much from us. A story from his life expresses this well. Barth returned to war-torn Germany in 1946 to lecture on the Apostles Creed, which later became his popular little book, *Dogmatics in Outline*. In the city of Bonn, he taught in the semi-ruined Kurfürsten Schloss (the Electoral Palace, which had been taken over by the university). Barth recounts a small but meaningful act:

> We began by singing a psalm or a hymn to cheer us up. About eight o'clock we became aware of the rebuilding in the quadrangle from the noise of the demolition crane which was breaking up the ruins. (Incidentally, my curiosity led me to discover, among the rubble, an undamaged bust of Schleiermacher, which was rescued and restored to a new place of honour.)[22]

The restoration of Schleiermacher's statue to its rightful place of honor is an ironic testimony to Barth's own contribution to Schleiermacher-studies. We could not accurately describe Barth as either an enemy or an ally of Schleiermacher's theology, but this ambiguity does not negate Barth's steadfast conviction about Schleiermacher's significance. In his own way, Barth's massive influence has resulted in a revival of interest in Schleiermacher. I can personally attest to being among those brought to Schleiermacher because of Barth. Terrence Tice summarizes this revival well:

> Although there are fundamental difference not only in temperament but also in both method and doctrine between Barth and Schleiermacher, many of the widely accepted, positive contributions of Barth actually constitute a revival of the genuine Schleiermacher—especially the renewed understanding of the church orientation of dogmatics and of its radical grounding in the personal Word of God spoken by grace in Christ.[23]

Barth and Schleiermacher are far closer than they seem.[24] They share a common non-speculative approach, a dedication to Jesus Christ and redemption, and a Church-oriented perspective. Both theologians attempted to revive and refashion the doctrines of election, God, and the Trinity, and the ways in which they worked out these alterations are too similar to ignore.[25] As we have seen, they also both held a common conviction regarding the usefulness of philosophy in theology, in spite of Barth's misreading of Schleiermacher to the contrary. In short, Barth and Schleiermacher are best understood, not according to their superficial disagreements in matters of form, but according to their fundamental congruency in matters of substance.

Barth concluded his 1968 "Unscientific Postscript" by reflecting on this question:

> Could [Schleiermacher] not perhaps be understood differently so that I would not have to reject his theology, but might rather be joyfully conscious of proceeding in fundamental agreement with him?[26]

In my reading, the answer is a clear and unmistakable *yes*. Barth may not have seen it in his own day, but he was, indeed, Schleiermacher's truest theological heir. As this study has shown, they share far too many convictions to ignore their congruency. Barth and Schleiermacher, far from being theological opposites, are allies traveling down a non-speculative path. They do not always arrive at the same place, but they are heading in the same direction. So we are not forced to choose sides between them; indeed, there is an essential harmony between Barth and Schleiermacher.

Conclusion to Part I

1. CF §33.3, 197.
2. OG, 45.
3. *Christian Faith*, first edition (1821/22), §2, note b. Quoted in Gerrish: *Continuing the Reformation*, 151. Chicago: The University of Chicago Press, 1993.
4. *Tradition and the Modern World*, 31. Chicago: The University of Chicago Press, 1977.
5. *Commentary on True and False Religion*; placed in the heading of *CF* §33.
6. *Evangelical Theology*, 51. Grand Rapids: Williams B. Eerdmans Publishing, 1979.
7. Ibid., 58.
8. Kierkegaard, for example, was an early philosophical influence on Barth, particularly strong in *The Epistle to the Romans*. Sartre is discussed at some length in the doctrine of creation (*Church Dogmatics* III/3, §50), Plato receives just as many references as Origen, and Hegel is referenced more than Turrettini. Schopenhauer, Heidegger, Kant, and many others are also discussed in various places. While none of this proves anything particular about Barth, it goes to show that he was well informed regarding philosophy. See Kenneth Oakes' monograph, *Karl Barth on Theology and Philosophy*.
9. T. F. Torrance, in the editor's introduction to *Church Dogmatics* I/2, summarizes this critique: "Thus instead of binding theology to the philosophy of one age, like an Aquinas or a Schleiermacher, Barth has sought to give theology such an expression in our thought that the living Truth becomes the master of our thinking, and not thinking the master of the Truth" (ix).
10. James Gordon argues this point well: "Schleiermacher's theological method and formulations are just as anti-speculative as Barth's." See "A 'Glaring Misunderstanding?'" *International Journal of Systematic Theology*, Vol. 16, number 3, July 2014; 313-330.
11. OG, 87.
12. CF §16.PS, 124.
13. *Continuing the Reformation*, 170. Chicago: The University of Chicago Press, 1993.
14. *Christian Faith*, first edition (1821/22), §2, note b. Quoted in Gerrish: *Continuing the Reformation*, 151. Chicago: The University of Chicago Press, 1993.
15. Philosophy is included in the eternal covenant, as Ebeling notes, "Schleiermacher is of the conviction that theology and philosophy, however sharp they are to be distinguished, nevertheless in principle do not contradict each other, but must agree" ("Schleiermacher's Doctrine of the Divine Attributes," *Schleiermacher as Contemporary* [ed. Robert Funk], 135. New York: Herder and Herder, 1970).
16. "Understanding God as Triune," *The Cambridge Companion to Friedrich Schleiermacher*, 181. Cambridge University Press, 2005.
17. Included in Barth's rejection of natural theology is the conviction that human nature has no capacity for God apart from grace. So to know God is at once to be reconciled to God and to share in God's knowledge of Godself. Barth writes: "The reconciliation of the world with God accomplished and consisting in Him is revelation in its very reality. [...] That reconciliation is also revelation means that in its accomplishment, which establishes, orders and guarantees peace between God and man, it also reveals and proclaims itself as divine-human truth" (*Church Dogmatics* IV/3.1, 165; Peabody: Hendrickson Publishers, 2010). See further, *Church Dogmatics* IV/3.1 §69.3.
18. It has been suggested that Barth actually has *two* doctrines of the Trinity. First, the somewhat speculative, Hegelian Trinity from *Church Dogmatics* I/1, and a more thoroughly Christological Trinity, the co-suffering Godhead of Christ's reconciliation, presented in *Church Dogmatics* IV/1-3. See Bruce McCormack's essay in *Trinitarian Theology after Barth*, 87-120. It may be a fruitful study to compare Barth's "second" Trinity with Schleiermacher's to see if they are not more alike. I do not doubt that essential differences remain, but I am merely suggesting that their methodology is not as polar-opposite as it is often supposed.
19. Barth: "The being of God is either known by grace or it is not known at all" (*Church Dogmatics* II/1, 27; Peabody: Hendrickson Publishers, 2010); "The fact that we know God is His work and not ours. [...] He is and remains the light visible and seen only in His own light" (ibid., 40). The potential examples from Barth which might show his non-speculative impulse are far too numerous to list. For Schleiermacher, see CF §50.1.
20. The most significant difference is how they form the content of the doctrine. For Barth,

revelation, not speculation, is its basis. He writes, "*God* reveals Himself. He reveals Himself *through* Himself. He reveals *Himself.* […] God, the Revealer, is identical with His act in revelation and also identical with its effect" (*Church Dogmatics* I/1, 296; Peabody: Hendrickson Publishers, 2010). So the structure of revelation is Trinitarian: Revealer, Revelation, and Revealedness.

Barth's critique was that the Trinity bears no constitutive significance in Schleiermacher's dogmatics, but while the content of the doctrine differs drastically for both, they share the conviction of its essentiality.

As previously noted, revelation and reconciliation go hand in hand for Barth. By basing his doctrine of the Trinity on revelation, he presupposes Christ's reconciling work, just as Schleiermacher saw. Both Barth and Schleiermacher ground the doctrine of the Trinity in redemption/reconciliation, even while they are worlds apart in how they form the doctrine itself.

21. Quoted in Gerhard Ebeling: "Schleiermacher's Doctrine of the Divine Attributes," *Schleiermacher as Contemporary* (ed. Robert Funk), 128. New York: Herder and Herder, 1970.
22. *Karl Barth: His Life from Letters and Autobiographical Texts*, 334-7. Philadelphia: Fortress Press, 1975.
23. *Barth and Schleiermacher*, 55. Philadelphia: Fortress Press, 1988.
24. As James Gordon concluded: "[O]ne need not pick a side between Barth and Schleiermacher, for the two stand closer than is commonly recognized" ("A 'Glaring Misunderstanding'? Schleiermacher, Barth and the Nature of Speculative Theology," 330; *International Journal of Systematic Theology*, vol. 16 number 3, July 2014).

Their closeness, however, should not be confused with total uniformity. Barth and Schleiermacher still disagree over many vital issues, even if they are closer than commonly thought. They travel a similar path, but they do not always end up in the same town, even the same country.

25. In brief: They both argue that election is community-centric, even though Barth stressed the election of Jesus Christ above all else, both made brilliant use of the hiddenness and revealedness of God in their doctrines of God, and both initiated a revival of Trinitarian theology.
26. *The Theology of Schleiermacher*, 275. Grand Rapids: Eerdmans Publishing Co., 1982.

PART II

MAJOR WORKS

6

ON RELIGION

SUMMARY: The *essence* of religion is neither doing nor thinking but what Schleiermacher calls "feeling." This must not be confused with an emotional state but, instead, indicates an immediate existential perception of the self in relation to another, to God—a "sense and taste for the infinite." But Schleiermacher's argument does not conclude with this; instead, his point is to show how religious feeling develops into faith-communities (the Church) and religions.

IN SCHLEIERMACHER'S OWN WORDS:

> If, therefore, you have paid attention only to these religious dogmas and opinions, you do not yet know religion itself at all, and religion is not what you are objecting to. Why haven't you gone deeper to find the kernel lying inside these outer layers?[1]

> First of all, remember that no feeling counts as a genuine stirring of piety simply because we have met with some particular event in the world. It is only pious insofar as the whole confronts us as the revelation of God in and with that feeling. Thus it is not something finite and particular that enters into our life in religious feeling. It is God himself. [...] In short, it is the immediate presence of the divine in us.[2]

SECONDARY QUOTES:

> Schleiermacher's aim in these addresses is to penetrate the excrescences and the corruptions of so-called religion to reach its vital heart so as to clarify what religion essentially is, to suggest how it is to be found, to consider how it may be cultivated, and perhaps also to stimulate a responding chord of sensitivity and devotion among his hearers.[3]
>
> — Terrence Tice

Introduction

Schleiermacher's first major book, *On Religion,* is arguably his best known. There are three English editions of the text that I am aware of (Owen, Tice, and Crouter) and much has been written about its significance. But the book itself is not an ideal representative of Schleiermacher's mature thought. It remains an early work, brilliant, indeed, but in no way does it offer a complete understanding of Schleiermacher's theology.

The difficulty with *On Religion* is that it was intended for a particular audience and had a set goal in mind, both of which—somewhat alien to us today—we often fail to recognize. Furthermore, it was written in a rhetorical style that readily lends itself to being misunderstood if overlooked. It has been misread as a text establishing the heart of Schleiermacher's entire thought, but this is not the case. It is indeed a vital work for Schleiermacher, but it is not *the* essential piece of his corpus.

So before we examine the content of this book and its significance, first we must stress the actual situation in which it was written. Then we will work through a brief summary of each speech before addressing some of the misconceptions about it. It is common to focus on the second speech, but this is not the best way to interpret the text. The work actually culminates in the fourth and fifth speeches because it is there that Schleiermacher reveals his full intentions.

Who were the Cultured Despisers?

Schleiermacher was clear about what drove him to write: "I feel I cannot help but speak. To me, what seems a divine impulse makes it impossible to withdraw my overture inviting precisely you, the cultured detractors of religion, to hear me out" (OR, 40). We must remember that *On Religion* was written for a particular audience, who bore with them a set of presuppositions regarding religion we no longer share. Schleiermacher describes the cultured despisers as those "exalted above the commonplace" and "imbued with the wisdom of our age" (OR, 39). So Schleiermacher's goal was simple: to convince these cultured despisers about the value of religion. In other words, his goal is to identify and explain the innermost heart of the religious impulse, and to then explain why and how it develops into the external expressions they despise, namely, faith-communities and developed religions.

On Religion was an apologetical book, though not in the sense that it was attempting to prove anything about God but to defend religion itself. Schleiermacher writes in a poetic and rhetorical voice throughout the book, leaving him open to unfair criticisms from those who failed to recognize his tone. It is vital we acknowledge both the audience and style of this work if we do not want to fall prey to poor misreadings of it.

Who were the cultured despisers of Schleiermacher's time? In Berlin, he befriended two significant individuals: Henriette Herz and Friedrich Schlegel. Herz's home was a central meeting place for the cultured members of Berlin society, and Schlegel helped introduce Schleiermacher to the world of artists, writers, and literary critics. Through the deep friendships he developed, Schleiermacher entered the world of these "cultured despisers." But as a preacher, he remained somewhat like a foreigner among them, although those who knew him best defended his Christian faith against those who might quickly pass judgments on him for it.

On Religion is directed towards these individuals. Schleiermacher hoped to show why they should not scoff at religion. On the contrary, he argues they should be the most prone to it. To prove this, Schleiermacher strips away all that is foreign to religion and presents its innermost essence. The external appearances of religion are what Schleiermacher thinks they are truly refusing when they scoff at religion. But he is convinced these cultured despisers will see religion in a new, favorable light when all that is stripped away and religion itself is placed before them. Schleiermacher states it best, "I want to lead you into the innermost depths from which every religiously oriented experience and interpretation takes form" (OR, 51). From this, however, Schleiermacher shows why and how the religious impulse develops into faith-communities and unique religions. It is a plea to look beyond the external and see the internal, but then to see that these externals are determined by the interior. One should not despise the external factors that frame religion and imagine this is true religion without also considering its inner core.

Summary

The first speech describes the cultured despisers and begins to offer an apologia for religion. Schleiermacher hints towards two important principles still to be developed. First, he presents a theory about the two drives of every individual. The first drive is the very longing to be an individual, but the second consists of "the longing to surrender to something greater, to absorb oneself in it, and to feel both grasped by and determined by it" (OR, 42). It in this second drive that Schleiermacher places religion, though never at the expense of the first. The second principle Schleiermacher hints towards is the important notion of the "One and All" (OR, 45). Julia Lamm explains it well:

> For Schleiermacher, the *One and All* is at once an expression of the relation between divine transcendence and immanence and a regulative principle which guides us in our speech about God. The fundamental experience of God is not that of some abstract or lifeless *One*; rather, it is the experience of having been redeemed through the communication and impartation of divine love.[4]

The second speech continues with a description of the essence of religion. Religion is neither knowing (doctrine) nor doing (ethics) but *feeling*, particularly, "true religion is sense and taste for the infinite" (OR, 82). Schleiermacher writes:

> The contemplation of pious men is only the immediate consciousness of the universal being of all finite things in and through the infinite, of all temporal things in and through the eternal. To seek and to find this infinite and eternal factor in all that lives and moves, in all growth and change, in all action and passion, and to have and to know life itself only in immediate feeling—that is religion. Where this awareness is found, religion is satisfied; where this awareness is hidden, religion experiences frustration and anguish, emptiness and death. And so religion is, indeed, a life in the infinite nature of the whole, in the one and all, in God—a having and possessing of all in God and of God in all.[5]

The motif of "One and All" is shown here more fully. It is the interconnectedness of all finite things and their being-in-relation with the infinite, with God. As we have seen in our study of *Christian Faith*, "feeling" cannot be a mere subjective state of being or emotion. Feeling itself is not God, nor does it attempt to grasp God like an object. Instead, feeling signifies a being-in-relation with God, a feeling determined by and originating from God in grace.

Religion, in its essence, is this feeling of the infinite in the finite. There is an oscillation, or dialectic, between unity and multiplicity at the heart of religion. The first speech established the idea of a twofold drive in human nature, of the individual to be one and yet the to take part in the whole. This is carried further with this notion of the dialectic of the infinite and finite. Religion is the desire to feel united with the infinite even in the midst of our finitude.

Feeling is not a general experience with the world but is "only pious insofar as the whole confronts us as the revelation of God in and with that feeling" (OR, 146). That is, the "One and All" principle is not about the experience we have with the world or with something finite. It is "not something finite and particular that enters into our life in religious feeling. *It is God himself* [...] it is the immediate presence of the divine in us" (OR, 146-7).[6] Schleiermacher continues:

> How, then, can anyone contend that I have depicted a religion without God? Actually, what I have been presenting is precisely the immediate and original being of God in us through feeling. Isn't God the sole and highest unity?[7]

It is not a *concept* of God that is the essence of religion but our immediate existential being-in-relation with God. Schleiermacher reminds us that "God's being can only be active, not passive" (OR n18, 171). This feeling—the sense and taste for the infinite—as the essence of religious piety, is receptivity for the activity of God in and through the world. It is a *relational* metaphor.

The third speech then asks the question, "How does religion develop?" After describing the essence of religion, Schleiermacher continues by considering its concrete expressions. This is why focusing only on the second speech is a grave mistake. Schleiermacher has not reached his goal by merely describing the essence of religion but is attempting to show the value of religion in its concrete form. Namely, he aims to demonstrate the value of the Church.

The fourth speech explores the communal nature of religion. Here Schleiermacher proposes an understanding of the Church from the inside out. He states: "Religion must be social if it is to exist at all" (OR, 208). Just as the very essence of religion is incomplete without this communal expression, so Schleiermacher's work is misread if we ignore this aspect of his argument. He hopes to subject the concept of the Church to a "fresh investigation, reconstructing it from the center outward" (OR, 208). This is done by his emphasis on the inherently communal aspect of religion.

Finally, the fifth speech explores the diversity of religion in "the religions." This argument presupposes that "no one can possess all religion completely in himself" (OR, 275). Therefore, to assert that only one religion contains the whole truth of all religious expression is a mistake. Schleiermacher compels us to see religious diversity as a good thing, though not something wholly without difficulties. Ultimately, this speech does not give *validity* to the variety of each and every religion but recognizes the necessity of diversity in organized religion. But Schleiermacher also acknowledges that it must be in relation to *one* religion, as the focal point of all religions, that this diversity is viewed. He is not deluded into thinking that every religious expression is entirely valid, but subdues each under the Christian faith. And within this framework, there is value in the diversity of religions.

Schleiermacher writes:

> We all exist 'somewhere.' Therefore these religions of man to the whole have varying degrees of proximity to each other, and because of their difference in overall relationship each feeling is bound to arise differently in the life of each person. We all exist as 'someone.' Therefore each person has a greater receptivity for some religious perceptions and feelings than for others. In this manner every person's experience is different. Obviously, then, no single relationship can do justice to every feeling.[8]

Schleiermacher places Christ as the high mark for religion when he writes, "Jesus has brought into being the most glorious things that have yet appeared in religion" (OR, 314). There is some hesitancy in *On Religion* for Schleiermacher to give exclusivity to Jesus as the mediator of divine redemption, but in *Christin Faith* he removes any such doubt. For Schleiermacher, Jesus is *the* Redeemer. In the fifth speech, however, Schleiermacher affirms the diversity of religious consciousness, even if that diversity is best seen in relation to Christianity. He writes, "Nothing is more irreligious than to demand general uniformity among humanity. Likewise nothing is more unchristian than to seek uniformity in religion" (OR, 321). Ultimately, these sections might be read as Schleiermacher's attempt to preach the Gospel among the cultured. He does not feel the need to *make* them Christians, believing instead that it is God's work to "draw all to Himself" (John 12:32), and he merely attempts to restore the dignity of the Christian faith specifically and religion generally.

So, as we can see, the second speech is undoubtedly vital to Schleiermacher's argument, but it is incomplete without the remaining three speeches, especially the critical conclusions that are drawn from the fourth and fifth speeches. To ignore the diversity of religion or its communal nature would be to misunderstand Schleiermacher's overall goal. He intends to show that these cultured despisers have more in common with religion than they thought and that their tendency to scoff at religious expressions misses the true essence of religion. Yet they cannot ignore these expressions (the Church and religious diversity) and resign themselves only the essence of religion in some subjectivist isolationism. The two are intertwined, the internal and external. The basis of Schleiermacher's argument may be found in the second speech, but its real goal is fully expressed in the fourth and fifth. Schleiermacher's point is that we *cannot* have the essence of religion without its external developments in faith-communities and religions.

The common misreading of *On Religion* that religion is about some private emotional state of being is the very opposite conclusion Schleiermacher hoped his readers would reach. To the contrary, he aimed to show why we cannot have religious feeling apart from the Church and organized religion. It is not a private experience. Religion in its truest state is shared.

Conclusion

When combined with his mature reflections on religious self-consciousness in *Christian Faith,* Schleiermacher's philosophy of religion is one of the first successful systematic attempts to develop a theory of religion from an empirical standpoint. That is, he develops it from the actual experience of religion and not merely its speculative ideal. As Terrence Tice writes, "[T]he addresses remain virtually unsurpassed in their presentation of the groundwork for an adequate theory of religion" (OR, 10). At the very least, this innovative approach should be appreciated for what it is. Though it may be problematic at times, it remains a notable contribution. Most of all, it should also be thought of as a "counter-cultural" text, as James M. Brandt writes:

> Schleiermacher's *Speeches* must be seen as a counterculture work deliberately swimming against the tide of rational religion and its moralism. Schleiermacher insists that religion in its essence be identified as intuition rather than as either morality or knowledge.[9]

So much of the controversy surrounding Schleiermacher's theology comes from misreading *On Religion.* While the Introduction to *Christian Faith* is carefully argued, the style is more rhetorical and poetic in *On Religion.* In his forward to the third edition, Schleiermacher writes, "The rhetorical form has been almost universally ignored, despite its use throughout the book" (OR, 37). Schleiermacher added a significant number of clarifying notes to the third edition in the hopes of avoiding many of the persistent misunderstandings about the work.

On Religion is a book that should be read with caution. It is not a properly *theological* text, nor is it necessarily a fair representation of Schleiermacher's full views on "the feeling of absolute dependence," as he later expressed it so well. Instead, it should be read like a book with a particular historical purpose. It should also be interpreted with an awareness of its rhetorical mode of expression. And it must be read in its entirety. Only then will the book be appreciated for what it is—even if we ultimately disagree with a few of its points. But we should avoid any unfair judgments regarding its value until we have carefully understood it.

---

1. OR, 55.
2. OR, 147.
3. "Introduction," OR, 9.
4. *The Living God*, 228. The Pennsylvania State University, 1996.
5. OR, 79.
6. Emphasis mine.
7. OR, 147.
8. OR, 281.
9. *All Things New*, 5. Louisville: Westminster John Knox Press, 2001.

7

CHRISTIAN ETHICS

SUMMARY: Schleiermacher's theology has sometimes been called ethically deficient, but the opposite is true: He hoped to elevate Christian ethics to a place of high esteem in the field of theology. From his early work on ethics to his unfinished *Christian Ethics,* Schleiermacher's thought was profoundly aligned towards the ethical. Just as faith seeks understanding so faith must produce good works.

IN SCHLEIERMACHER'S OWN WORDS:

> In Christianity the will of God does not come to us so much as it arises within us through the union in which Christ stands with God. Each individual is in the Christian church only to the extent that there exists between him and Christ a unity of will like that between Christ and God. The true essence of Christianity and the way in which redemption should be conceived in moral terms is this: The will of God arises within us through communion with Christ. [...] The principle of all Christian ethics, upon which rests everything that is to be presented in Christian ethics, is none other than the *pneuma hagion* [Holy Spirit].[1]

SECONDARY QUOTES:

> Where the orthodox theologians understand ethics in terms of obedience to the command of God and appeal to the Decalogue, the Sermon on the Mount, or

other biblical injunctions, Schleiermacher proposes a descriptive ethics that lays out the 'distinguishing characteristics of the Christian life' as they are appropriated in the current context. He asserts that the actions of Christians are 'actually continuations of the action of Christ himself.' The actions of Christ 'establish the reign of God, at which all Christian action aims, and indicated its characteristics, so that all action of the Christian church is nothing but the realization of these characteristics.' Thus Schleiermacher departs from orthodoxy and its imperative, biblical ethics; instead he lays out a descriptive ethics that is focused on the continuing action of Christ in and through the Church.[2]

[F]or Schleiermacher, Christian thought culminates in Christian ethics.[3]

— James M. Brandt

Introduction

Schleiermacher's *Christian Ethics* was intended to be a complementary work to *Christian Faith*. Dogmatics and ethics are inseparable, and the one is incomplete without the other. Unfortunately, he died before completing a manuscript for publication, and all we have are his own notes and drafts alongside the lecture notes of his students. These notes in their entirety are still untranslated, which, in addition to their incomplete character, has resulted in the mistaken perception that Schleiermacher's theology is ethically deficient.

But the truth is Schleiermacher's theology was thoroughly ethical. In this chapter, we will briefly work through some of the insights from *Christian Ethics* (CE) and the *Introduction to Christian Ethics* (iCE). The primary goal, however, is to confront the myth that his theology was ethically deficient.

Faith and Action

Just as faith seeks understanding (dogmatics), so faith naturally produces good works (ethics). This thought is what joins Schleiermacher's *Christian Faith* inseparably together with his *Christian Ethics*. Arising from the same concrete situation—namely, the Christian self-consciousness of redemption in and through Christ—Christian ethics is a reflection on the reign of God. Schleiermacher developed this connection already in *Christian Faith*:

> [G]ood works are natural effects of faith [...] The reason is that once we allow ourselves to be taken up into community with Christ, we are deeply stirred, with him, by the union of what is divine with the human nature in

Christ's person, and our consent to this situation becomes a steadfast, active will to hold firm to this union and to spread its impact further.[4]

In the community of Christ, we are compelled to take part in the reign of God, which is the love of God towards us and from us towards others. So faith becomes active, becomes love for neighbor and God.

While Schleiermacher never prepared a manuscript for publication, he lectured on Christian ethics twelve times from 1806 to 1831. In these lectures, the same connection has been made, though more explicitly. The *Introduction to Christian Ethics* offers a parallel to the Introduction of *Christian Faith,* in the sense that here he sets out the place and boundary-lines for what proper Christian ethics should be.

On the very first page he begins with this connection, writing, "Christian ethics and Christian theology are very closely related" (iCE, 33). Just as Schleiermacher established theology as a non-speculative, historical discipline, he placed Christian ethics in the same position. He claims "there cannot be [...] a universal Christian ethics" (iCE, 39). Just as no one dogmatic system can or should articulate the entire consciousness of the Christian faith, so no one Christian ethics can adequately present universal ethics for all Christians. These reflections, therefore, are inherently non-speculative, as Schleiermacher writes, "The propositions of Christian ethics, like those of theology, are only expressions of the Christian consciousness observed in its particular manifestations" (iCE, 42). Christian ethics belong to the historical situation of the Church.

Ultimately, Christian ethics are for *Christians,* and as such, they have only the Word of God as their normative guide. Schleiermacher writes, "[T]he Christian church should use nothing other than the authority of the Word" (iCE, 44). This is what separates Schleiermacher's *Christian Ethics* from his more speculative and general *Philosophical Ethics.*

Out from the Shadow of Dogmatics

Schleiermacher considered ethics and dogmatics to be two sides of the same coin: "The primordial Christian consciousness is precisely Christian faith, and that has two aspects existing side by side, one aimed toward the thought, the other toward the act" (iCE, 47). But if such a connection exists, why did Schleiermacher treat ethics separately? Why did he consistently uphold the need for *independent* Christian ethics?

Brandt explains:

> Christian ethics requires independent treatment so it can come out from the

shadow of dogmatics. By being presented separately, each discipline can be seen in its own interconnectedness.[5]

Christian ethics, when treated *within* dogmatics, becomes a sub-discipline robbed of its own proper standing, which results in the perception that ethics is less critical than theology. It was Schleiermacher's intention, instead, to set Christian ethics on equal footing with dogmatics. He hoped to construct a book with equal force and systematic coherence as his *Christian Faith*, but instead of focusing on the *thoughts* of faith, he would focus on the *actions* of faith. If Schleiermacher had lived to complete his visionary project, perhaps he would not be known today as the father of modern theology but as the father of modern ethics.

While it is far too speculative to say anything definite about what might have been, it is still worth noting Schleiermacher's intentions. His reasons for treating ethics as an independent disciple should not be misconstrued as its neglect. It was in the hopes of returning ethics to a place of honor directly alongside the doctrines of faith that he proposed its separate treatment. Even in its incomplete form, Schleiermacher's ethics remain a high-water mark.

Overview

Detailed notes from five students that attended Schleiermacher's lectures on Christian ethics have survived and were compiled and published by Ludwig Jonas, at Schleiermacher's request. The following overview is from these 1822/23 lecture notes, selected and translated by James M. Brandt. Schleiermacher's brilliance is apparent even in the limited picture these notes offer.

Schleiermacher divided his *Christian Ethics* into two parts, which articulates three actions arising from Christian religious self-consciousness. The first deals with "efficacious action," and the second deals with "presentational action." Efficacious action is further divided into "restoring (or purifying) action" and "broadening action." Every action is then related to a specific sphere, either the Christian community or within the "not yet Christian" community, the secular world. For example, restoring action takes the form of Church discipline in the Christian community, and in the public sphere, it takes the form of civil justice.

The following chart may help explain Schleiermacher's outline:

```
                                              Church as school
                        Broadening action   /
                       (grow Spirit's influence)
                      /                     \
                     /                        Schooling / Instruction
    Efficacious action
                     \
                      \                       Church discipline
                        Restoring action    /
                       (overcome flesh's influence)
                                             \
                                              Civil justice
                                              (e.g., abolish death penalty)
Faith
                                              Worship
                                            /
     Presentational action
                                            \
                                              Social Presentation
```

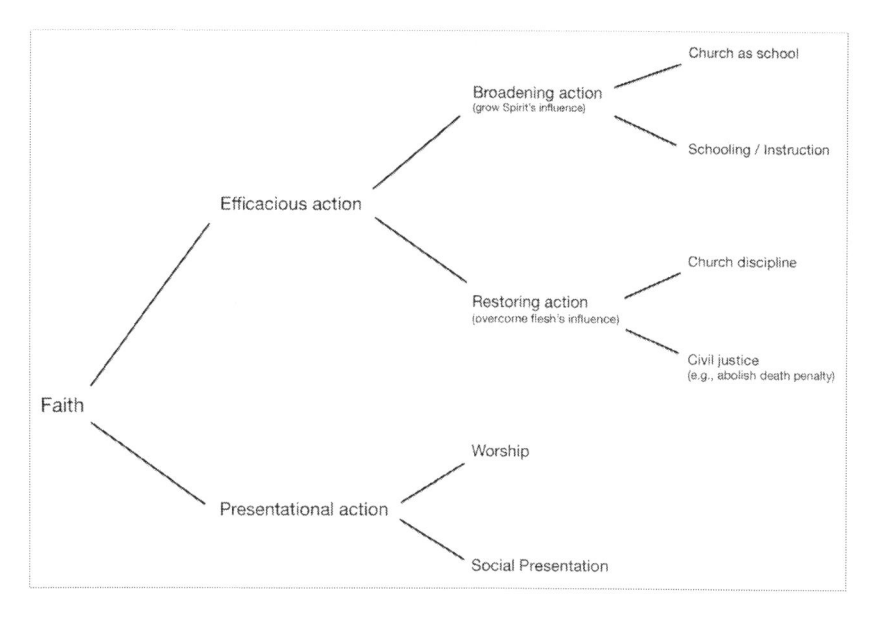

Fig. 1 - An outline of the kinds of actions that arise from faith.

Schleiermacher stressed that "all three forms of action can never be absolutely separated in reality" (CE, 145). Each action is considered independently only to be logically understood, not because of any real division. Christian ethics arise from *one* source, namely, Jesus Christ our Redeemer.

Efficacious actions arise from the consciousness of sin and grace, aiming either to grow the Spirit's influence (broadening action) or diminishes the flesh's influence (restoring action). In the Church, restoring action looks like Church discipline. In the public sphere, it takes the form of civil justice.

It is worth mentioning—and celebrating—that Schleiermacher was an early opponent of the death penalty, and he even considered it the obligation of all Christians to work towards its abolishment. He writes:

The Christian must strive resolutely for the death penalty to be abolished.[6]

This is what a Christianization of the state looks like. The death penalty is immoral and unnecessary. The very purpose of civil punishment is *restorative*. So it is unethical for a state to engage in the unchristian attitude of retribution or revenge. The goal of the penal law is to maintain obedience to the rules, but this is impossible if death is its penalty.

Furthermore, the death penalty contradicts the very essence of the Christian faith, which is founded upon the redemption of Jesus Christ. It is redemption, not re-payment, which is the goal of restorative actions, even in civil law. Opposition to the death penalty is a Christian obligation.

Broadening actions are also directed towards overcoming the flesh with the spirit, but the emphasis is now placed on *growing* the spirit's influence rather than *diminishing* the influence of the flesh. Here Schleiermacher makes an important connection: The broadening actions of the Church are the continuation of Christ's life on earth, the acts of Christ's body. He argues that "all actions of the Christian are as such actually continuations of the action of Christ himself. These actions have established the reign of God, at which all Christian action aims" (CE, 99). Whereas restorative actions are negatively applied to overcome the flesh, broadening actions *increase* the spirit's influence, which is at once the reign of God. Broadening actions bring about the reign of God and continue the mission of Christ. This is why Schleiermacher considered these actions inseparable. A broadening action can be restorative as it increases the spirit's influence, and a restorative action can be broadening as it diminishes the flesh's influence.

In the Christian community, broadening action takes the form of the Church as a school, both in the sense that it perpetuates the tradition of the faithful but also in the sense that it instructs and guides believers. The Church works towards Christian maturity. In the state, broadening action also takes the form of instruction. Ultimately, Christian ethics have one purpose and goal in mind: the reign of God. We hope for a time in which all humanity will be included in the Christian community. So even in the public sphere, broadening action takes the form of a school, which aims at maturing individuals.

Part two, presentational action, arises from the state of blessedness. This is a purely internal state, neither moving towards the spirit nor away from the flesh, but it is expressed externally because "an individual can in no way be conceived without community" (CE, 143). Accordingly, blessedness is always communicated. In the Church, this takes the form of worship, and in the public sphere, it takes the form of social presentation. Both aspects include the "narrower" and "broader" sense of each. And both aspects are essentially "Christian worship," but in its inner and outer form, as Schleiermacher writes, "The general type of this action [presentational] is everything that we bring together under the name of Christian worship" (CE, 47).

Conclusion

The convictions that made *Christian Faith* so ground-breaking, namely, Schleiermacher's Christomorphism and non-speculative approach, are also present in his *Christian Ethics*. He is adamant that every action in the Christian life must be connected with the redemption of Jesus Christ. Schleiermacher writes, "Christian ethics is a description of Christian ways of acting insofar as these are traced back to the Redeemer" (CE, 37). And just as Schleiermacher refused to accept speculative dogmatics, so Christian ethics cannot engage in empty speculation.

Brandt notes the strength of this procedure:

> Schleiermacher beings with a theologically defined moment—the experience of blessedness in redemption—and sees this as grounding the ethical moment as it initiates a process that is express by means of action and that drives toward a goal—the reign of God.[7]

In contrast with the more traditional kind of Christian ethics—Biblical ethics—Schleiermacher's *Christian Ethics* is phenomenological (or descriptive). It is rooted in the actual experience of redemption rather than in the arrangement of Biblical texts. That is, ethics are not *externally* derived, as a set of rigid, legalistic rules, but presuppose the living activity of God in the community of Christ. It is in communion with Christ by the common spirit of the Church that Christian ethics arise. With this, Schleiermacher stresses the *continuing* action of Christ in the Church rather than merely referring to past examples. In short, Schleiermacher takes the Spirit-filled Church seriously as the body of Christ and relates everything in the Christian life back to our communion with God. These are ethics of the *spirit*, not the *letter*.

---

1. iCE, 65-6.
2. "Translator's Introduction," *CE*, 5.
3. *Schleiermacher and Sustainability* (ed. by Shelli Poe), 11. Louisville: Westminster John Knox Press, 2018
4. CF §112.1, 742.
5. *All Things New*, 7. Louisville: Westminster John Knox Press, 2001.
6. CE, 87.
7. "Translator's Introduction," CE, 7.

8

HERMENEUTICS

SUMMARY: Understanding does not occur as a matter of course; in fact, *misunderstanding* is our default position in relation to the world around us. The "art of understanding"—hermeneutics—is vital, not only for reading texts but for understanding other people. Understanding must be pursued rigorously, it is not automatic. Schleiermacher is the father of modern hermeneutics because he was the first to propose general rules for interpretation, thereby broadening hermeneutics to the study of understanding itself.

IN SCHLEIERMACHER'S OWN WORDS:

> At present there is no general hermeneutics as the art of understanding but only a variety of specialized hermeneutics.[1]

> There is a more rigorous practice of the art of interpretation that is based on the assumption that misunderstanding occurs as a matter of course, and so understanding must be willed and sought at every point.[2]

SECONDARY QUOTES:

> Hermeneutics: The general art of getting an accurate, authentic interpretation of discourse of any kind, written or spoken. [...] It is comprised of two parts: the 'grammatical' part, which investigates and author's use of what is available through the styles and structures in a given

language tradition [...] and the 'technical' or 'psychological' part, which investigates the author's own distinctive language and thought.[3]

— Terrence Tice

To orient hermeneutics to understanding has proved to be Schleiermacher's lasting contribution to the history of hermeneutical theory. By virtue of this achievement he can lay claim to the title of 'founder' of modern hermeneutics.[4]

— James Duke and Jack Forstman

Introduction

The ancient Greeks credited the god Hermes with the invention of language and writing. Hermes was the messenger god who transmuted the insights of the gods into terms humans could understand. This is why we call the art of interpreting written or verbal communication "hermeneutics."

Schleiermacher stands out as the father of modern hermeneutics, constructing a new discipline with his ground-breaking work. Of course, many before Schleiermacher read and interpreted texts, and even developed principles on how to do so. Before Schleiermacher, however, this task had not yet received any general, universal guidelines. Hermeneutics was previously only *specialized*. Schleiermacher is credited for establishing the first comprehensive set of hermeneutical rules, and as a result, he initiated an entirely new discipline that has drastically shaped the modern era. Palmer notes, "For the first time hermeneutics defines itself as the study of understanding itself."[5]

Before we look at Schleiermacher's principles for hermeneutics, there are a few points worth considering more generally about the discipline.

First, interpretation is both an art and a science. Schleiermacher called it the "art of understanding" the "discourse of another person correctly."[6] It is both an art and a science because, like a science, it has set rules to follow but, like art, there are no established standards for how to *apply* those rules. Therefore, much of the hermeneutical process is left up to the interpreter.

Second, there is no such thing as an "objective" or "plain" reading of a text. We cannot, therefore, read a text "literally" without inevitably misreading it. No matter what period the text was written in, there are incalculable factors involved, including culture, linguistic usage, and personal experiences, which hinder a plain reading of any text. In other words, we will always read *ourselves* into a text, and this is only minimized if we take the time to practice sound hermeneutics. Fundamentalism is, in essence, the maximized effect of this error. Hermeneutics is its cure.

Finally, what "meaning" is and how we determine it is an extremely complicated question. Apparently, the goal of reading and interpreting a text is to learn what it means. But because of the extreme distance between ourselves and its author—whether geographical, cultural, economic, linguistic, or social—we are hindered from discovering its meaning without considerable research.

Hermeneutics forces us to take reading and interpretation seriously. That is, to lose our naive ignorance about how difficult it actually is to understand another person's thoughts. We are inclined to think that we can pick up a book and understand it at face value, but hermeneutics is a constant reminder that this is not true. And the older the text, the less likely it is we will understand it without considerable effort.

Biblical hermeneutics should immediately come to mind with all of this. A biblicist reading of the Bible is a flippant misreading. We have to take the Bible seriously enough to question ourselves and consider our distance from it. Before we ever attempt to understand what Paul, John, or Moses have written in the text, we have to reckon with its strangeness,[7] we have to read and interpret the Bible on *its own* terms, according to the original intentions of its authors, not our own preconceived ideas.

In this chapter, I want to explore some of Schleiermacher's ideas about hermeneutics. Now that we have discovered what it means and why it is crucial, Schleiermacher can help us fill in some details regarding how exactly we bridge the distance between ourselves and the author of a text.

One of the criticisms often brought against Schleiermacher's hermeneutics is his notion of "divination," which is essentially the idea that we should understand a text as well as and then better than its original author. But this is often misunderstood, and so we will correct a few of the problems surrounding this idea.

The Art of Understanding

"Understanding comes as a matter of course" is a common presupposition, but it is a *false* one. In contrast, hermeneutics presupposes that "*mis*understanding occurs as a matter of course." It is easier for us to misunderstand than it is to understand, misunderstanding is our default position. It takes diligent effort to ensure we understand the text or discourse of another person rightly. The discipline of hermeneutics is aimed at precisely this goal.

Schleiermacher's principles for hermeneutics comprise of two interlocking parts: the grammatical and technical.[8] If we wish to understand a text, then we must consider both aspects. Schleiermacher summarizes these:

Grammatical interpretation. To understand the discourse and how it has been composed in terms of its language.

Technical interpretation: To understand the discourse as a presentation of thought. Composed by a human being and so understood in terms of a human being.

Grammatical interpretation. The person and his activity disappear and seem to be merely an organ of the language.

Technical interpretation: The language and its determining power disappear and seem to be merely an organ of the person, in the service of his individuality, just as in grammatical interpretation the personality is in the service of the language.

Grammatical interpretation. Not possible without technical interpretation. Technical interpretation: not possible without grammatical interpretation.[9]

Here Schleiermacher distinguishes between the inner and outer characteristics of a text. He calls the inner the "technical" and the outer the "grammatical." The inner thoughts that preceded the text itself may be known through a kind of "divination" of the original idea of the author. Schleiermacher writes, "The task is to be formulated as follows: 'To understand the text at first as well as and then even better than its author.'"[10] Divination strives to discover the motives and aims the author held before writing the text, which shaped and molded it. The external form the text takes, however, may be interpreted through its grammatical or stylistic appearances. This means considering the expressions the author's thoughts take. Only by oscillating between the inner and outer aspects of a text will we come to understand what we are reading. The inner thoughts are never without their expression in grammar and style, but neither is the written expression alone without its basis in the innermost thoughts of the author. They are bound together.

Schleiermacher more concisely summarizes these two approaches:

> [U]nderstanding a speech always involves two moments: to understand what is said in the context of the language with its possibilities, and to understand it as a fact in the thinking of the speaker. [...] Understanding takes place only in the coinherence of these two moments.[11]

This ebb and flow, the co-inherence of the grammatical and technical, results in a kind of circle. "For Schleiermacher, understanding as an art is the reexperiencing of the mental processes of the text's author. It is the reverse of composition."[12] Not only must we understand what the language (the external expression of the original idea) meant to its original audience, but we must understand what it meant to the author. Jumping into this circle is vital for understanding the text on its own terms. We cannot import foreign notions onto the author or their language but must step into their world, so to speak, and see with their eyes.

But the problem is we can only understand something *new* with reference to something *old,* something previously understood. This is why the hermeneutical circle requires a "leap." We have to recognize the whole and the parts of the whole as an interconnected circle. For example, even as you read this sentence now, you are oscillating between the individual words used and the sentence as a whole. Furthermore, the sentence is then placed within its paragraph, and its paragraph is situated within its particular chapter. Finally, the chapter is positioned within the whole scope and purpose of the book. The individual parts always depend on the whole just as the whole always depends on the individual parts. This is why we must oscillate between the particular and the whole whenever reading a text. Every interpretation requires a hermeneutical leap.

Schleiermacher writes:

> Complete knowledge is always in this apparent circle, that each particular can only be understood via the general, of which it is a part, and vice versa.[13]

Likewise, James Duke and Jack Forstman explain:

> Certainly no metaphor for the movement in hermeneutics is more important than that of the circle. The hermeneutical circle, that is, the logically vexing proposition that the whole is understood from its parts and the parts from the whole, means that interpretation is at base a referential procedure. Though not coined by Schleiermacher, this proposition is applied at every crucial point in his theory.[14]

The hermeneutical circle stresses the importance of *re-reading*. Because of this continual oscillation between the parts and their whole—the co-inherence of the grammatical and technical—the best way to navigate difficult texts is to read them several times and in their proper context (namely, the life and times of the author). Why this is true should be obvious. If the parts depend on the whole and the whole on the parts, then we leap into this circle by reading until we have the whole picture before us. Then we read again and begin to piece together the various connections and, as a result, dive into the intentions of the author. From this, we come to a relative place of understanding the text better than the author themselves, because of the unconscious elements of the text they could not perceive. And then we can derive meaning from their work.

An Example

For an example of how I personally implement this method, allow me to explain my writing processes as it pertains to this series of books.

I read and reread as much as possible until I can get "inside" an author's head, so to speak, and understand their work charitably and on their own terms. I follow a relatively simple process: For at least five or six months I read *only* that author, and because I read quite diligently, six months of reading means digesting around fifty or sixty books. I move between primary texts, which I always spend the most time with, and secondary texts from experts to help make sure I am on the right track in my thinking. I do little else but think about the author I am currently studying, and I take copious notes in the margins of books or on my computer about the author. I try to read all the essential texts at least twice, such as *Christian Faith* and *On Religion* for Schleiermacher. Although, there is truly no primary text that I do not, at least in part, look back over when I am compiling my research. In short, I strive to immerse myself in their world as thoroughly as I possibly can.

The goal of all this is to recognize the various connections between individual ideas and their relation to the whole of an author's thought. That is, to understand the parts as they relate to the whole, and then in turn to newly understand the whole in the light of its parts. As a result, I attempt to discover the impulses of an author so that I might "intuit" their meaning through a series of connections. I am always looking for these connections so I can relate what I already know to what I do not know. For me, I think of it as a kind of "knowledge by osmosis." This is not a perfect example of Schleiermacher's point, but it may help clarify what the hermeneutical circle can look like in practice.

The hermeneutical circle strives after an inner knowledge of the whole corpus of an author, which includes the author's driving thoughts and intentions. Each part is always joined to the whole and vice versa. Ultimately, the more fully immersed we are in the whole, the better equipped we are to comprehend the individual parts, and likewise, the more we understand those parts, the more we can perceive the whole. That is, in essence, the hermeneutical circle. It demands only time, diligence, and re-reading from us, but it is essential for right understanding. Above all, we must be gracious towards the author and lend a humble ear to genuinely hear, understand, and appreciate what they are trying to communicate.

But the task of hermeneutics is unending. At best, we may only achieve relative success. We are not God, we will never be able to perceive all the spoken and unspoken intentions of an author, nor will we ever understand their meaning fully. Understanding is an ongoing process, not a goal we will ever achieve in this lifetime. As Schleiermacher writes, "[T]he task is infinite."[15]

Difficulties: Divinatory Method

All of this brings us to the difficult method of "divination," which is the result of Schleiermacher's technical reading of a text as it corresponds to the grammatical. Whenever we read a text, we attempt to step into the thoughts of its author. The controversial aspect of this method is its stated goal: that we might understand a text *better than* the author understood it. Schleiermacher writes:

> The task [of hermeneutics] is also to be expressed as follows, to understand the utterance at first just as well and then better than its author.[16]

How is this possible? Schleiermacher clarifies:

For because we have no immediate knowledge of what is in him, we must seek to bring much to consciousness that can remain unconscious to him, except to the extent to which he himself reflectively becomes his own reader.[17]

That is, an author is often unaware of their own impulses when they write a text, and therefore, a reader may pick up on those drives and understand their work better than they understood it themselves.

Richard Palmer was especially critical of Schleiermacher's method, claiming he falls into "bad metaphysics" by overly psychologicalizing hermeneutics.[18] His entry-level textbook on the subject is widely read, which has caused many to repeat his criticisms of Schleiermacher. But it is not a fair assessment of his work. We have to remember Schleiermacher never prepared a publishable manuscript on hermeneutics, and so we should be more charitable towards his intentions since all we have are rough outlines and notes.

Critics often ignore a key qualifier to this method. Immediately following the proposition that we "understand the text at first as well as and then even better than its author," Schleiermacher writes, "Since we have no direct knowledge of what was in the author's mind, we must try to become aware of many things of which he himself may have been unconscious."[19] Therefore, the goal of technical interpretation "can only be approximated."[20] Schleiermacher writes:

> Despite all our progress we are still far from the goal. [...] Not only do we never understand an individual view exhaustively, but what we do

understand is always subject to correction. [...] [W]e are quite far from our goal.[21]

The stated goal of the divinatory method is one we will never reach. It is important to acknowledge this point because it qualifies everything Schleiermacher has said so far about the possibility of understanding a text better than its author. This is something we can only strive for *approximately*. It is our goal, but it is a goal we will never obtain.

Another example makes this clear:

> The divinatory method is the one in which one, *so to speak*, transforms oneself into the other person and tries to understand the individual element directly.[22]

This quote is often used to justify the "psychologizing" critique, but that is possible only if we intentionally ignore the little "so to speak" phrase in italics. The text's translator notes that this is a "vital clarification" regularly omitted by Schleiermacher's critics, but it is "definitely in Schleiermacher's hand-written manuscript."[23] There should be no doubt, then. It is not that we *actually* transform into another person, but that we strive to understand an author's work as they understood it themselves. Accordingly, this may be seen as a textual re-interpretation of saying we must walk a mile in someone else's shoes before we judge them. Likewise, we must, *so to speak*, transform ourselves into the author and read their text through their own eyes. This is Schleiermacher's point, not some psychological trickery or speculative metaphysics. He has no illusions about trying to become omniscient like God and know the innermost thoughts of a person, but he recognizes that understanding another person means striving to relate ourselves to their perspective as much as possible. Of course, we will never escape ourselves. But we owe it to every individual we meet to strive to understand them as fully as possible.

The presupposition behind this method is not that we can know the thoughts of another person, but rather, that all knowledge is formed in the same way. As Andrew Bowie notes, "Even though we 'cannot know whether the other person hears or sees as we do' [...], we assume that knowledge is constituted in the same way in everyone for there to be knowledge at all."[24] That is, we *can* make some assumptions about how an individual thinks because we share the same technical basis for knowledge. As Theodore Vial explains:

> The divinatory is not a mystical leap but the principle that if you know yourself to some extent then you already know at least a little bit about others. Knowledge of yourself is the basis on which you can begin to make

judgments about the motivations or goals of someone else (just as broad knowledge of others is the basis for the comparative method of beginning to make these same judgments about a speaker).[25]

Because we know ourselves and understand how we know things, we can make a leap into the minds of another person and grasp *something* of how they know things, too. We can strive to understand the meaning behind their communications, whether that is in oral speech or written text. We actually do this every day in our interactions with friends and family. We often say to each other, "Yes, I know what you mean." We immediately connect their linguistic fragments to the whole of their intended thoughts, and this is because we know how *we* think ourselves and can relate it to how we suppose they must think as well. As we stated above, we only learn new things by relating them to what we already know. The hermeneutic circle in which we leap into the thoughts of an author relies on the fact that we know how we think and can relate it to how others think.

Conclusion

Hermeneutics as a discipline is extremely important for the world today—especially with the rise of fundamentalism, nationalism, racism, and other forms of social woes. These are primarily rooted in our failure to cultivate an understanding of others. We are racist because we fear other races, and we fear them because we do not understand them (or because we *think* we know them, albeit wrongly). The same is true for national and religious fears. Personally, I think the discipline of hermeneutics should be taught and studied more widely. High school students should at least be aware of its fundamental points before entering the adult world. This would drastically limit the bigoted tendencies so many foster when they fail to slow down and understand others. If we only took the time to understand each other, recognizing the differences and distances between us, and no longer allowed ourselves to fear what we do not understand, then the world would be a much better place. So we must look first inside ourselves and seek to actively counteract our natural tendency, which is to misunderstand each other. Misunderstanding is natural, it is our default position. We have to *work* at understanding. This is the task of hermeneutics.

---

1. *Hermeneutics: The Handwritten Manuscripts*, 95. Missoula: Scholars Press for The American Academy of Religion, 1977.
2. Ibid., 110.
3. *Schleiermacher (Abingdon Pillars of Theology)*, 60. Nashville: Abingdon Press, 2006.
4. "Translators' Introduction," *Hermeneutics: The Handwritten Manuscripts,* 15. Missoula: Scholars Press for The American Academy of Religion, 1977.

5. *Hermeneutics,* 40. Northwestern University Press, 1969.
6. *Hermeneutics and Criticism,* 5. Cambridge: Cambridge University Press, 1998.
7. This is why Barth talked about the "strange new world within the Bible." We all have to arrive at such a place before we can give the text a fair reading. If we assume familiarity with the text, we will only turn it into a projection of our own presuppositions.
8. These may also be called the linguistic and the psychological.
9. *Hermeneutics: The Handwritten Manuscripts,* 161. Missoula: Scholars Press for The American Academy of Religion, 1977.
10. Ibid., 112.
11. Ibid., 98.
12. Palmer: *Hermeneutics,* 86. Northwestern University Press, 1969.
13. *Hermeneutics and Criticism,* 23. Cambridge: Cambridge University Press, 1998.
14. *Hermeneutics: The Handwritten Manuscripts,* 5-6. Missoula: Scholars Press for The American Academy of Religion, 1977.
15. Ibid., 112.
16. *Hermeneutics and Criticism,* 23. Cambridge: Cambridge University Press, 1998.
17. Ibid.
18. See *Hermeneutics,* 91-4. Northwestern University Press, 1969.
19. *Hermeneutics: The Handwritten Manuscripts,* 112. Missoula: Scholars Press for The American Academy of Religion, 1977.
20. Ibid., 149.
21. Ibid.
22. *Hermeneutics and Criticism,* 92. Emphasis mine. Cambridge: Cambridge University Press, 1998.
23. Ibid., 92n4.
24. *Hermeneutics and Criticism,* "Introduction." xxviii. Cambridge: Cambridge University Press, 1998.
25. *Schleiermacher: A Guide for the Perplexed,* 52-3. New York: Bloomsbury T&T Clark, 2013.

9

LUKE AND THE LIFE OF JESUS

SUMMARY: In his own day, Schleiermacher was a leading Biblical scholar. His brilliance in the field has often been overshadowed by his other works, but it is no less significant. Schleiermacher was also the first, in 1817, to offer public lectures on the life of Jesus.

IN SCHLEIERMACHER'S OWN WORDS:

> When rightly understood, the infinite significance of the Holy Scripture is not in contradiction to its hermeneutical limitations.[1]

SECONDARY QUOTES:

> Schleiermacher determines Christ's priority over Scripture in such a way as to establish a non-competitive relation between an ecclesial use of the Bible and a scientific investigation of the New Testament canon. [...] [He] reversed the Christ-Scripture correlation without detriment either to the scientific investigation of the Bible or to the integrity of the Christian faith. Scripture was grounded in Christ and not the other way around (CF §128).[2]
>
> — CHRISTINE HELMER

Introduction

The first of Schleiermacher's works to appear in English was his critical essay on Luke (1825).[3] For ten years, until Moss Stuart's 1835 translation of his Trinity essay, *Luke* was the only work of Schleiermacher's available to English speakers. It was another fifteen years before a third text appeared, William Farrar's 1850 translation of *Brief Outline*. Forty years passed before the *Christmas Eve* dialogues appeared (1890) alongside a collection of twenty-seven sermons translated by Mary Wilson that same year. *On Religion* did not appear in English until 1893, and Schleiermacher's masterpiece, *Christian Faith*, was not available until 1928 (and even then, the task of its translation was placed into the hands of some of his harshest critics, notably, the Barthian Scotsman, H. R. Mackintosh).

The reception of Schleiermacher's work in English is a fascinating history. The popularity of Barth's theology was likely a significant cause behind the "Schleiermacher renaissance" that took place from 1959-1987, wherein a number of his works received fresh translations, and an overall interest grew surrounding his theology.[4] But the complexities of this history aside, it is notable that Schleiermacher's critical investigation into the Gospel of Luke was the first of his works to appear in English. It is to this text, alongside *The Life of Jesus*, that we now turn.

Luke advocated the historical-critical method of Biblical interpretation, a task famously expanded by Rudolf Bultmann and his program of demythologization. And *The Life of Jesus* was a forerunner in the "quest for the historical Jesus." Yet strangely, both texts are often under-appreciated for their innovation. Part of the reason may be because their research has been superseded by modern scholarship, but in their own way, each book displays Schleiermacher's unique scholarly brilliance and creativity.

Schleiermacher's critical and biographical examination of Jesus' life in *The Life of Jesus* was an altogether new approach. It is not by accident that one of Schleiermacher's most famous students was also a pioneer in the "quest for the historical Jesus" movement: David Friedrich Strauss. Much of what Strauss is famous for doing in his own *Life of Jesus, Critically Examined* (1835/36) could be seen as a critical continuation of what Schleiermacher already lectured on as early as 1817. Strauss criticized Schleiermacher quite fiercely, but it was also clear he owed a debt to his work. Strauss' critique has likely led to the lack of interest in Schleiermacher's *The Life of Jesus*, at least in English, since both texts were translated within a year of each other. But it remains yet another example of how much Schleiermacher was ahead of his time.

These two books together will offer insight into Schleiermacher's work as a Biblical scholar. In his own time, Schleiermacher was widely considered to be a foremost authority on the New Testament. We have already noted that he lectured on Paul and the New Testament more than any other subject, even dogmatics. His theology was profoundly guided by this life-long dedication to the Scriptures. Though not a "Biblical theologian" in today's sense, he was, indeed, a faithful servant of the Word.

Luke

Schleiermacher's book on Luke is somewhat dated, and modern scholarship is unlikely to agree with its conclusions, but it is also quite contemporary in its motivation and approach. Schleiermacher may not have had the same resources modern scholars have, but he implemented many of the techniques used still today. In this sense, he tilled the ground for modern scholarship.

Personally, I must confess that I am not as up-to-date on modern trends of Biblical criticism as I should be, and so I cannot offer much guidance in terms of how Schleiermacher contrasts with those working in the field today. But I am informed enough to recognize Schleiermacher's important role. Others more versed in this field will be able to say how relevant (or outdated) his ideas are.

Schleiermacher breaks Luke into four sections and offers a series of literary and historical observations about it. For example, he did not consider the census of Luke 2 historically accurate, but he did think Luke's account of the shepherds returning home was based on authentic records. He considered the Annunciation account poetical, not historical. But it should be respected still for its importance to the Christian tradition. Luke's account of the Last Supper was his most original contribution. And the tearing of the veil at Christ's death was poetic rather than historical, but Schleiermacher notes that this fact does not negate its importance.

Finally, Schleiermacher concludes:

> [Luke] is from beginning to end no more than the compiler and arranger of documents which he found in existence, and which he allows to pass unaltered through his hands. His merit in this capacity is twofold: first, that of the arrangement [...] But the far greater merit is this, that he has admitted scarcely any pieces but what are peculiarly genuine and good; for this was certainly not the effect of accident, but the fruit of a judiciously instituted investigation, and a well weighed choice.[5]

William Baird aptly called *Luke*:

> [A] brilliant display of Schleiermacher's ability to analyze the form and content of a text. Rather than beginning with some hypothesis about the

Gospel, Schleiermacher begins with the text itself and, observing details that most readers miss, constructs a theory about its origin and nature.[6]

Furthermore, the freedom Schleiermacher displayed in relation to the text brought about a new "epoch in the history of English theology," according to Jack Verheyden.[7] As such, the book remains a novel approach and a sure sign of Schleiermacher's innovative genius.

Luke is not the only example of Schleiermacher's work on the New Testament, which includes various other textual studies, especially on the letters of Paul. Schleiermacher was among the first to express doubt regarding Paul's authorship of Ephesians, a theory the majority of scholars agree on today. He also doubted attributing the authorship of James to the disciple James, Hebrews to Paul, and Revelation to John. The Catholic Epistles received the most severe criticism, as Schleiermacher argued: "[I]t should not be maintained that it would be a great loss if this whole section were lacking from our canon."[8] He considered John's witness trustworthy, so trustworthy that forty-one percent of the time he preached from one of the four gospels, it was from John.[9]

All of this reveals a brilliant and critical mind at work, but Schleiermacher was also a careful critic. He read the Biblical texts more seriously than most. It may be easy to criticize the historical-critical method, but no serious student of the Bible can read it without discovering some contradictions worth investigating further. It is important to remember Schleiermacher highly regarded the Scriptures, and he considered the New Testament, even in its present state, an authoritative norm for the Church. His work is in no way motivated by the desire to disregard the importance of the Bible, but rather, it is *because* he takes the Bible as seriously as he does that he was compelled to criticize it so freely. We tend to be the most critical and passionate about what we love the most, and the same is true for Schleiermacher's textual investigations of the New Testament.

The Life of Jesus

Schleiermacher was the first theologian to offer public lectures on the life of Jesus, according to Church historian Karl Hase. The published version of these lectures mostly comprised of notes from his students, but Schleiermacher's own, brief notes were also included. The lectures that became the text for *The Life of Jesus* were given in 1832. The book was published posthumously in 1864 (English translation, 1890).

One of Schleiermacher's primary goals for his biography of Jesus was to "seek for the unity of the particulars and the inward of the externals."[10] In other words, he hoped to distinguish between "what is inward in what is external."[11] He writes:

> The task is to grasp what is inward in the man with such certainty that it can be said: I can say with a measure of assurance how what is outward with respect to the man would have been if what affected him and also what he affected had been different than was actually the case, for only then do I have an actual knowledge of what is inward in him, because I can also construe it as the constant factor to different results.[12]

Schleiermacher admits there are limitations to such a task, but within that limit, we may have something valid to say about the inner life of Christ from observing His external circumstances. Schleiermacher argues strongly for "true human development in Christ" because this makes it possible to assert His genuine humanity.[13] Christ developed as a man of his time, being affected by and affecting His environment. As Schleiermacher notes, "No individual can be torn loose from his time, age, and people."[14] Therefore, a person who does not develop over time is not truly human at all.

Schleiermacher divides Christ's life into three periods: the period before His public appearance, the period of His public life ending with His arrest, and the period between His arrest and ascension. Many interesting remarks and observations are made in these sections, but we will not attempt to explore them all here. Two are worth briefly noting, however.

First, as we have seen, Schleiermacher argued that we must account for development in Christ's life if Christ was truly human. We cannot ascribe anything divine to His life, such as omniscience. So if we were to ask a speculative question—such as, "Did Jesus know the Earth revolves around the Sun?"—then we cannot answer "yes" on the basis of His divinity. Instead, we must recognize his limitations as a human being like us in every way. Likewise, Schleiermacher argued that Christ's miracles were not necessarily factual or historical, even though they have significance for how we perceive Christ, particularly the being of God in Him.

Second, *The Life of Jesus* offers further examples of how Schleiermacher understood Christ's absolutely strong God-consciousness. He writes:

> Christ was always conscious of being within the relationship of the divine will, where this relationship as consciousness must be thought of as something always gradually developing: And so Christ represents himself as always looking to the will of the Father [...]
>
> [Christ] was conscious himself of what in him was plainly operative [..., namely,] he was aware that to do everything only under the form of the divine will and to see everything only in relation to God was what was

operative in him. Consequently God was really what was operative in him, and all individual aspects proceed from this.[15]

Schleiermacher notes that this way of thinking about the being of God in Christ "would be the same thing" in content with what the Church's creedal formulas tried to say. That is, Schleiermacher thinks his Christology is faithful to the intentions of the early creeds regarding Christ's divinity.

With this Schleiermacher has found the inner truth of Christ's life: the being of God in Him. It is Christ's unbroken adherence to the divine will of the Father that makes Him so significant, and it is what deems Him worthy of our faith. Christ's absolutely strong God-consciousness is developed more explicitly in Schleiermacher mature work, *Christian Faith*, but it is here already an essential feature of his critical biography of Jesus.

Overall, this text is an insightful look into Schleiermacher's theology, which reveals that he was an innovative forerunner to the quest for the historical Jesus of the late nineteenth and early twentieth centuries. It is, above all, yet another example of Schleiermacher's creativity and brilliance, which spans across so many disciplines. Whether or not modern scholarship would agree with him, it is clear he was far ahead of his time.

Eternal Covenant

Schleiermacher's concept of an eternal covenant between faith and science is not limited to the natural sciences. On the contrary, as these two texts show, any critical investigation into the truth exists in a partnership with Christian faith, including textual criticism, linguistic analysis, and historical research.

Science, in all its forms, can (and should) be an ally to the Church and its mission. As Pedersen argues, the eternal covenant is not a peace treaty, nor simply a way to keep science and faith at a distance from each other. No: "Instead, it amounts to a cooperative union, a friendship, between theology and science in pursuit of a shared perfection."[16] Seeking to uncover if Paul wrote Ephesians, if Christ's miracles were factual, or if the New Testament is reliable is a natural pursuit of honest faith. Such critical examinations of the Biblical texts are not merely permitted but necessary. If faith does not seek understanding, is it really faith? If faith does not pursue a scientific understanding of the Bible and theology, is it anything more than a self-given ideology?

Fundamentalism has tried to convince us that by questioning the supposedly "infallible" text of the Bible, we are excluded from faith—as if faith and doubt are mutually exclusive. It has corrupted our ability to question the Bible or the doctrines of our tradition without feeling like we are renouncing our faith in the process. But Paul Tillich has shown convincingly well, following Schleiermacher's example, that faith is always uncertain and cannot remove its inherent uncertainty. Tillich writes:

> But faith is uncertain in so far as the infinite to which it is related is received by a finite being. This element of uncertainty in faith cannot be removed, it must be accepted. Faith includes an element of immediate awareness which gives certainty and an element of uncertainty. To accept this is courage.[17]

Because we cannot escape ourselves and our finitude, faith remains a certain uncertainty. To be courageous in the face of uncertainty does not look like turning a blind eye to doubt, but accepting our finitude and going on anyways. Tillich even argues that "serious doubt is *confirmation* of faith."[18] The possibility of faith without doubt is an *illusion* created by fundamentalism, an ideology. We will never escape our humanity, and thus, we will never be free from uncertainty.

Questioning the Bible's accuracy is a freedom *of* faith. There is no contradiction between faith and the quest for truth.

Schleiermacher reversed the conventional way of thinking about the Bible. The Bible is not the foundation of faith, faith is the foundation of the Bible. While Schleiermacher *does* place the Church under the authority of the Biblical account of Christ, he does not place the Bible's authority above Christ's, who is ever-present by the common spirit of the community.

This recalls Schleiermacher's point about the presuppositional authority of Scripture (which we discussed in the sidebar to chapter four). What is in the Bible does not determine what is Christian, but instead, what is Christian determines what is in the Bible. Schleiermacher writes, "[T]he ground of faith must be the same among us as among the first Christians" (CF §128.1, 835). If this is true, then the Bible cannot be the foundation of faith. Only Christ's self-proclamation in the Christian community—which is always God's own self-proclamation by the common spirit of the Church—can be the source of faith.

But Schleiermacher also writes, "[E]verything must be referred to the conception of Christ that comes from Scripture" (CF §133.1, 858). This defends Christianity from separatists. As always, Schleiermacher is concerned with the community-centric nature of Christian faith, writing that "the union of an individual with Christ is not imaginable without one's union with the faithful" (CF §141.1, 905). This means that neither a person's private experience with Christ nor private reading of the Bible can determine the whole of Christianity. We are bound to one another. The latter distortion is the error of fundamentalism, and the former is the error of liberalism. Neither point is Schleiermacher's. He rejects the privatization of Christianity wholly.

It is in this context that we can appreciate Schleiermacher's Biblical criticism. His work as a scholar is a seamless expression of his theological convictions, which are at once modern and faithful, *scientific and ecclesial.*[19] He prioritized the Christ behind the text of the New Testament, whose influence first led to the text's being written but who remains active in the community still today. The Church is bound to the first account of Christ in Scripture, but it is nevertheless free to criticize the texts themselves with the knowledge that Christ's presence persists still today. The Bible is an important authority but the Church has only one Lord.

---

1. *Hermeneutics: The Handwritten Manuscripts,* 55. Missoula: Scholars Press for The American Academy of Religion, 1977.
2. "Schleiermacher's exegetical theology and the New Testament," *The Cambridge Companion to Friedrich Schleiermacher,* 230-1. Cambridge University Press, 2005.
3. Trans. by E. C. Thirlwall.
4. For a brief summary of this history, see Terrence Tice: *Schleiermacher: The Psychology of Christian Faith and Life,* 53. Lanham: Lexington Books, 2018.
5. *A Critical Essay on the Gospel of St. Luke,* 313-4. Public domain. London: 1825.
6. *History of New Testament Research, Vol. 1,* 215. Minneapolis: Augsburg Press, 1992.
7. "Introduction," *The Life of Jesus,* xxix. Philadelphia: Fortress Press, 1975.
8. Quoted in Baird, *History of New Testament Research, Vol. 1,* 215. Minneapolis: Augsburg Press, 1992.
9. Catherine L. Kelsey, *Schleiermacher's Preaching, Dogmatics, and Biblical Criticism,* 31. Eugene: Pickwick Publications, 2007.
10. *The Life of Jesus,* 6. Philadelphia: Fortress Press, 1975.
11. Ibid.
12. Ibid., 8.
13. Ibid., 15.
14. Ibid., 8.
15. Ibid., 101, 103-4.
16. *The Eternal Covenant,* 167. Berlin: Walter de Gruyter, 2017.
17. *Dynamics of Faith,* 16. New York: Harper & Row Publishers, 1957.
18. Ibid., 22. Emphasis mine.
19. See CF §17: "Dogmatic propositions have a twofold value, an ecclesial one and a scientific one; their degree of completeness, moreover, is determined by both of these values and by their relationship to each other" (125).

10

BRIEF OUTLINE OF THEOLOGY AS A FIELD OF STUDY

SUMMARY: Schleiermacher devised an original three-part schema to organize the field of theology: philosophical, historical, and practical. *Brief Outline* reveals how Schleiermacher thought about the various tasks and goals of theology.

IN SCHLEIERMACHER'S OWN WORDS:

> Theology is a positive science, the parts of which join into a cohesive whole only through their common relation to a distinct mode of faith, that is, a distinct formation of God-consciousness.[1]

> [A] presentation that remains the same for all time is totally impossible.[2]

SECONDARY QUOTES:

> Schleiermacher regards the essential contents of the System of Faith not as a concluded *letter,* but as a free, *spiritual* stream, diffused through the entire historical life of the Church, and attaining to its complete development thereby.[3]

— FRIEDRICH LÜCKE

Introduction

Schleiermacher's brilliance, in many respects, comes from his unique ability to structure and organize a wide range of disciplines. His "architectonic" scheme for organizing theology was so masterfully constructed that even his critics admit its merit. T. F. Torrance, for example, writes, "I was captivated by the architectonic form and beauty of Schleiermacher's method and his arrangement of dogmatics into a scientific system of Christian doctrine."[4] Torrance follows a familiar Barthian critique that Schleiermacher "lacked objectivity" and was fundamentally "wrong." It is noteworthy, however, that Torrance—and others have admitted the same—can not help but find himself amazed at the structure of Schleiermacher's great work.

Schleiermacher's constructive strength is displayed best in *Christian Faith*, but it is also profoundly implemented on a larger scale with *Brief Outline of Theology as a Field of Study*. His writing style is comparable to the architectural geniuses of history, perhaps akin to someone like Gaudí with his faith-inspired, naturalistic designs. Although, an organic metaphor is more appropriate than an architectural one because of the interconnectedness of Schleiermacher's thought.[5]

In this chapter, we will focus on how Schleiermacher organized theology as a field of study. This may seem trivial at first, but it actually offers an insightful look into how Schleiermacher thought about theology as a discipline. As such, it will be a fitting way to conclude this book.

What is Theology?

Schleiermacher divides the field of theology into three parts: "philosophical theology," "historical theology," and "practical theology." Philosophical theology includes apologetics and polemics. Historical theology includes exegetical theology, Church history, and the present condition of Christianity, which includes dogmatics and Church statistics. Finally, practical theology includes Church service and government.

Schleiermacher begins by asking general questions about the task of theology, its nature and aim, and its place within historical Christianity. Of particular interest is Schleiermacher's overall definition:

> Theology is a positive science, the parts of which join into a cohesive whole only through their common relation to a distinct mode of faith, that is, a distinct formation of God-consciousness.[6]

Terrence Tice breaks this into three notable points. First, theology is a *positive* science. This means theology is "not merely empirical or speculative

Brief Outline of Theology as a Field of Study 161

or theoretical in character but rather (a) refers directly to actual historical experience, (b) within a given set of social circumstances, and (c) in order to serve a definition practical function" (BO, xv). The strength of Schleiermacher's *Christian Faith* is its dedication to the historical experience of Christians. As we saw, this is an experience God initiates, it is a being-in-relation with God by grace, in and through the redemption of Christ. This emphasis on the historical experience of Christians is not a relativist, subjectivist method, but more appropriately that of a grace-centered theology.

For Schleiermacher, it is a false dichotomy to argue that theology must begin with either God *or* humanity. If we start with a God unrelated to human beings, then we resign ourselves to empty speculation about our self-made concepts of God, we have a false sense of objectivism but without any real verification. On the other hand, if we begin with human beings, we end up with a false subjectivism. In both cases, we fail to speak of God adequately. For Schleiermacher, then, it is improper to begin with God alone or humanity alone. Instead, we begin with the actual relationship established by grace, that is, we do theology from the relationship God has established with humanity in and through Christ.

As a "science," theology uses "rational and orderly methods" to assemble "a particular kind of information, one that can be validated in experience" (BO, xv). Schleiermacher treats religious consciousness as something universal to the make-up of human nature. Theological information is validated by this experience, namely, the experience of redemption in and through Christ. Again, it is important to remember this is not a self-given experience. This is the experience of God's grace. It is not fair to deem such experiences invalid because these are essential to our being-in-relation with God. Therefore, it would be foolish to ignore the experience of grace as if it were self-given.

The second point of note about Schleiermacher's definition of theology is its cohesiveness. Schleiermacher's *Christian Faith* is one of the most tightly constructed works of theology ever written. This is why it is nearly impossible to understand his dogmatics without multiple readings.

For Schleiermacher, "Dogmatic propositions have a twofold value, an ecclesial one and a scientific one" (CF §17, 125). The scientific and ecclesial aspects of theology are inseparable and mutually dependent. The ecclesial character of theology is in harmony with the rigors of its scientific investigations. Several practical implications follow from this. Often, theology is split apart from other disciplines in the Church, such as Biblical scholarship and even ministry itself. Schleiermacher's point is that no special discipline is complete without a basic understanding of *all* the disciplines of our faith. Schleiermacher writes:

Therefore, if one is to deal with any one of the theological disciplines in a truly theological sense and spirit, one must master the basic features of them all.

Only when each person in a general way comprehends the whole, along with one's own special discipline, can each and all communicate. Only thus can each person exert an influence upon the whole through one's main field.[7]

Accordingly, the three parts comprising the whole field of theology are interrelated. Schleiermacher himself engaged in most of the specializations mentioned in his outline. Not everyone will be capable of such a wide range of interests, but nevertheless, everyone should have a basic understanding of each part of the whole field. A specialist in Biblical studies cannot afford to be ignorant of dogmatics, nor should a practical theologian who ministers in the Church be ignorant of philosophical theology.

Finally, the third feature of note about Schleiermacher's definition is that theology is for the Church. Theology strives to provide a greater understanding of the distinct nature of Christian faith. Philosophical theology helps establish the boundary for what is distinctly Christian, against what is distinct for other communities of faith. Historical theology creates the norm for Christian faith through its exegetical and dogmatic reflections, as well as through its presentation of statistics about the current state of the Church. Practical theology applies this understanding to Church leadership. All three parts serve the same goal differently. They *establish, normalize,* and *apply* an understanding of the distinct nature of Christian faith to the Church. This is the "distinct formation of God-consciousness" Schleiermacher refers to in his basic definition of theology. All theology, therefore, is directed towards this end, towards the formation of God-consciousness in the Church.

Schleiermacher's outline is formal and preliminary. It does not offer much in terms of content. But he nevertheless placed at the center of his theological vision, in its threefold form, the *one* central fact, namely, that "within Christianity everything is referred to the redemption accomplished through Jesus of Nazareth" (CF §11, 79). As a whole, the outline he presents is an original attempt to define a field of studies systematically. As Tice notes, "Even to this day, this is a task that has rarely been achieved in such a thoughtful, systematic way in any academic or professional area" (BO, xvii).

1. Philosophical Theology

The first division of Schleiermacher's outline is *philosophical theology*. This contains two sub-divisions: apologetics and polemics. According to Schleiermacher, philosophical theology "utilizes the framework developed in philosophy of religion in order to present" what makes Christianity a "distinctive mode of faith," the "form in which the Christian community subsists," and "the manner in which each of these factors is further subdivided and differentiated" (BO §24, 11). These three tasks are the work of philosophical theology, achieved through apologetics and polemics.

Apologetics is outward-focused and establishes what is distinct about Christianity in contrast with other religious expressions. Polemics is inward-focused and determines what is proper to Christianity in contrast with its diseased conditions. In *Christian Faith,* this is where Schleiermacher presents the four natural heresies of Christianity: the Docetic and Nazarean, the Manichean and the Pelagian (CF §22, 144). For Schleiermacher, apologetics is not the task of *proving* Christian faith. Instead, it is a legal term for pleading one's case. Therefore, the goal is not to convince anyone to be a Christian, but rather to "bring others to the point where they can let Christianity run its course" (BO §39n8, 18).

Philosophical theology relates to historical theology because it presupposes knowledge of its content. But it also lays a "foundation for attaining a properly historical perception regarding Christianity" (BO §65, 29). It does this by establishing what is distinctively Christian, against other expressions of faith, and what a healthy Christianity looks like by its polemics against a diseased Christianity. In relation to practical theology, philosophical theology is directed toward practical matters, against historical theology, which is primarily aimed at observation and description.

2. Historical Theology

The second division of Schleiermacher's outline is *historical theology*. This contains three subdivisions: exegetical theology, Church history, and the present condition of Christianity. These disciplines gather "information about primitive Christianity, information about the total career of Christianity, and information about the state of Christianity at the present time" (BO §85, 36).

Within these divisions, there are further subdivisions. Exegetical theology includes the canon, higher and lower criticism, original languages, hermeneutics, and New Testament background. These all strive to study the primitive state of Christianity. Church history includes the Church's life and the Church's doctrine. These aim to examine the total career of Christian faith and theology. Finally, the present state of Christianity includes dogmatic theology and Church statistics. It is arguably the most unique aspect of Schleiermacher's outline that he places dogmatic theology here.

By placing dogmatic theology within the sub-discipline of observing the present state of Christianity, Schleiermacher has made a remarkable statement about the very nature of dogmatics. Dogmatics is not a timeless reflection but historically bound to its present time and situation. There is no such thing as a universal dogmatics, of a theological system that remains valid for all times and all places. As such, Schleiermacher brilliantly invalidates every attempt to create a "system" or a "school" around a figure or movement in the Church's history, even himself. Certain classifications may be helpful to identify where someone is coming from theologically, but they are ultimately founded upon a false understanding of dogmatics. For example, the idea that we might become "Calvinists" or "Schleiermacherians" is nonsensical, according to Schleiermacher's outline. We may be indebted to Calvin and exist within the tradition of the Reformed faith, as Schleiermacher's own self-understanding attested, and thus we might be classified as "Calvinists." But to pledge dogmatic allegiance to the theology of another period would be to deny the very nature of dogmatics. Dogmatics is historical, it is bound to the present situation of the Church. We have quoted it once already, but it is worth repeating Schleiermacher's famous declaration: "The reformation still goes on!"[8]

The redemption wrought in and through Jesus Christ is the historical reference point for all dogmatics, even in its ever-changing, time-bound nature. No one individual or group may claim to have exclusive rights to truth claims except for Jesus Christ. Dogmatics is a human endeavor, and therefore, it is bound to its own situation and time. This conviction is likely why Schleiermacher did not consider his work "original" but merely a reflection on the present state of theology in the Church. He writes, "Both the form and content of my *Glaubenslehre* [faith-doctrine, CF] are conditioned by the presupposition that the notion of God set forth in it is not original, but develops from reflection on the higher self-consciousness" (OG, 85). Dogmatics is descriptive, not creative.

Heterodoxy and Orthodoxy

Truth and error always co-exist. There is no such thing as absolute truth or absolute error—in the sense that we, as human beings confined by our limitations, will ever fully apprehend truth or be thoroughly deceived by error. Truth and error do exist in reality, but our apprehension of reality is never entirely free from one or the other. This does not equate to relativism but recognizes that truth and error are always included in our perception of reality. Schleiermacher writes:

> [U]nderlying the entire presentation of doctrine that is being introduced here is the maxim that error never occurs anywhere in and of itself but always exists only in relation to what is true, and that error will never have been

completely understood until one has found its connection with truth and with whatever that is true to which the error is affixed.[9]

For Schleiermacher, heterodox theology is just as necessary to dogmatics as orthodox theology. He defines the orthodox character of a doctrine as, "Every feature of doctrine that is construed in the intention of holding fast to what is already generally acknowledged, along with any inferences that may naturally follow" (BO §203, 76). And he defines the heterodox character of a doctrine as, "Every feature constructed in the inclination to keep the body of doctrine mobile and to make room for still other modes of apprehension" (ibid.). Heterodox and orthodox theology are counter-balancing and thus of equal importance to dogmatics.

The orthodox features of a doctrine remain unmoved and unite together the majority by "holding fast" to the status quo. In contrast, the heterodox features of a doctrine move it forward, keep it mobile, and create space for new modes of apprehension. Both holding fast and pushing ahead are vital for theological development. Schleiermacher warns against an unequally balanced theology, which results in either "false orthodoxy" or "false heterodoxy." He writes:

> It is false orthodoxy to wish to retain in dogmatic treatment what is already entirely antiquated in the public pronouncements of the church and does not exercise in its scientific expression any definite influence on other points of doctrine. [...]
>
> It is false heterodoxy in dogmatic treatment to inveigh [protest] against those formulations which have well grounded support in pronouncements of the church and the scientific expression of which does not create confusion regarding their relation to other points of Christian doctrine.[10]

In the first edition of *Brief Outline,* he explained the difference more succinctly:

> To want to retain in the body of doctrine what is already antiquated and thus to obstruct progress is false orthodoxy.
>
> To want to change things without preserving what is essential in Christianity as well as in its present period destroys the unity of its appearance in history and is false heterodoxy.[11]

The balance between holding fast to a well-established doctrine and moving forward to new modes of apprehension is essential for Schleiermacher's conviction that dogmatics is historically bound to the changes of time. Those who dogmatically hold fast to a past thinker or a former doctrine are practicing "false orthodoxy." Think, for example, of fundamentalism, which refuses to acknowledge modern scientific or even theological breakthroughs, and attempts to live in the twenty-first century as if it were the fifteenth. This is false orthodoxy. On the other hand, it is equally dangerous to deny all orthodoxy, to deem even the purest doctrine false, and to innovate not *from* the old but by first *destroying* the old. Such is a false heterodoxy.

Interestingly, Schleiermacher admitted that his own theology pushed the boundary towards the heterodox. He acknowledged that it was his tendency, or perhaps his "bad habit," to shift his weight from the orthodox to the heterodox whenever the majority of those on the boat stand on the other side so that the whole will not capsize (OG, 68). This image of a boat in balance is useful for what he has in mind. To over-emphasize either orthodox or heterodox features in a doctrine would be to capsize it entirely.

Schleiermacher's stated intention is to extend orthodoxy, in contrast with those who so rigidly expel even the most subtle differences of opinion. He writes:

> In contrast to the contending parties, who attempt from their own perspectives to restrict the area of orthodoxy more and more so that the real danger arises of dividing the church, I am interested in *extending it*. My intention was to demonstrate [in CF] in as much detail as possible at every key point how much distance there is between the theses of the church and those of heresy and that within this open area how much friendly agreement is still possible on points common to both the heterodox and orthodox.[12]

I once had a conversation with a self-proclaimed Calvinist about Karl Barth. His opinion was that because Barth denied the inerrancy of Scripture, he was a heretic and thus not even a Christian. For this individual, affirming that the Bible is infallible in every way was *the* test for one's orthodoxy. To use Schleiermacher's analogy, he turned the "open area" of a generous orthodoxy into a closed, VIP only space where admittance is granted solely to those who ascribe to this limited definition of orthodoxy. Sadly, this tendency is not uncommon. For many today, doing theology means pledging allegiance to a set of dead, unmovable doctrines. To question or challenge any of these would be a sign of unbelief or sin. Yet, this is a *false* orthodoxy that perpetuates itself through a misplaced sense of security under the guise of objectivism. But ultimately, such a limited and limiting perspective is detrimental to faith.

On the other hand, it is just as detrimental to engage in a kind of false heterodoxy, in which we reject our dependence on the historical Church. We may not follow their every decision or decree, but we are just as bound to the Church of the past as we are to the Church of the present because it is *Christ's*

Church just as much now as then. It is Christ who sustains the Church, and it would be a denial of Him and His Spirit to renounce all ties to the historical Church.

Schleiermacher's insight that dogmatics needs both orthodox and heterodox features is a profoundly practical way to implement his convictions about dogmatics. Furthermore, it offers insight into Schleiermacher's understanding of his own work. He writes self-reflectively:

> I am firmly convinced, however, that my position is an inspired heterodoxy that in due time will eventually become orthodox, although certainly not just because of my book [CF] and perhaps not until long after my death.[13]

Looking back with almost two-hundred years of theological history between Schleiermacher and us, this statement has more truth to it than perhaps he even knew. The massive influence of Schleiermacher's theology is evident, and many of the significant developments over these last two-hundred years are, undoubtedly, the indirect by-product of Schleiermacher's mission to extend orthodoxy.

Katherine Sonderegger aptly summarizes what it is like to do theology post-Schleiermacher:

> Always we return to Schleiermacher, for though we may not see this at first, we have always, in our day, already begun with him.[14]

It would be an overstatement to say that *every* doctrine in modern theology owes a debt to Schleiermacher, but he is appropriately called the father of modern theology because we have, indeed, always begun with him. He set the course for modern theology more than any single figure.

3. Practical Theology

The third division of Schleiermacher's outline is *practical theology*. In the 1811 edition of *Brief Outline,* Schleiermacher called practical theology the "crown of theological study" (BO §25n35, 12). In the final edition, his language is altered to remove this exact phrase, but the point remains. Practical theology is that which both philosophical and historical theology point towards and support. Theology, in other words, serves the Church and its mission.

Practical theology is divided into two parts. First, "Principles of Church Service," and second, "Principles of Church Government." Everything, however, is directed towards one simple goal: the care of souls. Schleiermacher writes, "[A]ll deliberate influence on the church that is exerted so that

Christianity may be more purely presented within it is nothing other than care [or guidance] of souls" (BO §263, 99).

A "theory of practice" articulates how the Church may preserve and protect its integrity in these two areas: service and government. Schleiermacher produced his own practical theology, though only a small portion of it has been translated into English. There Schleiermacher writes:

> Practical theology is the crown of theological study because it presupposes everything else; it is also the final part of the study because it prepares for direct action. Thus systematic and historical theology are presupposed by practical theology, and can in this respect be distinguished from it.[15]

The scope of practical theology includes every action the Church might engage in. It is not limited to the task of ministry but consists of every action that falls within the context of "caring for souls." As he writes, "All the specific tasks related to church leadership are part of what the Greeks called *psychologia* [... i.e.,] guidance of souls.'"[16] Even the political and social responsibility of the Church is contained in practical theology as it pertains to the care of souls.

Interestingly, as a side-note, Schleiermacher was one of the first theologians to stress the importance of separating Church and state. The Church can and should act as a mediating agent for the care of souls in the public sphere, but it must remain separate from the state in order to fulfill its task correctly. It must be engaged in politics but cannot confuse its responsibilities with those of the state.

Conclusion

Schleiermacher's *Brief Outline* remains not only a novel approach to the field of theology, but it offers us profound insight into his self-understanding as a theologian. As such, it provides a fitting conclusion for this book.

Ultimately, Schleiermacher's theology is an *invitation* to a lively dialogue. He never stands above us as an instructor we must sit before in silent awe, but as partners with us in the life of faith. We rightly perceive ourselves to be in the presence of a master, but he has been gracious enough to invite our passionate responses. Even if we walk away from Schleiermacher feeling frustrated with his conclusions, we cannot leave unchallenged by his keen mind. And ultimately, there is more value in a teacher who challenges our preconceptions than in one who reinforces our long-held ideals.

---

1. BO §1, 1.
2. CE, 24.

3. *Reminiscences of Schleiermacher,* 41. Columbus: Beloved Publishing, 2018.
4. *How Karl Barth Change My Mind,* 52. Grand Rapids: William B. Eerdmans Publishing, 1986.
5. For this distinction, see Robert Sherman: *The Shift to Modernity,* 28-33. New York: T&T Clark, 2005.
6. BO §1, 1.
7. BO §16, 8.
8. Quoted in Martin Redeker: *Schleiermacher: Life and Thought,* 198. Philadelphia: Fortress Press, 1973.
9. CF §7.3, 49.
10. BO §206-7, 77.
11. BO, 77n155.
12. OG, 68; emphasis mine.
13. OG, 53.
14. *Systematic Theology: Vol. 1, The Doctrine of God,* 183. Minneapolis: Fortress Press, 2015.
15. *Christian Caring,* 99. Philadelphia: Fortress Press, 1988.
16. Ibid., 109.

AFTERWORD

I have said enough already about my Barthian perspective and the possibility of appreciating *both* Barth and Schleiermacher. I have also made it clear that even if we disagree with where he ended up on every issue, we cannot ignore the path Schleiermacher has left behind. But instead of repeating these points, I want to end on a more personal note about how Schleiermacher can be a comfort to the theological doubter in all of us.

I have found Schleiermacher to be a compassionate and empathetic theologian. What I mean is simply this: Schleiermacher extends the boundary lines that are so often rigidly defined and closed off, the lines of what can and cannot be believed as a faithful Christian. Accordingly, Schleiermacher is a theologian for doubters. He is a reminder that even if we find ourselves in the situation he did, wherein "the childhood images of God and immortality vanished before my doubting eyes" (*OR*, 48), we may still find our way back to the grace and love of God. Or, more appropriately, God may still find a way back to us even in our doubt.

Theology can be therapeutic. But it can also be terrifying. It provides comfort by restoring our trust in the love and grace of God for all humanity, yet it can just as quickly shatter every man-made idol we previously called "God." Even though these idols are false images, they have perhaps been a comfort to us, and giving them up, no matter how important that is, remains difficult. As such, theology can be existentially unnerving. The cherished beliefs of our childhood (if we grew up in the faith, as I did) can vanish before our eyes as we begin to think them through critically. Giving up our illusions about God can feel like giving up an imaginary friend. There's a reason why people often look back and long for the good old days of that "old time religion."

But when all that fades, Schleiermacher's work is a reminder that what lies ahead of us is always greater than anything we have left behind. Growth is painful, at times, but it is necessary. The Church has to grow—we *must* grow. Holding fast to the doctrines of old without forging ahead to discover new pathways means failing to follow the Spirit who is always doing a "new thing." The Church of the Spirit does not have this option.

Yet, when we find ourselves doubting everything we once believed, there is comfort in knowing some truths remain fixed: God is love, redemption is secure in and through Jesus Christ, the Church is His body, we are the elected people of God, and in Christ, there is a new creation. Or we could state these truths existentially: We are loved, redeemed, included in a fellowship, chosen, blessed, and made new. These remain, even if the packaging we were once so familiar with changes. Faith remains, even if the thoughts of faith fade away.

Schleiermacher is a theologian for the doubter in all of us. Everyone has doubts from time to time about the doctrines of faith. Admittedly, the doctrines we confess *are* a bit wild—the belief that God became human and operates still today in our midst through the Spirit is simply astounding when you stop to think about it. So it seems only natural to find a bit of doubt in the hearts of the faithful. Schleiermacher lends a sympathetic ear to our doubt and reminds us just how deep and wide and inclusive this faith of ours can be. He reminds us that our Lord did not shame or excommunicate poor old doubting Thomas, but invited him to come closer and see for himself. Doubt is often left unspoken because we fear exclusion, but doubt should be the very thing that brings us closer to Jesus. It is what draws us in to taste and see that the Lord is good.

Schleiermacher saw that "whenever people among us have lost interest in knowing of God, it has always been due to the prevailing exposition rather than to the idea itself" (OG, 52). For the Church today to stand up and publicly express doubt in the prevailing expositions of God may be exactly what the world needs. Because faith is not about adhering to a set of dogmatic formulas but about the gracious God to whom we are absolutely dependent and through whom we are redeemed.

I do not find myself convinced by everything Schleiermacher says, but I do find him extremely compelling. And most of the time I think he is more right than I once imagined he could be. I find myself in the same position Barth described: "An inner voice always spoke to his advantage." This book is not my full endorsement of Schleiermacher's theology, but neither is it a critique. There are many things I simply do not understand enough to criticize, but there are also far too many benefits to ignore his brilliance. Ultimately, he is a gentle reminder that even when we feel our theology is shaken, our faith is not grounded upon ideas but upon the living God of love who meets us and redeems us. Faith is neither theology nor ethics, thinking nor doing. Theology is faith seeking understanding, a sense and taste for the Infinite. Faith is solely God's work in us, God's gracious willingness to be in a relationship with us. Therefore, we stand on an unshakable ground, in the assurance of God's grace, even when our theology feels uncertain and our eyes harbor doubts.

KEY THEMES

Several key themes and motifs shape Schleiermacher's theology. These do not provide *content*, per se, but *shape* content into its distinctive form. Understanding these will drastically improve our ability to recognize Schleiermacher's goals and intentions, and to read him more accurately. The themes and motifs explained here are neither exhaustive nor final, but I hope they will be helpful. They are the tools and tips of a beginner, not an expert, and should be taken as such. Refer back to this section whenever you feel overwhelmed by the density of Schleiermacher's theology and need a helping hand.

Centrist — Schleiermacher is often called a "liberal" theologian, but in his own mind, he was a centrist, one who always sought a *mediating* position between reductionistic conservatives and revisionist liberals, or, in his own time, between the supernaturalists and the rationalists. He disowned the liberal label whenever it was applied to him, and so, while the term may be helpful to some, it should be avoided when speaking accurately about Schleiermacher.

Christomorphic — Coined by Richard R. Niebuhr,[1] this indicates the end to which Schleiermacher's theology points and the basis from which it originates, its organizational center: Jesus Christ our Redeemer. Every doctrine is theologically "morphed," or shaped, around the person of Christ and the experience of redemption wrought in and through Christ's life. A key expression of this theme is that "Christ had come to be determined in the way he was only because and insofar as the whole given interconnection of things was also determined in a certain fashion, and, in reverse, the whole given interconnection of things would have been determined in the way it was only because and insofar as Christ too would have been determined in a certain fashion" (CF §120.3, 790). The interconnected process of nature—through which God acts in creation—is Christomorphic, yet Christ is part of the natural process. Schleiermacher writes, "[O]ne could also just as rightly say that already Christ was also coming into being, even as a human person, at the same time as the world was coming into being" (CF §67.2, 595). The creation of humanity is completed in Christ. While these examples seem to point to a mutuality between Christ and creation, it is Christ who takes up the determinative role in creation and redemption. The whole organic process of nature is determined by Christ. Likewise, all theological reflections must be determined by Christ.

Christian religious immediate self-consciousness — Schleiermacher rarely used this phrase in its entirety. It is often reduced to shorthand phrases such as "consciousness," "Christian self-consciousness," "religious self- consciousness," "immediate self-consciousness," or basically any other combination of these terms.

This theme indicates Schleiermacher's aim for an empirical dogmatics, one free from speculation. As such, it is vital for understanding Schleiermacher, especially his methodology, yet it is also one of the most difficult terms to define because it is so multifaceted. Terrence Tice indicates five dimensions (which I have put into my own words here).[2]

At the most basic level, this can mean 1) piety, or more simply, a relationship with God. 2) It also refers to the *modification* of that relationship in faith, that is, to the further *development* of religious self-consciousness by the grace of God. Every human being has a capacity for God-consciousness, or piety, but not every person's self-consciousness has been modified by grace to develop into something higher. 3) The highest stage of the modification of piety is the "feeling of absolute dependence." This highest stage of human consciousness is a state in which we relate ourselves and feel ourselves related to God in a relationship of total, utter dependence. We "live and move and have our being" in and through Christ and thus in communion with God. 4) This highest stage of self-consciousness—our being in unbroken fellowship with God—is therefore synonymous with *blessedness*. It is our being in a relationship with God in and through Jesus Christ, which manifests in the experience of joy and satisfaction, or "bliss." 5) Finally, this stage of consciousness is bound to the experience of the "common spirit" of the Church. It is not an individualistic concept, in other words, but it is bound to a concrete, historical, and communal expression of piety.

Schleiermacher notes that "all Christian piety rests on the appearance of the Redeemer"—thus removing any doubt about the true source of Christian self-consciousness.[3] He continues, "[N]othing touching upon the Redeemer can be set forth as genuine doctrine that is not tied to his redemptive causality and that does not permit of being traced back to the original and distinctive impression that his actual existence made" (CF §29.3, 182). In other words, Schleiermacher's emphasis on religious self-consciousness is an indication of his Christomorphic thought. It is *because* Christ has made an "original and distinctive impression" on us—namely, redemption—that the task of dogmatics is to explicate and describe the Christian religious self-consciousness.

Community-centric — Almost everything in Schleiermacher's theology is marked by a fiercely community-centric commitment. It is arguably one of the most striking themes of his theology.

For an example of just how uncompromising this commitment is in Schleiermacher's thought, consider what he writes about those who remain unbaptized and have not been taken up into the Christian community: "[S]uch a person could have no true part in Christ's perfection and blessedness. This would be so because the person would have no part in Christ's activity of founding community, also no part in that blessedness of Christ which is grounded in the community's shared consciousness" (CF §137.2, 882).

This theme is connected to the *Naturzusammenhang*, the interconnected process of nature, because it stresses the interdependence of all finite things and our inability to conceive of the world in isolated parts without considering its coherence. Schleiermacher is not merely committed to a community-centric theology in theory, but he systematically removes the possibility of conceiving of the world apart from its organic interconnectedness.

The interconnected process of nature (*Naturzusammenhang*) — This term could also be translated "coherent system of nature" or "nature-system." Tice writes that "humanity is part of the one indivisible web of being," with reference to this concept.[4] It designates the interconnectivity or coherence of nature as a whole and its absolute dependence upon God. Schleiermacher writes, "Being-conscious-of-oneself-as-part-of-the-world is one and the same thing as finding-oneself-placed-in-a-general-interconnectedness-of-nature" (CF §34.1, 198). This does not result in determinism since Schleiermacher includes a relative degree of human freedom within this process. Instead, the nature-system is an interdependent organic whole, inconceivable according to its isolated parts but only in its unity.

This idea becomes vital for understanding how Schleiermacher conceives of both God's acts and self-revelation. The interconnected process of nature is closely connected with the supernatural becoming natural theme because it is *how* God expresses Godself and how God acts in the world, it is the naturalization of God's decree. The supernatural event of God's activity becomes natural through the interconnected process so that we could rightly say the natural and supernatural coincide. Even Christ is included in the natural process, although Christ is at once its determinant. Redemption takes places within this interconnected process so that the world is rightly called the "theater of redemption" (CF §169, 1013), in which everything exists "only insofar as it could be an object of divine love" (CF §169.2, 1017).

Shelli Poe notes: "As part of the organic whole of the *Naturzusammenhang*, which God has shaped in relation to Christ, humanity is already permanently united with Christ. Consistent with the focus of Schleiermacher's theology in general, the incarnation is the key to salvation."[5] This means that the incarnation has *always* been God's plan, not an afterthought in the light of some historical fall. The whole interconnected system/process of nature is determined by Christ and redemption was its goal from the beginning.

Non-speculative (or anti-speculative) theology — Together with Barth, Schleiermacher rejected natural theology and speculation as an invalid approach to Christian dogmatics.[6] Even though Schleiermacher does find some value in speculation as a logical tool (especially in his philosophy, *Dialectics*), he nevertheless refused to develop a speculative dogmatics. It is perhaps *the* central theme of his work, and it is one of the best ways I think we can accurately understand his controversial methodology. Schleiermacher argued and consistently showed that the shaping of dogmatics propositions "does not depend on any philosophical form of school, or has not proceeded from any speculative interest in any respect. Rather, it has proceeded only from the interest of satisfying immediate self-consciousness, which is mediated by the genuine and unadulterated foundation endowed by Christ alone" (CF §16.PS, 124). His method is not philosophically or speculatively based but founded upon the Christian self-consciousness of redemption in and through Jesus Christ, that is, on the Gospel. Included in this concept is **the non-objectifiablity of God**, which is a core conviction Schleiermacher shares with twentieth-century dialectical theology.[7] "God is to be placed above all being and nature" (CF §96.1, 585).

Phenomenological theology, or **the complete coincidence of God's being and act**, or **God hidden and revealed** — This multifaceted theme manifests itself most clearly in Schleiermacher's consistent reminder that God's being is pure activity: "God's being can be conceived only as pure activity" (CF §94.2, 576).[8] Predating modern phenomenology, he was devoted to speaking of

God's being in active and actualized terms, as that which corresponds to the phenomenon of being, or we might say the explication of the feeling of absolute dependence. This theme includes the complete coincidence of the God hidden and revealed, of positive and negative theology, which we discussed in chapter two in connection to Schleiermacher's Trinitarian theology. While this is based on a constructive reading of Schleiermacher's dogmatics—he rarely, if ever, used this exact terminology—nevertheless, it has shown itself to be a helpful interpretive perspective.[9]

Relational redemption — As opposed to reconciliation or atonement, redemption is the defining theme of Schleiermacher's soteriology. This results in a relationally-focused, or community-centric, doctrine. By focusing on redemption, Schleiermacher moves the emphasis away from "transactional" salvation—in which we are saved *from* God in an exchange of blood to satisfy God's wrath—and focuses instead on the relational implications of Christ's life and work. Redemption is the transference from the collective life of sin to the life of grace, in union with Christ and communion with the Spirit-filled Church. It is a thoroughly relational metaphor, which connects this theme with Schleiermacher's community-centric tendencies.

The editor's of the new edition of *Christian Faith* helpfully explain redemption: "[A]t its root *Erlösung* (redemption) does not mean payment or exchange so much as release (becoming freed or loosed from) in contrast to the typical meaning of the English word" (CF §8n23, 87). And elsewhere they write, "This concept literally refers to a process of being loosed or liberated from, hence there is no prima facie, built-in sense of substitutionary payment made in punishment sustained or sacrifice offered on behalf of sinners, as in customary atonement theories" (CF §71n29, 432). Redemption is purposely chosen to distinguish Christ's work from any transactional, penal atonement theory.

Spirit and letter or the **inner and outer dialectic** — This indicates Schleiermacher's aim to distinguish what is essential and non-essential in theological propositions. He often removes the superfluous elements of faith in favor of the "spirit," or the inner, essential truths at the heart of a doctrine. He prioritized the spirit of an idea over its dogmatic formulation. This can be seen in so many of his revisions to theology, especially his doctrine of the being of God in Christ. Here Schleiermacher believed he was faithful to the *spirit* of the Chalcedonian formulas while revising the *letter* of their definitions. Terrence Tice feels that this is one of *the* most essential themes in Schleiermacher's theology.[10]

Schleiermacher writes that "greater attention must be paid to the spirit of these symbols than to clinging to their letter"—referring to confessional symbols and formulas (CF §27.1, 169). Prioritizing the spirit of a doctrine over its letter, its dogmatic formula, is a theme that recurs throughout Schleiermacher's dogmatics.

Supernatural becomes natural — Schleiermacher considered it a maxim of his dogmatics that "the reign of God is supernatural but becomes natural as soon as it appears" (CF §100.3, 627). It is a theme that bears a definite stamp on much of his theology, especially his doctrines of Christ and the Church. The Church is a natural, historical phenomenon with its basis in the unfolding of the divine government, that is, the reign of God. Christ's community follows the same pattern as Christ Himself, namely, the uniting of the divine with human nature, or the being of God in Him. Just as the incarnation resulted in the supernatural becoming natural, so the being of God is present and active in the Church, the supernatural becomes natural, in the form of its common spirit. The supernatural and the natural seamlessly coincide. Schleiermacher writes, "Whenever I speak of the supernatural, I do so with reference to whatever comes first, but afterwards it becomes secondly something natural. Thus creation is supernatural, but it afterwards becomes the natural order. Likewise, in his origin Christ is supernatural, but he also becomes natural, as a genuine human being. The Holy Spirit and the Christian church can be treated the same way" (OG, 89).

Teleological — Christianity is a "monotheistic mode of faith belonging to the teleological bent of religion" in Schleiermacher's famous definition from *Christian Faith* §11. Specifically, this necessitates that "everything is referred to the redemption accomplished through Jesus of Nazareth." *Telos* means "goal" or "purpose." For the Christian faith to be teleological means everything is oriented towards a divine purpose and goal, namely, redemption in and through Jesus Christ. Furthermore, this means that the development of humanity towards its ideal state—the "new creation" in Christ—is a crucial feature of Schleiermacher's understanding of Christianity.

Included in this theme is Schleiermacher's theological and ethical orientation towards the reign of God, which is the sovereign government of God in Christ that orders and preserves all things for redemption in Him. Schleiermacher avoids the more common phrase "Kingdom of God" because of its anthropomorphic connotations.

---

1. See *Schleiermacher on Christ and Religion*, 210-214. (New York: Charles Scribner's Sons, 1964.) Alister McGrath and B. A. Gerrish also use this term to describe Schleiermacher. See McGrath: *The Making of Modern German Theology*, 26. (New York: Basil Blackwell, 1986.) Gerrish clarifies the term, "In the apt expression of Richard R. Neibuhr, Schleiermacher's manner of theological thinking was 'Christomorphic,' not in the Barthian sense

Key Themes

'Christo-centric'" (*Continuing the Reformation,* 176. Chicago; The University of Chicago Press, 1993).
2. See *Schleiermacher (Abingdon Pillars of Theology),* 50-1. Nashville: Abingdon Press, 2006.
3. This further supports the argument that Barth and Brunner misunderstood Schleiermacher, falsely labeling him a subjectivist. Personal emotions are not the content of religious self-consciousness. In the truest sense, Christian religious self-consciousness is, indeed, *Christian*—that is, it is Christ-originating.
4. *Schleiermacher and Sustainability* (ed. by Shelli M. Poe), 95. Louisville: Westminster John Knox Press, 2018.
5. *Schleiermacher and Sustainability,* 38. Louisville: Westminster John Knox Press, 2018.
6. CF §51.1, 29.2, 83.3.
7. Prominent figures include Karl Barth, Rudolf Bultmann, Paul Tillich, and Emil Brunner. Lesser-known figures, but of no less importance, are Friedrich Gogarten and Helmut Gollwitzer.
8. The editor's of the new critical edition note: "God is always both *Sein* and *Seiendes*" (CF §94n9, 576). That is, *being* and *be-ing* (activity). This is a key aspect of what makes Schleiermacher's theology phenomenological. God's self-revelation is never a *given* but a *giving*.
9. In my estimation, scholars tend to agree with the basic concepts behind Robert Williams' reading. My research has not found any substantial critique of it, at least. Julia Lamm seems to approvingly cite Williams' text, as does Terrence Tice and C. W. Christian. Sheli Poe, most of all, takes his argument further by exploring the coincidence of Schleiermacher's apophasis (negative, hidden) and kataphasis (positive, revealed) understanding of God. See *Essential Trinitarianism,* 137-8 particularly and chapter 6 more generally. But she is also critical of Williams on some points.
10. See Tice's unpublished dissertation, *Schleiermacher's Theological Method* (1961). Also see *Schleiermacher (Abingdon Pillars of Theology),* 21-2 and 62. Nashville: Abingdon Press, 2006.

A BRIEF READING GUIDE

From page one, the purpose of this book has been to equip and encourage you to read Schleiermacher for yourself. So it is vital we end by offering a brief reading guide for how to tackle Schleiermacher's difficult corpus. Here I will offer up a reading plan for *Christian Faith,* discuss the editions of *On Religion,* list the most helpful theological and philosophical texts by Schleiermacher, and the most useful secondary recourses for studying him.

Christian Faith

Schleiermacher's *Christian Faith* is one of the most intricate and cohesive pieces of dogmatics ever written. Schleiermacher says more in a few pages than what most theologians of a lower caliber say with entire books. This makes *Christian Faith* like a beautiful tapestry—both on account of its interconnected logic and precise style. But it demands so much from its readers that it is also one of the most challenging pieces of theology I have ever read. How should we go about reading such a masterful work?

It is unavoidable that you must read *Christian Faith twice.* One reading of the text may be enough if you are only casually interested in Schleiermacher (and I will recommend a plan for a single reading at the end), but if you are serious about understanding Schleiermacher, then it is important to read *Christian Faith* more than once.

But you do not have to read the text in order. Schleiermacher constructed it in such an interconnected way that any section can serve as a suitable entry point. Over and over again he refers to previous or future propositions, which makes his work deeply intertwined. For example, Schleiermacher may deal with the doctrine of creation briefly in Part One, but the true force of what Schleiermacher thinks about creation, especially as it relates to preservation, is unveiled in the doctrine of God's wisdom, which orders the world for the sake of redemption. Schleiermacher's doctrine of God is another good example. The doctrine of God is explicitly discussed in four separate places, though it is also implicit in many others. It is, therefore, possible to read the parts and sections of *Christian Faith* out of their original order.

There are three reading plans that I recommend. The first two are for those who know they are willing to read it twice, and the third is for those who know they will not. No matter which method you choose, it is vital that you read slowly and patiently. Also, please note that not every idea Schleiermacher entertains he finally adopts as a set doctrine. The propositions themselves (in bold at the beginning of each section) accurately reflect what Schleiermacher holds to be true, but what he discusses under each heading is not always what he finally endorses.

Of the two English editions of Schleiermacher's *Christian Faith*, the new critical edition translated and edited by Terrence N. Tice, Catherine L. Kelsey, and Edwina Lawler is superior. The old edition of 1928 is dated and lacks the precision of the new edition. And as previously noted, that edition was also translated by *critics* of Schleiermacher, and so while they may not have intentionally mistranslated the text, it is possible they did not give it as much care as the new editors have given it. So I highly recommend the two-volume critical edition published by Westminster John Knox Press (2016) above the H. R. Mackintosh and T. S. Stewart translation of 1928 (T&T Clark).

With all that said, here are three potential reading plans for *Christian Faith*.

First, read the book "backwards," beginning with Part Two then circling back to the Introduction and Part One. (Read §§62-172, then §§1-61.) Preferably, read uninterrupted and finish within a few months. When you are reading the Introduction, try to remember that Schleiermacher considered it preliminary. Reading the Introduction and Part One *after* Part Two will cause you to see it in its proper light and context, and as you read, try to recognize the connections between the parts. Part Two is the true heart of the book, and you should encounter it first. Part One is an *abstraction* from the particular doctrines of Part Two, though it also has its place within the whole organic system.

Your goal for this first reading is to become acquainted with Schleiermacher's ideas. Do not try to master every section. If you get stuck or confused, remember you will return to that section again and move on. Therefore, this first reading should be rather quick, though never rushed. Take some of your own notes in the margins or underline passages that stick out to you, but overall, do not put too much stress on yourself for this first reading. You will come back to the text soon enough.

The next thing I recommend is that you take a break and read something else from Schleiermacher. The best text for understanding *Christian Faith* is undeniably Schleiermacher's own defense, *On the Glaubenslehre*. This book is indispensable for understanding his dogmatics. Other texts might be read in between your first and second readings of *Christian Faith*. Schleiermacher's essays on the Trinity or Election would compliment it well, as would Schleiermacher's sermons or his *Brief Outline*.

After a bit of time, return for your second reading. This time, we are going to read it normally, as Schleiermacher intended. We are also going to spend more time reading it. But we should still try to read as consistently as we can, without long interruptions. Reread the Introduction and Part One with the knowledge that Part Two is the true heart of the book. Spend more time thinking through what Schleiermacher is attempting to do in these sections. In the light of your first reading, you can appreciate these for what they are without trying to discover some hidden impulse behind their propositions.

Ultimately, this method reads *Christian Faith* like a sandwich. The true heart of the book is like the bread that holds the sandwich together, Part Two. With this method, you begin and end with those sections most essential to the whole book so that they are the first and last impressions you have from Schleiermacher's text.

With this reading, you should have a reasonably solid grasp of Schleiermacher's thought. But you will also know there is so much still to discover.

The second method for reading is basically the same as the first but in reverse. Begin by reading the text in the order Schleiermacher intended it to be read. Take some time to read *On the Glaubenslehre* and a few other texts, then return and read the book by reading Part Two first and ending with Part One. This approach is less preferred than the first, simply because I want you to read *Christian Faith* with the heart of the text in mind from beginning to end. But it is still a perfectly adequate way of understanding *Christian Faith*.

Finally, for those who intend to read *Christian Faith* only once, the best way to do it is like this: First, skip everything else and read the sections in Part Two on the doctrine of God as love and wisdom (§§164-169). These could easily be read in one sitting. In my opinion, this is the high point of the whole work. After that, you might consider reading a few of the sections from

Schleiermacher's Christology, such as those in §§91-105. This is a longer section, but it is well worth becoming acquainted with.

After you've explored some of these later sections, you should read the whole text from beginning to end, while trying to stay consistent in your reading schedule. Do not skip over the sections you have already read on God's love and Christology when you come to them because now you will be able to understand them in their proper context. These sections were necessary to read first so that you keep in mind the goal Schleiermacher is leading you towards so that whenever you encounter tough sections from the Introduction and Part One, you won't miss the forest for the trees. Keep in mind all the things we have discussed about Part One and the Introduction as you read them. The Introduction is preliminary, and Part One is an abstraction of Part Two. Part One is, indeed, a *Christian* reflection—do not make the mistake of thinking it is purely speculative—but it is Christian in a more *implicit* sense and thus relies on Part Two for its fullest expression. Above all else, take your time and read slowly. And once you've finished, try to read *On the Glaubenslehre* as soon as possible, or perhaps even beforehand.

On Religion

There are three English editions of *On Religion*. I used Terrence Tice's translation in this book (published by John Knox Press in 1969). Unfortunately, this version is out of print, though used copies are available online. This is my preferred translation and the one I recommend for you to read if you read only one version. It will soon be updated by Tice, as he plans to expand his earlier translation so that it includes a critical comparison of all of Schleiermacher's revisions from 1799 until 1821. He will base it on the final edition but, in the footnotes, will compare the editions. This is similar to what Tice has done with *Brief Outline* and *A Christmas Eve Celebration*. It is not available yet, and I do not know who is publishing it, but it will supersede the out of print edition.

There are two other translations worth considering. The John Oman translation is the most common edition, published in 1893, which means it is in the public domain and thus freely available online. There are also many inexpensive reprints. Oman's translation is of the final, 1821 edition, which includes Schleiermacher's lengthy explanations.

Richard Crouter's translation is unique, in comparison with the other two, because he based it on the first edition of *On Religion* in 1799. Crouter's introduction is detailed and helpful. While reading the first edition is not necessarily essential for understanding the text, it can be helpful for anyone wanting to study the work in depth. Crouter's translation is also the most recent one, so it is perhaps more readable than Oman's.

Reading *On Religion,* no matter the translation, is a fairly straight-forward task. In chapter six, I hope to have shown why the second speech should not be overemphasized. The fourth and fifth speeches are just as important as the second. The second speech is directed towards the fourth and fifth so that its argument is not fully realized until those later speeches. I say all this to stress that you cannot *only* read the second speech, as is sometimes commonplace. The whole work is interconnected.

Theological Texts

The following theological texts are arranged in order of how valuable I personally found them in my reading of Schleiermacher. Certainly, each of these texts are important for understanding his thought, but I was personally helped by certain texts more than others.

1. *On the Glaubenslehre* - As I have already mentioned above, this text is essential for rightly understanding Schleiermacher's dogmatics.

2. *Brief Outline of Theology as a Field of Study* - Be sure to pick up Tice's translation, which compares the third edition with the first and second. This work is important for placing Schleiermacher's dogmatics within his larger vision for theology. It is somewhat dry—mostly because it is a series of short propositions with very brief comments or explanations—but it is important.

3. *Christmas Eve Celebration* - Again, Tice's translation is preferred. This book was underwhelming when I first read it (it was the first of Schleiermacher's texts I read), but after reading more of Schleiermacher's work, I began to recognize its value. It is a short piece but an enjoyable one.

4. *An Essay on the Trinity* - A new translation of this text is supposed to be in the works by Tice, but until then, pick up the reprint of Moss Stuart's 1835 translation.

5. *On the Doctrine of Election* - Although it is somewhat limited by its historical context—since Schleiermacher wrote in direct response to an essay from one of his contemporaries—this is still an enlightening book on the doctrine of election.

6. *Selections from Schleiermacher's* Christian Ethics.

7. *The Life of Jesus.*

8. *Luke: A Critical Study.*

9. *Introduction to Christian Ethics.*

10. *Christian Caring* - This book translates sections from Schleiermacher's *Practical Theology,* and so it mostly deals with the pastoral issues of Schleiermacher's time and environment.

11. *Schleiermacher's Soliloquies* - This book was written soon after *On Religion,* and it reflects Schleiermacher's rhetorical period of writing. Personally, I

thought it was quite dull to read and not very helpful. Others might disagree, and I will admit that it could be read alongside *On Religion*. But it was my least favorite primary text.

Sermons and Letters

Perhaps the best introduction to Schleiermacher's life and thought is to read his sermons and letters. We have already noted how important preaching was for Schleiermacher, but he was also a prolific correspondent.

There are two volumes of Schleiermacher's letters in English. These were published under the title *The Life of Schleiermacher as Unfolded in his Autobiography and Letters*. It was translated by Frederica Rowan in 1860, and so it is in the public domain and thus freely available online.

Schleiermacher sermons, however, should be counted among the most important of his works. There are a few collections available in English. Unfortunately, most of these are out of print. The earliest translation is Mary Wilson's 1890 *Selected Sermons of Schleiermacher*, which is in the public domain. Another collection is Dawn DeVries' *Servant of the Word*, published by Fortress Press in 1987 and reprinted by Wipf and Stock Publishers in 2004. This was my favorite of the two collections. Finally, Terrence Tice's newest book on Schleiermacher, *Schleiermacher: The Psychology of Christian Faith and Life*, translates a Christmas sermon from 1820. It is a valuable book for that sermon alone.

Besides these, a few other collections have been translated, but they are expensive and harder to find, being published by a specialty academic press, Edwin Mellen. If you can gain access to them through an academic library or via inter-library loan, then they are well-worth reading:

1. *The Christian Household: A Sermonic Treatise.*

2. *Reformed but Ever Reforming: Sermons in Relation to the Celebration of the Handing over of the Augsburg Confession.*

3. *Fifteen Sermons of Friedrich Schleiermacher Delivered to Celebrate the Beginning of a New Year.*

4. *Friedrich Schleiermacher's Interpretation of the Epistle to the Colossians: A Series of Sermons (1830-1831).*

Philosophical Texts

Schleiermacher's contribution extends far beyond the Church. His philosophical texts are worth considering for their own sake, but they also shed light, in a more implicit sense, on Schleiermacher's thought. These are a few of the notable texts available in English:

1. *Hermeneutics: The Handwritten Manuscripts* and *Hermeneutics and Criticism*. These two texts translate Schleiermacher's lectures on hermeneutics. The first relied only on his handwritten notes, and it is the more reliable source. The second used the notes from his students alongside handwritten notes. I recommend the handwritten manuscripts. Follow the reading guide that the translator's articulate, which suggests reading manuscripts three and four first.

2. *Dialectic or, The Art of Doing Philosophy* - translated by Terrence Tice from Schleiermacher's 1811 lecture notes. This text offers useful insight into Schleiermacher's philosophy, and Tice's notes are superb. It will be of particular interest to those acquainted with Kant's philosophy. Schleiermacher takes a radically unique stance against the philosophical trends of his time. He sets himself apart as a *critical realist*, rather than an idealist.

3. *Philosophical Ethics* - Schleiermacher's philosophical ethics are distinct from but congruent with his *Christian Ethics*. Christian ethics are the particular form of a general philosophical ethics. Schleiermacher's philosophical ethics aim to do something similar to Kant's ethical theory, but he also distances himself from Kant in significant ways.

4. *Schleiermacher's Introductions to the Dialogues of Plato* - Schleiermacher's translation of Plato remains among the most significant editions of the text in German. He wrote extensive introductions to each dialogue (amounting to over four-hundred pages in English), which sheds profound light on both Schleiermacher's appreciation for Plato and on Plato's work itself. Read this text if you are interested in Schleiermacher's work as a Plato-scholar.

The remaining texts were published by Edwin Mellen Press and are thus expensive or hard to find:

5. *On Freedom* - An early example of Schleiermacher's philosophy.

6. *Occasional Thoughts on Universities in the German Sense* - If you are interested in Schleiermacher's work in forming the University of Berlin, this text would be of value to you.

7. *On What Gives Value to Life* - This was one of Schleiermacher's first major pieces of writing, which he composed from 1790-1792.

General Secondary Texts

Because Schleiermacher is so difficult to read, secondary texts were essential for my own study of his thought. There is so much confusion surrounding Schleiermacher's work that one cannot read him directly and rightly understand him without a bit of help. So I do recommend the following books from experts. I have arranged these from the most helpful to least, though they have all been very beneficial to me. I have also broken these down into three categories. First, general introductions. Second, subject-specific books.

And finally, books dealing with the relationship between Barth and Schleiermacher.

These are the general studies I recommend:

1. *The Cambridge Companion to Friedrich Schleiermacher* - edited by Jacqueline Mariña. If you read only one secondary book on Schleiermacher, then it should be this text because of how well it articulates a broad overview of Schleiermacher from a wide range of voices.

2. *Thinking about Christ with Schleiermacher* by Cathrine Kelsey. While it is not technically an overview—this book deals with Schleiermacher's Christology—it was one of the most helpful books for my own reading. Kelsey articulates so clearly the core ideas of Schleiermacher's doctrine of Christ, emphasizing how he developed these ideas and why, which makes it extremely beneficial for newcomers to his theology.

3. *Schleiermacher (Abingdon Pillars of Theology)* - by Terrence Tice. This is a shorter introduction but it packs a lot in its pages. Notably, Tice, the master translator, defines key terms from Schleiermacher's corpus.

4. *Schleiermacher: Life and Thought* - by Martin Redeker. Schleiermacher's biography is essential for rightly understanding his work. This is currently the only book-length biography available in English.

5. *Friedrich Schleiermacher (Makers of the Modern Theological Mind)* - by C. W. Christian.

6. *Schleiermacher: A Guide for the Perplexed* - by Theodore Vial.

7. *Friedrich Schleiermacher* by Richard Crouter.

8. *Schleiermacher on Christ and Religion* - by Richard R. Niebuhr.

9. *A Prince of the Church* - by B. A. Gerrish. I do not entirely agree with Gerrish's reading, but this is still a helpful introductory text.

10. *Reminiscences of Schleiermacher* - by Friedrich Lücke. Dr. Lücke knew Schleiermacher personally and offers a reflection on his life and work. It is especially worth reading for his moving account of Schleiermacher's final hours.

If you can read German, the two best biographies of Schleiermacher are available only in that language. Redeker's text is the closest English alternative, but it was an attempt to follow Dilthey's (now somewhat dated) biography. If you can read either, they will provide the most precise and scholarly look into Schleiermacher's life and context. Nowak's text is considered the better of the two.

1. *Leben Schleiermachers* by Wilhelm Dilthey, edited by Martin Redeker (Berlin: G. Reimer, 1966).

2. *Schleiermacher: Leben, Werk und Wirkung* by Kurt Nowak (Göttingen: Vandenhoeck & Ruprecht, 2001).

Subject-Specific Secondary Texts

Miscellaneous:

1. *The Eternal Covenant* by Daniel Peterson. An excellent investigation into what precisely Schleiermacher meant by the "eternal covenant" between faith and science, which is an extremely relevant idea for doing theology in the modern world.

2. *The Living God: Schleiermacher's Theological Appropriation of Spinoza* by Julia Lamm.

3. *All Things New* by James M. Brandt. An essential study on Schleiermacher's *Christian Ethics* and its place in his overall corpus.

4. B. A. Gerrish's historical theology studies are always insight and worth reading, but they are especially helpful in situating Schleiermacher within the Reformed faith. These include: *Thinking with the Church* (part one and chapter eight), *Continuing the Reformation* (parts three and four), and *Tradition and the Modern World* (chapters one and four).

5. *Schleiermacher and Sustainability* ed. by Shelli M. Poe. A collection of essays towards an ecological-theology in conversation with Schleiermacher.

6. *Embedded Grace* by Kevin M. Vander Schel.

7. *Christian Ethics According to Schleiermacher* by Hermann Peiter.

On the Trinity/doctrine of God:

1. *Schleiermacher the Theologian* by Robert R. Williams. This was one of my favorite texts to read of all the secondary literature available. Although it only deals with Barth briefly, this text proved to me just how similar Barth and Schleiermacher's essential impulses are—especially their mutual dedication to a non-speculative doctrine of God.

2. *Essential Trinitarianism* by Shelli Poe.

3. *An Essay on the Trinity* by Friedrich Schleiermacher. Half of the book's length comes from Moss Stuart's introductory and closing remarks, which helps explain Schleiermacher's complex argument.

4. *Schleiermacher as Contemporary* - ed. by Robert Funk. Worth reading for Gerhard Ebeling's essay alone, although Niebuhr's is also insightful.

On election:

1. *Eternal Blessedness for All?* by Anette Hagan. A very fine historical overview of Schleiermacher's doctrine of election.

2. "An Introduction" by Iain G. Nicol and Allen G. Jorgenson in *On the Doctrine of Election* by Friedrich Schleiermacher.

On preaching:

1. *Jesus Christ in the Preaching of Calvin and Schleiermacher* by Dawn DeVries.

2. *Schleiermacher's Preaching, Dogmatics, and Biblical Criticism: The Interpretation of Jesus in the Gospel of John* by Catherine L. Kelsey.

Barth and Schleiermacher Studies

1. *Barth and Schleiermacher: Beyond the Impasse?* ed. by James Duke and Robert Streetman.

2. *Orthodox and Modern* by Bruce McCormack. See especially chapter three, "What Has Basel to do with Berlin?" McCormack is a leading expert in Barth's theology and offers a charitable reading of Schleiermacher from the Barthian perspective.

3. *Barth and Schleiermacher on Election* by Matthias Gockel.

4. *The Identity of Christianity* by Stephen Sykes.

5. *The Shift to Modernity* by Robert Sherman. This book compares the doctrine of creation in both Barth and Schleiermacher, arguing that they share the conviction of a Christological doctrine of creation.

6. *The Theology of Schleiermacher* by Karl Barth.

7. *Karl Barth: His Life from Letters and Autobiographical Texts* by Eberhard Busch. Barth's personal admiration for Schleiermacher is evident, and his biography proves that he remained a life-long conversation partner with his theology.

8. *Church Dogmatics* by Karl Barth. Barth refers to Schleiermacher often in his great work. Though most of the references are negative, there are also a surprising amount of favorable comparisons Barth makes. After Luther, Calvin, and Augustine, Schleiermacher is the fourth most-referenced author. See the index volume (V) for a complete list.

ABOUT THE AUTHOR

STEPHEN D. MORRISON is a prolific American writer, ecumenical theologian, novelist, artist, and literary critic. A strong sense of creativity and curiosity drives his productive output of books on a wide range of subjects.

This book is the fourth in his "Plain English Series." Previous volumes include *Karl Barth in Plain English*, *T. F. Torrance in Plain English*, and *Jürgen Moltmann in Plain English* (foreword by Jürgen Moltmann).

For more on Stephen, please visit his website. There you can stay up to date with his latest projects and ongoing thoughts.

WWW.SDMORRISON.ORG

ALSO BY STEPHEN D. MORRISON

Plain English Series:
Karl Barth in Plain English (2017)
T. F. Torrance in Plain English (2017)
Jürgen Moltmann in Plain English (2018)
Schleiermacher in Plain English (2019)

For a complete list of the projected volumes in this series, please visit:
www.SDMorrison.org/plain-english-series/

Other titles:
Welcome Home: The Good News of Jesus (2016)
10 Reasons Why the Rapture Must be Left Behind (2015)
We Belong: Trinitarian Good News (2015)
Where Was God?: Understanding the Holocaust in the Light of God's Suffering (2014)